From Southerner to Settler

For Avi, my everything.

First edition May 2023.
Published in New Jersey, United States.

Book design by the Virtual Paintbrush.
Photography by Susannah Schild.
Author photo by Kineret Rifkind.

ISBN 979-8-9883341-2-5 (hardcover)
ISBN 979-8-9883341-0-1 (paperback)
ISBN 979-8-9883341-1-8 (ebook)

www.hikingintheholyland.com

From Southerner to Settler

Unexpected Lessons from the Land of Israel

Susannah Schild

Table of Contents

INTRODUCTION

I MOVED TO ISRAEL two decades ago as a young mother, with my own youthful understanding of why Israel was important. In the years that followed, my appreciation of the Holy Land shifted and grew into something entirely different. The fact that I had changed became apparent to me over time, especially when I met with old friends from abroad, friends who had also planned to come to Israel, but had never made the move. During our time together, I became aware that their vision of the country hadn't changed much since those early years. And how could it possibly have shifted as mine had, when Israel wasn't a part of their everyday lives?

I so wished that I could express my experiences and explain the way they had changed my perspective, but our short hours of conversation together left me tongue tied. So, I decided to write this book, a personal memoir about the land, Religious Zionism, and the importance of Israel to the Jewish people.

I want to acknowledge that this is simply my perspective, the perspective of a Southerner turned Settler, a Religious

Zionist in Israel. There are many different types of Jews in Israel and outside of it, all with their uniquely wonderful sets of loves and ideals about our country. Their passions about Israel are important, their stories and dreams valid. The story of my experience does not negate their visions for the land.

This is a book about what Israel might mean to the Jewish people today. I believe that, together, we are writing the next chapter in the once ancient history book of our land and our people.

How will that story unfold?

I.

REFLECTIONS

March 24, 2020, during the first days of COVID-19.

W E COULDN'T WAIT. It didn't matter anymore that the official wedding date was only days away. The florist had cancelled, along with the hall and the band. Tomorrow morning, we would make a wedding for our daughter Elie, the earlier the better. Although Elie and her husband-to-be, Moshe, were both youngsters still completing their years of national service, they had been eagerly anticipating their marriage for months. Yet somehow it was also all happening before anyone was ready for it.

We made phone calls, planning, worrying. Moshe's parents called and suggested: Maybe we should have the wedding tonight? We reassured them. The new COVID restrictions weren't set to go into effect until tomorrow morning at the earliest. We could wait until then. But no longer. Most of our plans had already been scrapped because of this new virus that was sweeping the world. The expected arrival of family from America to celebrate with us would not happen. The original venue, an elegant Bedouin tent overlooking the beautiful Judean Hills, was impossible now. Friends could not attend. This last plan, a party of twenty—immediate family, the rabbi, the musician, one set of grandparents, and two friends to serve as witnesses—on our friends' remote hilltop farm, was going to happen. *Tomorrow.*

Pushing all of my feelings aside, I transitioned into power mode. What we had left were my daughter and her fiancé, isolated in their own homes, eagerly looking forward to beginning their new life together. We had a rabbi to officiate, a beautiful, simple wedding dress. What more did we really need? I threw myself into giving my daughter the best wedding day possible. After a few phone calls and messages, we managed to find flowers, one of my daughter's only requests. Because of the new travel restrictions, all of the local flower exporters were stuck with lots of beautiful blossoms with no place to go. We bought bushels from several different sellers—every wedding should have lots of flowers—and picked out the prettiest blooms to weave into a happy bouquet. We picked up a giant tallit from a neighbor. It would serve as an extra-large *chuppah* (marriage canopy), so that everyone could stand underneath, leaving space between the two families to comply with COVID regulations. The rabbi and witnesses would stand two meters away. At the local hardware store, we bought four wooden broomsticks to hold it up.

And so, it continued. All day, we pulled it together: the food, party items, the rest of our wardrobe. My friends pitched in, driving all over the place to find a random assortment of items: a garden bench belonging to a neighbor's sister became the bridal chair. A giant satin sheet from down the block became its adornment. My daughter, throughout it all, remained happy and totally go with the flow. How many modern Jewish brides are content to let a sixteen-year-old neighbor do their hair for their wedding day? Our bride sat in the living room that afternoon with a teenage neighbor, both of them masked, trying out hairstyles in front of the mirror.

Late that night, Elie, my husband Avi, and I sat in the living room after the younger kids had gone to bed, pulling together the finishing touches: candles for the ceremony; tablecloths for the small meal we would hold at home in our backyard afterwards. And then it was time to create the actual chuppah. We had a giant tallit and four broomsticks, but how were we going to make the thing actually hold together? Our destination wedding would take place in a wide-open area, the mountain cliffside of our friends' farm—this chuppah had to be completely windproof. Running through possibilities in my head, I came up with a potential solution. My kids' curtain poles had knobs on the end; if we could somehow secure those knobs to the broomsticks with screws, then tie string tightly around the tallit to hold it all together…we would have a chuppah!

I crept into the room shared by my two youngest sons, Gabi and Benzi, to retrieve the knobs. Climbing on to four-year-old Benzi's bed, I held my breath as I carefully unscrewed one knob. Then I tiptoed to the other side of his blond head to grab the knob at the other end. Two more knobs later, I hurried from the room and back downstairs with my prize.

Miraculously, the knobs fit! All we had to do was place screws into the holes at the edge of the knobs and secure each one to a broomstick, just as they had been secured to the curtain poles upstairs. We jimmied the whole thing together in fits of laughter. We had our chuppah.

The next morning, we ran around in a frenzy of preparations. As mother of the bride, it was my job to make everything as easy as possible for my daughter. The world was newly fearful of this thing called COVID-19. So, like everyone else, my Elie's friends were staying away. Keeping things smooth was my responsibility. I was fortunate that my friends and neighbors were eager to help. Before we left for the farm, I sent out one last WhatsApp to my friends, letting them know what was left to be done at home as I hurried upstairs to get dressed.

"How much time do you need?" asked Avi. We were already running late.

"Ten minutes," I answered as I rushed off.

Ten minutes to get ready for my first daughter's wedding. Ten minutes to throw on a dress, some jewelry, and shoes (no high heels—those weren't going to work at this new wedding venue on a farm). Today wasn't about looking perfect. I dressed quickly, trying to stay calm.

Ten minutes later we were on our way, crammed into our van with everything we needed for this makeshift wedding. I sat in the back seat, ducked under chuppah poles, having given up my customary spot in the front to the bride. And then there we were: at my daughter's wedding.

Green and rocky mountains spread out in waves all around us. The expansive view was one you could never get used to—a deep canyon down below, hills in the distance, and an open sky. On the farm itself, vineyards grew, just like in Tuscany. An ancient olive press sat at the edge of a field. A small, domed "meditation room" stood in the center, built from stones found all around the property.

When the groom's family and the clarinet player (also a close friend and mentor) arrived, we were ready to get started. In the distance, we saw our neighbor, Mendel, setting up cameras for video and Zoom. Beyond the cameras, some of our extended family had pulled up and were watching from their cars—like a wedding safari.

We passed out tambourines and the ceremony began. Ancient wedding tunes poured out of one lone clarinet, with the beat of tambourines and a darbuka played by members of our small wedding party completing the sweet music. As we made our way to the chuppah, my husband and I on either side of our firstborn daughter, holding her hands, I thought to myself that nothing could be more perfect. The simple wedding canopy, the striking setting. The rocks and hills and the mountains, dramatic and intense. Simple and imperfect and beautiful. This was my daughter and everything she stood for.

And nevertheless, this scene was deeply surreal. Nineteen years ago, when Elie was born in Englewood Hospital, New Jersey, I never could have imagined a wedding day like this one. On a farm, in the midst of sweeping mountains and valleys, in the hills of Judea and Samaria. Except for our family, every member of our small wedding party, from the groom to the rabbi to the witnesses, spoke only Hebrew. How did we get here?

II.

In Search of a Nation

"We have not lost our hope, the hope of two thousand years: to be a free nation in our land." –HaTikvah

I GREW UP IN a different world, very distant from the Land of Israel. Born and raised in the American south, I lived in Uptown New Orleans, in a big yellow house on a shady street lined with giant live oak trees. My mother, raised a Catholic, was born in the Portuguese colony of Angola, in Africa. She had come to America in 1965 at age twenty-five, after completing medical school in Montpelier, France. Her religious journey took off in New York, where she became attracted to the idea of finding a more authentic religion. After meeting my father, she left the Catholicism she had been raised with for his Reform Judaism. What began as a medical internship turned into a new life for my mother, one that would take her to places that she had never imagined. My father grew up in Chicago and Miami. His father, my grandfather, was a first-generation Jewish American businessman whose father had emigrated from Austria. His mother, my grandmother, was a Kentucky girl who had converted from Christianity and married my grandfather.

My parents met at New York French Hospital during their summer jobs. My father, a tall and handsome guy, was immediately attracted to my mother, an exotic foreigner. During their courtship, my American grandparents "adopted" my immigrant mother, buying her dresses, taking her out for meals and cultural events, and introducing her to the wonders of American convenience cooking. My parents' wedding picture shows my father with his piercing green eyes looking straight at the camera, a calm expression on his face. My mother looks elegant and happy, her hair piled high in a mountain of blonde extensions which I am sure my grandmother must have arranged for. (My mother reports that this was the last time she ever stepped foot into a beauty salon.)

After their marriage, my parents moved to the French Quarter in New Orleans to continue with their medical training at Tulane Medical School. They started their family by having Sharon and Jesse (my older brother and sister) in quick succession. Then, during the war in Vietnam, my father served in the U.S. Navy as a flight surgeon, moving to the naval base in Virginia Beach. When my father's service was complete, they all moved back to New Orleans, into the big yellow house that I grew up in, my parents eventually both becoming established neurologists.

As they built their lives in New Orleans, my parents became more connected to Judaism through their children's day school, and the Conservative synagogue. My second brother, Aaron, was born in 1978, and I was born in 1980, over ten years after our older siblings.

I remember many things about those early years. Before beginning preschool, I had a nanny, Willie Mae, a pleasantly plump Black woman who was almost like a second mother to me. She cared for me in the upstairs area of my parents' office, which they had converted to a cheery, yellow-wallpapered nursery. I remember the handwritten notes my mother included in my packed lunch, and Willie Mae giving me baths in the oversized kitchen sink. Every day, after naptime, Aaron showed up after his full day at pre-school. Willie Mae then drove us over to Lafreniere Park to play, stopping at the local Parkway for Yoo-Hoo chocolate milk. Sometimes she would stop for herself at the Popeye's drive-thru, passing me back the little plastic toys that came with her fried chicken. After these outings, we would return to the office, and my parents would drive us all back home to Uptown New Orleans in their brown and white station wagon.

At some point during my early childhood, my parents and older siblings discovered Chabad House of New Orleans, which happened to be less than a mile from our home. This was a convenient point in its favor as my parents embarked on the path to observance; they could walk to shul on Shabbat. My father, always a life-long student (to this day, he can often be found with his nose in a big book), was drawn to Torah study and the Talmud. My mother's ever-present inner spirituality recognized that living as an Orthodox Jew would lead to a deeper connection to God.

It was a process, but after much study and detailed consultation with the Chabad rabbi, our family became fully observant of the laws of Shabbat and Kashrut. By the time I was six years old, we had all undergone an Orthodox Jewish conversion—we were all officially Jewish, Orthodox, American Southerners, with Portuguese Angolan roots thrown in for good measure.

Our new Orthodox Jewish community at Chabad was tiny—just a few families and a handful of Tulane students attended the Shabbat services. There was no guarantee of a *minyan* (the group of ten men required for organized prayers) on any given Shabbat. So there weren't a lot of kids around town like me. Whether in school, or on the neighborhood streets, as an Orthodox Jew, I didn't exactly fit in in New Orleans, Louisiana. But I was totally fine with it—or at least I felt like I was. My parents and older siblings always taught me that nonconformity was a positive thing. One of Papa's most repeated rhetorical questions was the classic, "If everyone jumped off a bridge, would you jump too?"

Throughout the years of my childhood, Chabad House New Orleans hosted a motley crew of all different types. As well as the students from Tulane, there were occasional visitors from out of town, and random local Jews looking for a path to authentic religion. Every so often, a young family seeking a more observant lifestyle would join the community, and in that way, we gradually grew larger. As the only thriving Orthodox synagogue in the City of New Orleans, there weren't a lot of options for those looking for a more religious Jewish experience. Chabad was the place to be.

One Shabbat evening, Bob Dylan stopped by on his way through town, a woman on each arm. This type of blatant non-conformity was right at home at Chabad, and we loved to rehash the rock star's visit to our tiny shul whenever the opportunity arose.

I had friends at Chabad: the rabbi and his wife had nine children for me to play with. These were my "Shabbat friends," the ones I spent Saturday afternoon with, in their little white house on Pine Street. On my walks to their home in my frilly, flowered Shabbat dresses, I was attired very differently from the Saturday jogging shorts and t-shirts sported by almost everyone else on the streets. But New Orleans is known for its relaxed and eclectic atmosphere. I don't think most people around would have even guessed (or cared) that I was an Orthodox Jew.

Being so close in age (only two-and-a-half years apart), my brother Aaron and I did almost everything together. On non-Shabbat days, we played Nintendo, and made each other treasure hunts, and watched Disney movies together. We played team basketball one year and took archery lessons another. When I was eight years old, we would typically spend afternoons after school at our parents' office in Metairie, a suburb of New Orleans. One day, after the office had officially closed for the day, Aaron and I spent hours creating piles of colorful confetti with the office hole punchers. Then I accompanied my mother on her hospital rounds, while Aaron did his homework. It was a great day. Then it got even better. While we were in the car on the way home, my mother turned to us in the backseat to deliver some news; Aaron and I were going to be joining the swim team the following week—no more long afternoons of hole punching for us. We were thrilled and excited with this fun new development. Could it be true?! Would we really get to go swimming *every single weekday* from now on? To eight-year-old me, this seemed like the most exciting thing imaginable.

The next Sunday morning, we purchased rubbery blue swim caps and Speedo goggles, and on Monday, after school, my mother walked us over to the YMCA near her office. The gleaming, Olympic sized pool was filled with lap lanes and fast swimmers. Mama took us in and introduced us to Coach Chris, the head coach of the Metairie Y Aqua Jets, and gave us each a hug and a kiss before scurrying off to exchange her white doctor's coat and kitten heels for jogging clothes and rearrange her up-do into a long braid so that she could run laps around the track, leaving my brother and I alone to adjust to our new sport and teammates.

We took to swim team like a duck takes to water. We loved swimming. But swim practice itself wasn't pure fun. Coach Chris would blow his whistle, shouting commands in his stern and friendly way: "Gimme a fifty butterfly!" and then, "Okay y'all, now let's have a hundred freestyle with flip turns." We followed along with the team and did our best to keep up, day after day after day, all year long. In the summer, we woke up at 5:30 AM to make it to 6:00 AM practice every single weekday morning. Our team was the first group in the pool each day. It took intense willpower to get into the freezing cold water in the early hours of the morning, but we did it; my strategy was to dive in from the shallow end and then swim as fast as I could until my little body warmed up.

Much of swim team was great fun, for years of my child-hood—at least, the swimming and racing part was. What I *didn't* like was trying to socialize with my teammates: two Jamies, one Chris, a Stephanie, a Marie, a Timmy, a Tommy... and a whole bunch of others. Metairie, as opposed to the City of New Orleans, wasn't known for its eclectic atmosphere. Most kids on the team lived in cookie cutter houses and attended local Catholic schools. Before practice started, we would hold onto the side of the wall, splashing around in the water. And inevitably, whoever was next to me on the wall would start asking some variation on the same question:

"Do you believe in Jesus?"

"No," I would answer, honest instead of smooth.

But of course, that answer didn't satisfy anyone. It didn't make sense! My response bewildered them so much that all the kids had to take turns asking, each in a different way. First Chris, then Laura, then one of the Jamies. No, I didn't believe in Jesus. No, I didn't believe that he was the son of God. What more was there to say? I knew that my answer was wrong to these kids. I felt confident that my belief was the correct one, but also really confused as to why these kids couldn't process this simple bit of information.

One night at dinner I shared my frustrations with my parents. They got a big kick out of it. My father looked at me with a playful smile on his face, "Just ask them this: Are you a monotheist or a polytheist? That'll stump 'em."

At eight, I can't say I really had a good response to that. Papa chuckled under his breath, amused.

I knew it was okay to be an Orthodox Jew, to be different. It was okay on swim team, and it was okay in my private prep school. All it meant to me was that I followed a different set of rules. And at Chabad, we did have a kind of a community. But not in a way that made me feel like part of a united whole, a group with a common goal, like some of the kids on my swim team seemed to feel about their religion.

I'm not sure I was really conscious of what I was missing, or thought I was missing anything at all. I had my family, my few friends. As a child, I didn't suffer from any major angst or concerns about life. I was surrounded by people who loved me—my parents, my brothers and sister, my friends. And although they didn't live near us, I also had my grandparents.

I absolutely loved visiting my father's parents in sunny West Palm Beach during vacation. Vóvó and Vôvô Palmer, as we called them, borrowing the Portuguese terms for grandparents from my mother's family, were fun, fun-loving, and social people. They had a pretty, perfect little condo. We would play shuffleboard, and I would show off my form in the swimming pool. My grandfather played golf every morning with all of his old man friends in their condominium complex. I loved watching him on his return from the game, his tan skin glimmering past the short sleeves of his blue polo shirt and checked pants. My grandmother wasn't a golfer. She liked to shop and play mah-jongg. I always felt privileged to sit by her side to watch her games and listen to her chat with her friends as she shook the tiles.

On my mother's side, we had another Vóvó and Vôvô. They lived in Portugal, so we didn't visit them much, but they came to visit us once a year, bringing gifts of gold jewelry wrapped in intricate bags. My grandmother was an artist. After my grandfather died, she would still come to visit, often carrying gifts of artwork along with her. My grandmother, a lifelong Catholic, always sat with us at our Shabbat meals, totally respectful of our family's chosen religion.

Still, as much as I really did love my family and appreciate our uniqueness, there were times when I was a bit jealous of some of my friends. As I got older, I became part of a world where cheerleaders and football players ruled the school. Wealthy New Orleans socialites hosted Mardi Gras parade floats and exclusive balls. There were neighborhood Christmas light displays, haunted houses at the YMCA on Halloween, and Homecoming dances at school in the fall. Sometimes I tried to join in the fun, but mostly, I sat on the side-lines, growing up in a world that I could never truly be a part of.

Deep inside, I really did want to feel like I belonged. But that simply wasn't my reality, and I knew better than to question it, so I continued to live out my childhood making friends with other kids who didn't quite fit in at school and sticking it out at swim team. I won ribbons at every swim meet, except for the ones on Saturdays, which I couldn't attend.

One Tuesday afternoon after swim practice, my brother and I were standing by the soda machine, our last stop on the way out of the YMCA every day. As we rolled in our quarters and selected RC Colas and Fritos, we heard a teenage kid calling out from behind us.

"Hey brah," he called to my brother, "What's that beanie on yo' head?" The kid seemed genuinely curious.

Aaron explained unflinchingly, a nervous smile on his face, "It's called a yarmulka. I wear it because I'm Jewish."

The kid looked at my brother with confusion. He paused, then chuckled under his breath, having made up his mind. "I know ya lyin' brah. I can see you laughing."

Just another typical day in my life as a child. Orthodox Judaism was something so foreign, so atypical in the world I grew up in that, to this curious teenager, it just couldn't have been a logical explanation for my brother's unusual headgear.

Being different wasn't all that bad in a place like New Orleans, where the city streets were full of varied and colorful types. But moments like this one made a deep impression: I was not among my people.

III.

Wherefore Israel?

"If you want, then start to laugh. And if you must then start to cry. Be yourself, don't hide. Just believe in destiny." –Enigma, "Return to Innocence"

G ROWING UP IN New Orleans, moving to Israel was the farthest thing from my mind. I had other things to think about as a child of the Big Easy, like how many Mardi Gras beads my brother and I would have to string together to create a curtain for my bedroom door. Or, when I was older, whether my garage band was ready for its next performance at our local coffee house, The Neutral Ground. Travel, for me, extended as far as Florida…maybe Europe, on a really adventurous day. Israel played a barely noticeable role in my life. As an Orthodox Jew with very little knowledge of Hebrew, I'm not sure I even noticed how much Israel was mentioned in my daily prayers, which I recited more out of habit than understanding. The idea of Israel seemed far more mystical than practical. The Chabad camps and community that I was a part of placed an intense focus on Mashiach (the Messiah). When Mashiach came, I knew that we would all arrive in Israel *somehow*. I knew that modern Israel was the Jewish state. I knew that carob and falafel and strange-looking dried fruit came from that distant country. I had one red-headed Israeli friend, Sharone, who moved to New Orleans in second grade and then moved back to Israel a few years later. But that was the sum of my Israel experience. Throughout most of my childhood—at least before my teen years—I felt no personal connection to the land.

Then, however, I had the opportunity to travel to Israel a few times, during my still-formative years. On each of those visits, I experienced things which would eventually change my perspective on what it meant to be a Jew. And on Israel. The first time I visited was in June 1992, when we traveled as a family for a two-week trip. I was twelve. Israel was just another vacation for me. Of course, it was a place we had heard about and read about, but at first, it didn't feel any different or more special than a trip to Portugal or Florida. I stayed at the Sheraton Plaza in Jerusalem with my parents, my sister, Sharon, and my brother, Aaron. My other brother, Jesse, stayed behind, as he was finishing up his last year of college in Boston.

One thing I did absolutely appreciate was the novelty of eating kosher food at a hotel. Aaron and I devoured large ice cream sundaes with colorful floating umbrellas and mounds of whipped cream on top. We ate whole pizzas at a restaurant called Mamma Mia, just down the road, and more pizza at Cafe Rimon on Ben Yehuda. Our family tried the Moroccan buffet night at the King David Hotel and gorged ourselves on roast lamb, chicken with prunes, almond studded rice, and baklava. I was in food heaven. But aside from that, our trip to Israel was a lot like any other vacation.

My parents attended lectures at a medical conference all day, so Aaron and I swam in the hotel pool for hours at a time (with many ice cream breaks). When the conference ended, we went on a few guided tours. We visited the ancient ruins of Masada, which to the preteen I was, with no knowledge of history, was not so different from the ancient castles I had explored in Europe. I loved the Dead Sea, where I was unable to keep my body from floating to the top of the water. We visited museums and marveled over intricate Judaica, much like I marveled over Fabergé eggs in the New Orleans Museum of Art. It was a typical vacation—until we celebrated the holiday of Shavuot.

We remained in the Sheraton Plaza for the holiday. I was surprised and impressed by the beautiful display of fruit and flowers in the lobby at the beginning of the holiday. Having never been taught that Shavuot was an agricultural holiday, as well as the celebration of the giving of the Torah, this cornucopia of Israel's produce was a new feature for me.

After a delicious Shavuot dinner, we climbed the eighteen flights of stairs to our hotel room, preferring not to wait for the slow-moving Shabbat elevator. Then, to follow the Shavuot tradition of staying up through the night learning Torah, we sat down to read, and wait for morning. My parents had told us that if we managed to stay up all night, we would be going somewhere special for early morning *tefilot* (prayers). I sat on the floor with my family, my parents and siblings immersed in various forms of Torah study. With very little background in Torah study—at that point, I was at a non-denominational private prep school—there wasn't much learning that I knew how to do. I drifted off to sleep. A few hours later, I was awakened by my mother. It was nearly morning, but still completely dark, before dawn. My family was ready to go.

We climbed back down the eighteen flights of stairs and began our walk to the Kotel. At first, nothing seemed particularly out of the ordinary on the streets; it felt like we were just taking a night walk in Jerusalem. But as we neared the Old City, we saw other people walking alongside us; first a few, then a lot, and then absolute throngs. Towards the end of our journey, we sped through the alleys of the Old City, along with thousands of other Jews, all of us headed in the same direction.

When we finally arrived at the Kotel, otherwise known as the Western Wall, which I knew was the last remaining relic of our ancient Holy Temple, the sea of people before us was massive. My parents were afraid that we might get lost in the crowds, so we stuck close to them through all of the dawn morning service. My prayers that morning were the same as always—I barely understood the words, perhaps even less than I usually did, because of my exhaustion. But my prayers that day *felt* different. I had never seen so many Jews *together* before in my life. Not even close. It was the very first time I experienced what the Jewish people were like as a *nation*. It is only recently that I have begun to understand that mass march to the Kotel on a deeper level. Yes, the Kotel is the holiest place we've got, a place for deep prayers, stuffed with notes and supplications to God. It has been that for many, many years. But what the Kotel *really* represents is the lost Temple that it was once a part of; a Temple that is waiting to be rebuilt. As Jews we believe that, one day, the Temple will be rebuilt, in the same exact place.

Being one of the many Jews streaming towards the Kotel that Shavuot in 1992 was my taste of the *Shalosh Regalim*, the pilgrimage festivals. I did not realize it at the time, but on our walk we were Jews coming together as a nation to serve God: each one bringing our own small offering, making our own small sacrifice. For my twelve-year-old self, that offering came in the form of missed hours of sleep and the discomfort of being in a large crowd. And who knows what the many Jews who were there that day had sacrificed to be there, to be in Israel?

As Jews, we were coming together at the site of God's— our—ancient Temple, to offer our prayers and thanks. That Shavuot was my first exposure to the true soul of the Jewish people, my first chance to recognize our uniqueness and difference from the rest of the world. It was an experience that I was quite certain that my classmates at my non-denominational prep school would not appreciate or relate to. But I did—even at age twelve. That experience revealed to me that I was part of something different, and it left a tiny seed in my heart. Somewhere deep inside, I had begun to understand that our nation was special, and worth preserving.

My next visit to Israel came during the summer after ninth grade, when I was fifteen, on ISS—Israel Summer

Seminar. I'm not quite sure how I ended up on this summer touring program, but my sister had moved to Israel in 1993, after meeting Tzion, an Israeli who became her husband. Getting to visit her was at least part of the draw. I had no thought of moving there myself, yet, but I had no problem with the idea of another visit.

By that point, my parents had moved me from my private prep school in New Orleans to a Jewish high school in Memphis, Yeshiva of the South, where I dormed. I had become involved with NCSY, the most active Orthodox youth group in the United States. Most likely, my summer trip to Israel that year was the result of the efforts of a kind NCSY youth director named Roger who made it his mission to reach out to teens and bring them into the program.

Our group included about thirty kids. I made fast friends, some of whom I ended up treasuring for life. We were all together, *all* the time—on the bus, on our hikes and activities, and at night after we arrived at one more cruddy youth hostel, or occasionally at a beautiful kibbutz; there were lots of those, too. During our late nights, relaxing after the day's activities, I would gaze out at the wide, open sky with my new friends, munching Israel's national snack, the peanut butter flavored corn puffs known as Bamba (I thought they were gross). I felt free out in the Israeli countryside at night. The sky was like a sea of infinite blackness, and the stars seemed close, and plentiful. Those skies made for the best late-night conversations, and the most inspiring moments. Sometimes we would lie back in the grass and gaze up towards the heavens. Sometimes we would walk. But every night, I made it a ritual to look up at the stars and contemplate our tininess and the vastness of the universe, as every good teenager should. I felt a growing independence in my heart, and a desire to get to know every corner of this great, wide world.

My most memorable experience of independence occurred in Jerusalem. It wasn't at the Kotel, or during the solemn learning we undertook before the Fast of Av. It was a bus trip into the center of town, on a Saturday night.

I had just spent a free Shabbat with my sister, her husband, and her new baby, Meir. I loved hanging out with them in their tiny apartment in the Romema neighborhood of Jerusalem, but after a quiet Shabbat, I was looking for something more exciting to do. My sister suggested that I cross the street to the Central Bus Station and see if anything interesting was going on there. So, off I went.

I had grown up in a small Southern city, in a time when children were allowed to roam without fear: I was familiar with the feeling of being out by myself. But the Central Bus Station in Jerusalem was a totally different type of adventure than wandering my well-known neighborhood in New Orleans. I felt quite grown up just walking around, browsing the shops, and listening to the music of the Hebrew language flow around me. I was standing at one stall, browsing the rows of magnets, when out of the corner of my eye I saw someone familiar.

Standing nearby was an old acquaintance named Ben, the most popular kid at the sleepaway camp I'd attended. Despite being a few years older than me, Ben greeted me warmly, and asked what I was up to.

"I'm on ISS," I explained, "and I'm staying with my sister across the street. It's our off Shabbos."

Ben clearly considered it his mission to set me right. "You should go into town," he told me. "That's where everybody will be!"

"Really? Just, like, go to town?" I was somewhat skeptical of the simplicity suggested by his tone. "How would I even get there?"

"It's no problem," he insisted with a grin. "Just take a bus."

"I can't do that!"

"Of course, you can," he replied. "I'll go with you."

And so, Ben proceeded to escort me onto the bus and into town, where he waved me away with a smile and instructions to get on the last bus back to the Central Bus Station, at midnight, at the stop across the street.

I walked around town that night in kind of a daze. There I was, on a Saturday night, fifteen years old, and roaming the big city all by myself. In the cool dark of the Jerusalem night, I felt free, in a wholesome kind of way. The smell of pizza and schwarma filled the streets, so different than the rancid smell of spilled beer on Bourbon Street in my hometown of New Orleans. I bumped into a few friends—Ben was right, everyone was there—bought some watermelon-flavored bubblegum and, eventually, found my way back to the Central Bus Station on the last bus at midnight, just like Ben had instructed me.

He was right. It really was no big deal. But up until that night, I had never been on a bus in my whole life (New Orleans, where the legal driving age at that time was fifteen, wasn't known for its quality public transportation system). I had never gone to town in a foreign city on a whim. And that night I had done both of those things, all by myself.

In an era before cell phones were ubiquitous, I'm surprised that my sister wasn't even worried about me. But I guess she was already Israeli enough to know that '*yihiyeh beseder*'—all will be well. Children in Israel are given the permission and instruction to be independent. It's just what's expected— even for a fifteen-year old from another country. And that freedom to be autonomous was, and is, a wonderful thing.

After that trip, I can't say I really shared my sister's vision of making Israel my home. But I did begin to feel a connection to the country, one that came from having spent day after day physically exploring its length and breadth. Until that point, hiking had never been something I did or thought about. We just weren't that kind of family (and New Orleans isn't known for its hiking trails). But that summer in Israel, visiting Rosh HaNikra's grottoes and being soaked by the waterfalls of Ein Gedi for the first time, I felt a new space in my consciousness, one that included experiences of freedom and nature. Those moments in Israel's outdoors, from stargazing on kibbutzim to climbing ladders in a desert canyon, changed me in some indefinable way.

My next encounter with the Land of Israel began in 1997, my junior year of high school. I hated high school. Like, really hated it. I was bored with the low academic level, and I hated all of the rules—as a "dormer," I had so many more than my friends who were locals. Although I had good friends in Memphis, I felt as if I was just wasting valuable time. As far as grades, I was acing tests with ease. Sitting through classes where the teachers seemed to repeat themselves again and again, I felt like I was frittering my time away. I was ready to move on to the next phase of my life.

It wasn't just the boring classes that were making life difficult. As a teenager, my inner life was turbulent. On the outside, I was smart, pretty, and relatively popular. I sang a lot. But on the inside, I was full of teenage angst. My optimistic personality kept me from falling into a depression, but I spent many moments in a tempest. I would burst into tears at random, unable to deal with the ramifications of the questions and thoughts about the meaning of life that constantly flooded my brain. As far as I was concerned, there were too many things I didn't understand. The Torah we studied every day at school seemed full of confusing inconsistencies. I questioned my teachers relentlessly, repeatedly interrupting classes with debates (and never receiving any satisfactory answers). I constantly struggled with my inability to make sense of it all.

So, I filled my life with distractions. My close-knit group of friends (there were four of us), would get dressed in miniskirts or jeans, then drive around Memphis at night in a small white convertible, blasting music and feeling the wind in our hair. We'd meet the guys somewhere (including my twelfth grade boyfriend, Dovid), wander around from place to place, and eventually end up at the local Kroger at three in the morning in search of mint chocolate chip ice cream.

Compared to some of my earlier escapades in New Orleans, it was all fairly innocuous fun. Its main purpose, for me, was to keep me distracted from the fact that I felt life was absolutely pointless, and my soul hurt, thinking about it.

Not only that, but in Memphis, I felt like I had been labelled an outsider by the community. I repeatedly found myself being punished for small infractions by the school administration—things that no local would have been punished for. While my friends in the community were allowed to wander freely at all hours, or develop pot smoking habits, I got in trouble for staying out at my friend's parents' non-kosher restaurant (we weren't even eating, and that friend was in my class at school, one of the four in our convertible crew).

I needed a change.

I think it was my parents who suggested that I spend my last year of high school in Israel. I'm sure they figured it would be good for me to be near my sister, Sharon, and what could be bad about being in Israel? They looked for Israeli high schools and found an agricultural school in the northern town of Pardes Chana that included a boarding option. This idea seemed potentially acceptable to me, but I wasn't one hundred percent sure about it. What was an agricultural school, anyway? Would we be spending the day farming? That would be slightly out of my comfort zone; I had never expected pruning grape vines and picking oranges to be a part of my life. Still, I was *really* determined to get away from my small Jewish high school in Memphis and try something new. So, I considered the idea.

The first person I shared my thoughts with was Penina Salid. At Yeshiva of the South, there was no official dorm, but there were plenty of students from out of town like me, so the school had an arrangement with members of the community; local families would take in those students who needed a home away from home. I lived with the Salid family, and they treated me like one of their children. They made me feel loved at all times, especially when my confusion was deepest. Mrs. Salid was so wise; throughout my high school years, she guided me with utmost patience, always offering a listening ear, even when overwhelmed by small children and household duties. If I had a real problem, she was the clear address. So, to Mrs. Salid I went. I sat on the kitchen floor, as was my custom, and spilled out my plans. She paused, and considered, and questioned, while she juggled her babies and the dinner dishes…and then she very wisely guided me in a different direction.

I have no idea how she came up with a solution so quickly, but by the end of our conversation she had convinced me that rather than complete my last year of high school in Israel, I should apply for early admission to Stern College, a part of Yeshiva University, in New York City. Mrs Salid knew that I already had the grades and the SAT scores to gain early admittance to Stern, the most popular college choice amongst graduates of Yeshiva of the South. But she didn't want me to go straight away; she suggested that I defer my place for a year and attend a religious seminary in Israel (something many of my twelfth grade friends were going to be doing).

"But I don't want to go to Stern," I argued, aghast at the possibility, "I want to go to Columbia!" Getting my degree at an Ivy League college had been my plan for as long as I could remember. And there was no such thing as early admissions to Columbia University—standard acceptance was in no way guaranteed, even for someone with grades and SAT scores like mine. I didn't want to give up my chance to have an Ivy League education.

"You can figure that out later," she replied. As far as she was concerned, a religious Jewish college like Stern was a much better choice than Columbia. She must have known that my desire to be done with high school was strong enough to make this decision easier for me. Although I had no good plan for how to switch tracks after a year in Israel, I convinced myself that I would come up with some sort of solution. Mrs. Salid must have hoped that once I was on track to attend Stern, I would end up actually obtaining my college education there. (Spoiler alert: she was right.)

"At least this way," she continued, "You will be done with high school, accepted into college, and going to Israel."

Mrs. Salid had a point. I really was tired of high school. Wouldn't it be better to be done with it altogether? And who knew what the agricultural school in Pardes Chana would actually be like? Maybe a seminary in Jerusalem would be a better idea. My sister was there, and in truth, Dovid (my boyfriend) was also going to be spending the year in a Jerusalem yeshiva. Being near him was another point in favor of this new plan.

My conversation with Mrs. Salid took place in late March,

which was definitely not the ideal time to apply to schools for the following year, but she helped me through the process. Mrs. Salid chose a seminary for me (Michlelet Esther, a small offshoot of the larger seminary Neve Yerushalayim), and practically wrote my acceptance essay. She really wanted me to go to the right place. I knew nothing about Michlelet Esther, but Mrs. Salid must have known that it was ideal for girls from mixed backgrounds like mine. Rather than place a strong focus on Talmud study or simple accumulation of Torah knowledge, the school gave plenty of space for discussions of philosophy and existential thought. This would be perfect for me.

Within a few short weeks, I was accepted! To Stern, and to Michlelet Esther. My future was free of high school, and I was headed for a year in the beautiful land I remembered fondly from my previous visits.

A few months later, in August 1997, after purchasing the requisite wardrobe of long sleeve shirts and long skirts, I was on my way to Michlelet Esther, with no real idea what to expect. During the plane ride, I bonded with all of the "cool and rebellious" girls (they were easy to find, smoking in the back of the plane). After we landed at Ben Gurion airport, we were all whisked away on a bus destined for Kiryat Moshe, a neighborhood in the heart of Jerusalem. The apartment building where we would be learning and sleeping for the year was dilapidated but quaint. I swapped rooms with some of the other girls so that I could share a room with my new friends. And I settled in for a year of *fun*, enjoying my newfound freedom. Based on my previous experience at religious institutions, I wasn't really hoping for much more than that.

My year in Israel was unlike anything I had ever expected or experienced. To my complete surprise, I had landed in an amazing place, far better than anything I could have imagined. Michlelet Esther was a seminary that seemed particularly designed for someone like me: there weren't too many rules, but there was plenty of wisdom and patience (Mrs. Salid must have really known what she was doing!) The rabbis, teachers, and counselors were caring, and truly knowledgeable. These wise leaders gave me real guidance in the form of truth and deep understanding of the Torah. There were no pat replies to my searching questions; *all* questions were encouraged and discussed at length—which was exactly what I needed. And outside of school, there was my sister, who was always there for me, the very essence of a caring role model. Sharon and Tzion had moved to a new apartment just that year, in order to be closer to Tzion's parents who had lived in Ramat Eshkol since immigrating from Iran some thirty years earlier. I mastered the three-mile walk from Kiryat Moshe to Ramat Eshkol in only a few weeks.

I began my year in Israel with absolutely no desire to move there permanently. When I arrived, my heart was absent of the desire to do much of anything at all, in fact, except go into town and hang out with my boyfriend. Thursday nights were the expected 'go-to-town' nights, but for me, so were Saturday nights, and Sunday nights, and all the other nights of the week. Thankfully, our weekday curfew at seminary was quite generous. At Michlelet Esther, night-time classes were optional, which enabled me to wander around the city to my heart's content every evening as long as I was back before eleven (and if I wanted to stay out late on Thursday, I could always say that I was sleeping at my sister's). I drank in the delicious freedom that came with a *cartis noar* (bus ticket). I could hop on a bus *whenever I wanted to*. No one would stop me. There were no parents in the country to check in with, there was no Mrs. Salid, or nosy neighbors like in Memphis, so I could spend my free time as I saw fit. And to me, spending time as I saw fit meant hanging out at Second Cup (a coffee shop) or roaming Ben Yehuda Street with my friends. In Israel, as far as I could tell, there was no age limit on the purchase of cigarettes, so I promptly developed a light smoking habit to concretize my newfound freedom.

Beyond our free nights, Michlelet Esther also had many other optional classes, and days off around the holidays. On those days, I would take the bus out to Tel Aviv with my boyfriend, roam through the markets in Jaffa, and then spend the afternoon and evening on the beach unabashedly sporting my bikini (in the colorful world of New Orleans and the modern orthodoxy of Memphis that I grew up in, the Jewish laws of modesty seemed to be more of an optional choice than a hard and fast requirement). I got an impromptu nose piercing in the shuk one random night in December. I was living out my teenage dream, reveling in my first forays into the freedom of adulthood without any silly limitations (as I believed them to be at the time) on my behavior.

I wasn't a complete flake. I did attend my daytime classes diligently, searching for Truth with a fiery passion. I wish I could say that I sat and listened to my new rabbis and teachers with quiet humility, but usually I engaged in (disruptive) religious and philosophical debate with these wise and wonderful people. Finally, I had access to teachers who were prepared to engage with my questions and try to answer them.

Rabbi Smith, the head of our school, would sit and discuss Jewish philosophy and thought with me for hours. He made me feel, despite my youth and immaturity, that my questions were valuable and important. Over the course of our discussions, he helped me find answers to many things. Growing up, I had always felt intelligent and capable. I had believed that I could decipher and solve any problem if I just applied my intellect and patience. The most profound realization I had that year was that this assumption was untrue. No matter how much I thought about God, or tried to disentangle the meaning of the world, I could never *truly* comprehend the real meaning of life *because I was not God*. This concept was liberating for me. As a physical being, my ability to understand divine truths would always be limited. But that meant that I could rest easier knowing that I could deepen my understanding and come closer to Truth, even if I could never fully grasp it. It was Rabbi Smith's talks that brought me to this understanding.

I began to spend more time exploring the concepts of meditation and spirituality. Knowing that my intellect was, indeed, limited, tapping into the truth contained in my soul seemed like a good way to connect to the divine. And being exposed to this deeper side of Judaism eventually sent me on a journey towards Torah study and further halachic observance.

Often, I would spend Shabbat with my older sister. My relationship with her became just as transformative as the ones I was developing with my teachers. My sister had always been a loving, caring, and accepting person; when she was little, her nickname in school was Smiley. Sharon has always seen the world through rose-colored glasses. I could do no wrong in her eyes. Twelve years my senior, she had been out of the house by the time I was five or six years old, and when I was a child, she was my bubbly and happy older sister, sending me notes and packages full of candy from afar. When she came home to visit, she would fill the house with her melodious singing; in the shower, in the kitchen. Sometimes, she would take me into her room and give me a complete makeover, decking me out in layers of makeup like a child model.

That year in Israel, although I was seventeen, she took care of me like I was still a child, doing my laundry and cooking delicious meals specifically suited to my tastes, yet she treated me like an adult. I learned about life from spending time with her family. I began to understand what a value-driven existence looked like by watching her mother her two small children in her teeny tiny apartment in Ramat Eshkol. Sometimes she would send me to the park with Meir, the two-year-old, along with five shekel and instructions to buy him a popsicle at the store if he behaved. He was wild and fun. I *loved* him. And although my sister managed with Meir and his baby brother, Akiva, 24/7, I enjoyed my small opportunities to help her out and take care of the kids. For the first time in my life, I developed a true adult quality: the ability to care for people other than myself.

I met my teachers' families, too. They seemed different than the families I had known in America. They were raising their children in a less materialistic society than the one I had seen around me while growing up. It was easy to see the simplicity and gratitude that that kind of life instilled in people. Without the fancy toys, clothes, and baubles, they seemed far better off.

As I began to spend more and more time immersed in Torah study, my life felt richer. Change was not instantaneous, but for someone like me, it was inevitable. I was surrounded by real wisdom. And I possessed a thirst for knowledge and truth. Tranquility finally found its place inside my soul; I felt less like the rolling tempest I had been, thundering through the terrain of daily life. And I began to realize how rich and meaningful life could be with a steady dose of Torah and Jewish thought available at any time.

I felt happy and content in a way that I had never felt before. Throughout my years of day school, prep school, and modern orthodox high school, I had waited to experience a type of Judaism that I felt that I could connect to, profoundly and personally. For the first time in my life, I had easy access to what I believed to be a more thoroughly authentic Judaism, and true Jewish ideas, on the level that I needed. That experience shaped the way I felt about Israel. For me, Israel became the place where true spiritual pursuit was available, where religion was valued. All throughout the country, prayer and learning were accessible in a group setting, on a daily basis. Most of all, it was a place where great people, great teachers, and great leaders lived out their lives. It wasn't that the people I met lived charmed lives, at least not from a material perspective.

Most of them didn't have much in the way of possessions. But between their families and their Torah, they were living fulfilling lives, in the land that tied their beliefs all together in a complete package. And most importantly, their communities supported them in their way of life.

After my year in Israel, it seemed to me that, in this land, if you could just go with the flow and soak up some of the goodness all around, life would be okay. I grew to love small, poor, Israel. Having grown closer to my Jewish heritage and developed a deeper understanding of what I thought God wanted from me, I made some decisions about life. I decided that whenever I married and had children, Israel was where I wanted to raise them. I felt that Israel was really the only place that Jewish children *should* be raised. It's funny to think, looking back, that so simple a motivation could have convinced me to make such a huge move, but I was young and strong-willed. Once I made a decision that I believed in, I stuck to it.

At that point in my early adulthood, I didn't understand the complexities that come along with living in Israel. I only saw the good things about life there. But that good was *so* powerful and *so* profound that it seemed a worthy goal to make Israel my future home, no matter what small comforts I had to give up. And all comforts seemed small to me when compared to the deeper understanding of Torah I had found, that I wanted to share with my future children.

By the end of the year, I had begun to see beauty in halachic practices that I had never really ascribed much importance to. The small details of Shabbat, prayer, and modesty sudden-ly seemed to be profoundly important in the context of my life as a religious Jew. Torah study was no longer something I did in order to pass a test—instead, I began reading texts (in English) for enrichment, unearthing pearls of wisdom to add to my general understanding of life. I searched out mentors and role models, so much more readily available in the Holy Land, to guide me on my journey towards deeper observance. Finally, after completing my seminary year in Israel, I looked forward to a future guided by principles, one day living in Israel, as a Torah Jew.

The Blessing of Connection

ONE OF THE strangest realizations of adulthood is that hardship can actually bring a person closer to God. After my year in Israel, I had a sense that this country was different than my birthplace; the large and small struggles of life in Israel seemed perfectly designed to foster a relationship with the divine.

This idea of human struggle translating into a direct connection to God is a very old one, appearing just after the opening scene in our Torah. Following their sin in the Garden of Eden, God cursed man, woman, and snake. He cursed man with toil and labor; from now on, man would have to suffer to earn his bread. Woman received the curse of painful childbirth. And the serpent was given the following curse: "Cursed are you above all the livestock and all the wild animals! You will crawl on your belly, and you will eat dust all the days of your life" (Genesis 3:14).

At first glance, this seems like kind of a backwards curse. Is it a punishment to be able to be satiated with dust of the earth, food available just by slithering, while humans are forced to toil for their bread? But this *is* a real punishment, a punishment of rejection. After the serpent's sin, God wanted to have nothing more to do with it. With food readily available, the serpent would not have to turn to God for help—there would be no further connection to the divine. Humans, on the other hand, remained dependent on God to ease their pain and suffering. Forever, they would be obliged to turn their thoughts heavenward, whether to beseech God to alleviate suffering or to request greater blessing. This "curse" had a positive effect for humankind on their way out of the Garden of Eden; it ensured that there would be a long-lasting relationship between man and his Creator.

Similarly, when the Jews were freed from Egypt, they left behind a country where water had been readily available. The Nile overflowed at regular intervals, irrigating crops with its abundant water supply. There was no water shortage in Egypt; no need to ask God for rain. By contrast, the Land of Israel, the Jews' Promised Land, was entirely dependent upon rainwater for its sustenance. To be blessed with rain, the Jews were required to turn to God in prayer.

This dependence on the divine in Israel is not a curse, but rather a sign that God desires a closer relationship with the Jewish people. To this day, we pray to God three times a day during the rainy season in Israel with the words, "*Mashiv HaRuach u'Morid HaGeshem*—the One Who makes the wind blow, and the rain descend." We recognize that it is God Who causes the rain to fall, sustaining our crops and the water supply in our land.

Once the Jews were sent into *Galut* (exile), they lost this element of special connection to God. Most abandoned farming practices altogether. Our connection to the tangible results of our daily prayers for rain vanished, and our direct relationship with God changed.

Now, the Jews as a nation have returned to our land. Through this relocation, we have an opportunity to reconnect to God in a special way; our prayer for rain in Israel, *"Mashiv HaRuach u'Morid HaGeshem,"* has direct relevance in our lives once again. Living here, we pay close attention to the forecast after Sukkot, when the official rainy season begins. As we wait for the land's resources to be replenished, for the earth to turn green again, our prayers intensify. Rain matters. When we lack rain, we hear about it in the synagogue, on the news, and in conversation on the city streets. As a country, we are filled with gratitude when the rain starts to fall.

With our new independence and autonomy as a people in our own land, we can once again reap the blessings that God bestows on our people *as a unified nation*: rain in the wintertime, flourishing fields and orchards, and our very own cities and towns full of Jewish schools and synagogues, hospitals, and housing, nurtured by these blessings. All of this is ours in Israel, the land where our nation's close connection to God is palpable, something we experience each and every day.

IV.

To Follow a Dream

"In order to be a realist, you must believe in miracles." -David Ben Gurion

A FEW SHORT MONTHS later, I found myself immersed in life as an Orthodox Jew at Stern College, part of Yeshiva University. Now that I was no longer an angst-ridden teenager, I was able to focus during classes. The Jewish studies at Stern enriched my Torah knowledge, an area that I was sorely lacking compared to many of my college peers.

I settled quite happily into life in New York City, with old and new friends, missing Israel, but feeling that my time back in the United States was only temporary. With my credits from Michlelet Esther and credit from some AP classes in high school, it would only take about two-and-a-half years to complete the rest of my college education. I hoped to find a life partner, get married, and move to Israel for good within the next few years.

And that December, I met my husband, Avi, my roommate Leah's older brother. We were an unexpected match.

Avi came from an always-religious family in New Jersey, the heart of American Jewish modern orthodoxy; his grandparents were Holocaust survivors. I was from the tiny Jewish community of New Orleans, a real "out of towner" with a very colorful background. One weekend, Leah brought me home for Shabbat, and as we all settled down on the living room couches after dinner, Avi and I struck up a conversation. We found ourselves drawn to each other because of our similar ways of thinking – we were both on a quest to make sense of it all. I don't think it hurt that, for him, I was an exotic and different sort of Jew. And to me, he was classically Orthodox, someone who had grown up with Torah and traditional Judaism and could share that with me.

After Shabbat, he drove me back to my dormitory. We exchanged numbers right before he dropped me off. That winter, we began walking the streets of New York City together in the freezing cold, engaging in philosophical discussion. It didn't take much time before our long conversations had blossomed into a romantic relationship, one that swept us up and took over both our lives. We began seeing each other every single day. Thanks to our shared love of activity and the outdoors, we made several forays beyond the city streets and into nature. At that point, Avi was also in Yeshiva University, so we used Manhattan as our jumping point into all sorts of adventures. We went on early morning walks along the Hudson River, explored the bird sanctuary near Avi's home in New Jersey, and drove out to the beach.

Within a few months, we knew that we wanted to spend the rest of our lives together. There was only one potential issue—Avi wasn't sure that he wanted to move to Israel. He had grown up in an Orthodox, Zionist community, and making aliyah had actually been his dream too, just a year or two before we met, so much so that he had actually already tried to fulfill it, by going to Israel to study at an engineering college there. But after some time, he felt the pain of being isolated from his family, his friends, and his mother tongue. That was when he decided that perhaps the whole Israel thing wasn't for him, and he had returned to America. Still, it wasn't long before he came around to the idea of making aliyah; this time, with a life partner. Once we finished school and established a cash backup, we would go.

That summer, on July 25, 1999, we got married back home in New Orleans. Our wedding was a small and festive event, complete with New Orleans jazz, a kosher "seafood" buffet, and Mardi Gras paraphernalia. My in-laws' friends all flew in from their New Jersey community, ready to celebrate at an entirely different type of destination wedding. My friends from Memphis and Michlelet Esther flew in from around the country, along with my relatives from Italy and Portugal. Avi's friends all came too. Between the unique atmosphere and the closeness of most of the guests, it was a wedding to remember (just ask anyone who was there).

After the first joyous round of dancing, Avi and I washed for *hamotzi* and sat down in front of two massive challahs. Avi sawed away until he managed to cut the very end of the challah into pieces to share with our guests. Mendel Gottesman, a close friend of the family from back in Teaneck, arrived at our table at that moment, to grab the platter and stop for a chat.

"Great party," he shouted over the music. In the background, we could hear the members of our band, mostly flown in from New Jersey, playing traditional Jewish wedding music. Mendel was decked out in oversized Mardi Gras beads and a feather boa. I asked him where he'd got it all.

"We went on a French Quarter tour today, and picked up some stuff," he explained. "Hey, where's the jazz music?"

Just as he uttered those words, I heard the band switch their tune. When I realized what they were playing, I was mortified. And then, they started to sing. "Oh when the saints! Go marching in...oh when the saints go marching in...."

As a New Orleans native, I had known that the band had to play jazz at my wedding—it's what the guests were hoping for, after all! But as a newly serious Jew, I had requested that they *not* play "When the Saints go Marching in," a Christian hymn.

Mendel certainly didn't seem to mind. He put the challah platter back in its place as he stepped into a new line dance that had formed and was now weaving its way around the hall past our table. The line included my new in-law's friends, my father in-law, and yes, even the rabbi.

Afterwards, we stopped off in Memphis for one Sheva Brachot dinner, then continued on to our apartment in Teaneck, New Jersey, where we would settle down for the next couple of years.

Life really changed over those years. I had never before lived in such a large Orthodox Jewish community. Our apartment building was full of other young Orthodox couples, living similar lives. The streets nearby were lined with kosher pizza places, bagel shops, and one giant kosher store. Most of our friends and neighbors were decidedly comfortable living in this center of Modern Orthodoxy. I watched the women around me as they switched fashions at every season, buying new hats, dresses, and skirts to match the changing styles (which I could never seem to keep up with). Avi felt frustrated by the conversations at shul, mostly full of sports talk and stocks. But we found friends, people who seemed to share our values. And the best part about Teaneck was that my in-laws lived just a five-minute drive away, albeit in an entirely different community with its own shul.

By November time, I was pregnant with my first daughter. Avi had completed his studies at Yeshiva University and was beginning the last two, much more challenging, years of his engineering program at Columbia University. As a nineteen-year-old married and pregnant woman, I fit right in at Stern. There were lots of other women in the same life stage. I was happy that I had decided to stay there and abandon my once-cherished dream of an Ivy League education. My priorities had changed since high school.

I studied computer programming in the undergraduate business school, SySyms, another branch of Yeshiva University. Avi dropped me off every morning before driving on to the Columbia University campus nearby. My choice of major was born more out of necessity, than of any deep connection to the subject. I hoped that, as a programming major, I would easily be able to find a job working from home, should I decide to, and be available take care of my growing family.

In September of 2000, I gave birth to my daughter, Elie. Avi and I were both still in college. To my complete bewilderment, she came home from the hospital crying, and didn't stop for three months. I had no idea what to do. As a youngest child, I had absolutely no experience in baby management. Thank God for my mother, who flew in from New Orleans and moved into our apartment for two weeks, leaving her neurology practice behind so she could show me the ropes of motherhood.

Still, after my mother left, Elie continued to cry, all day and all night, whether we held her, bounced her, rocked her, or tried absolutely anything else. All of this crying made it a struggle for me to finish my last semester of school. This was especially true because Avi, as a full-time engineering student at Columbia, really had his hands full. My classes were far easier, so somehow, I was able to wing it and succeed by studying at home and showing up for tests.

Although there were times that I really didn't think we would, eventually we made it through those first really challenging months. Come mid-January, I had graduated, and Elie had *finally* stopped crying all the time. I remember feeling as if I was coming out of a deep haze. Suddenly, life seemed wonderful and peaceful again.

During my last months as a college student, I had considered what direction I should take after graduation. Being the daughter of two full-time physicians, I had just assumed that I would try to find some sort of employment. My good friend, Rivka, who lived in the apartment next door, had other ideas for me. She knocked on our door one evening with a stack of magazine articles and studies, all pointing to evidence that kids were better off when one parent stayed at home instead of working and putting their child in day-care during infancy and toddlerhood. Since Rivka had become a mother a year earlier than I had—she was practically a veteran!—I valued her advice and opinions. Soon, I was convinced—rather than try to juggle work (however light-weight) and childcare, I would give up on a career in order to be a full time, stay at home parent. We had enough money saved up to get us through Avi's final months of schooling, to the point where he would begin earning a regular salary. We were prepared to budget carefully and live on just one source of income so I could stay home with Elie.

Now, as my 'career' as a stay at home mom took off, for the first time I had nowhere I had to run off to—no more juggling motherhood with school. It was just Avi, Elie, and me, welcoming the end of winter and the approaching spring season from our little apartment in Teaneck. By Pesach time, we were ready to plan a post-newbornhood vacation, just the three of us. Israel was the obvious choice.

So, in May, we went to visit Israel for the first time as a married couple, with seven-month-old Elie in tow. I don't know if we thought of it precisely as a pilot trip at the time, but a five week trip to Israel (trying not to blow through the rest of our wedding savings along the way) seemed just the thing to do after Avi's graduation, before he started his new job in tech as part of the Management Associate Program in Citigroup Global Technology. Going to Israel was an im-pulsive thing to do. Had we been thinking practically, we probably would have come to the conclusion that it was a *bad* idea to go on a five week vacation with just fifteen thousand dollars in the bank. But our hearts were telling us to go to Israel. We needed a vacation, and we definitely needed some time in the Holy Land. And it turned out to be the best emotionally motivated decision we ever made.

We stayed in Jerusalem, in a beautiful apartment in Ramat Eshkol discovered by and booked for us by my sister. There were Japanese plum and other fruit trees in the yard, which made the place feel like a little paradise compared to our sterile apartment block in Teaneck. We spent those five weeks exploring the land and trying to recapture the magic of our prior years, when we had learned and lived in Israel. We took buses to museums and into the center of town, set off to the south to visit Masada and Ein Gedi once again, and toured archaeological remains in the Old City. I visited my old seminary and showed off my new baby daughter.

The trip was wonderful in a way that only vacation can be—but Israel wasn't some exotic, far-off destination we would never return to. It was where we wanted to build our lives! My baby daughter was getting to know her cousins who *lived* there. The trip reinforced our mutual desire to make Israel our home.

One weekend, we rented a car and drove up to Tzfat. A friend had given us the number of a family she knew who lived in Tzfat's old city—Americans, with grown-up children. They served us homemade chocolate croissants and took us to see their secret pool on the roof of their home. After a beautiful Shabbat, we went even further north, stopping at a winery in the Golan, and then turning back south to visit the Sea of Galilee.

For another of our five shabbatot in Israel, we visited Ramat Beit Shemesh, described to us as a "new American community," suggested by one of the young rabbis at my seminary. Ramat Beit Shemesh seemed like a dream to us. We stayed in a two-story apartment that had been vacated for Shabbat by the young family who lived there. It was clean, modern, and full of American toys for our daughter. We ate each meal with a different family, all of them incredibly generous and welcoming. Everyone we met just seemed so *friendly*, and they all spoke English. This new community was clearly the place to be for new immigrants. It was also the first time I had visited any community in Israel in which the residents didn't all live in small, cramped apartments. We had come to accept the fact that to live in Israel was to live in relative discomfort, so the idea that we might one day live in a duplex apartment or a house, and still live in Israel, seemed almost too good to be true. But there it was, we had found it—in Ramat Beit Shemesh. As we enjoyed the rest of our five weeks in Israel, we talked about what it would be like to live in Ramat Beit Shemesh one day in the future.

That summer, we arrived back home in Teaneck, New Jersey, inspired. The distance between Israeli culture and American culture felt even more pronounced after our trip, and our desire to raise our children in a less materialistic and more Torah-focused world had been reinforced. We began making concrete aliyah plans.

It was August of 2001. Avi had signed an eighteen-month

contract with Citigroup to be a participant on a special management program. The program would allow him to relocate to a different branch in another part of the world after the first nine months as an employee, and we hoped that different branch would be in Israel.

Unfortunately, when the first nine months were just about over, in the spring of 2002, we were disappointed to discover that Israel wasn't on the rotation list. Our two options for relocation were London and Hong Kong. Since by that time I was pregnant with our second, due in the fall, it seemed like a bad idea to fly off to another country that wasn't Israel. After my experience with Elie, I knew that newborns could be incredibly challenging, and this time around would perhaps be even more difficult since I would also have a toddler at home to take care of. It would be better if we stayed in Teaneck for another full year, getting the help we would need from my in-laws after the birth of our second child. So, we decided on a new date for our aliyah—the summer of 2003.

As time passed, slowly, it began to feel like Israel was a distant dreamland, one which I hoped to reach one day. Our next-door neighbors, Rivka and Elie Wildman, also dreamed of making aliyah. In the summer of 2002, we wished each other tearful goodbyes as they made aliyah with the very first Nefesh b'Nefesh flight. I was so happy that they were fulfilling this dream that I shared, but I also felt incredibly jealous.

We stuck around in Teaneck. I gave birth to our first son, Eitan, on October 28, 2002, and was very grateful that even if I wasn't in Israel, I was in close proximity to my husband's family, who constantly made themselves available to help with the many challenging tasks in the life of a stay-at-home mom with two small children. Eitan, thankfully, did not cry all the time, but he was still a typical baby, and we didn't sleep much. The snow fell relentlessly, and the cold weather seemed to drag on forever. My car seemed to get stuck in the snow more often than it successfully drove through it. It was a long, hard winter. Still, as the months passed, Elie was becoming a cute little person, and Eitan eventually grew out of the exhausting newborn phase.

In spring 2003, we *finally* began the aliyah process. Each step felt like an adventure, from going 220-volt appliance shopping to having our apartment's contents sized and priced to be moved across the ocean by ship. Life felt full and purposeful as we juggled paperwork, dealing with Israeli bureaucracy, and going to informative meetings about Israeli culture and real estate. At those events, we met other future olim and learned more about the small details of life in Israel. From a distance, my sister and the Wildmans instructed and assisted us with our aliyah plans. We learned what we should and shouldn't bring, what the moving process looked like, and even arranged an apartment rental from afar.

Came summertime and we couldn't believe that it was actually happening. We had been waiting for this moment our whole married life together, and we were almost there. We packed up our apartment into boxes and bubble wrap and sent it off, on a ship across the ocean, with a mixture of happiness and trepidation. Then we moved into my in-laws' house for a month, to wait for our departure to Israel on the second ever Nefesh b'Nefesh aliyah flight, in July 2003.

We were lucky that both Avi's parents and my parents were completely positive about our move to Israel. Avi's parents were Zionists; although it must have been hard for them to see their only grandchildren move so far away, they believed that our decision to move to Israel was right, and they supported us completely. My parents, already used to having my sister overseas, decided that they would come visit us in Israel every few months.

Arriving at the airport on July 8th, we could already feel that this flight would be like nothing we had experienced before. The terminal was buzzing with an unusual mixture of excitement and sadness. There were plenty of tears as everyone hugged their relatives and said goodbye… and dancing, as it dawned on all of us that our dreams were actually coming true. On the flight itself, no one around us slept. While I wouldn't have minded an hour of shut eye, we were all too jazzed up. Eitan, now eight months old, slept soundly in his car seat while Elie peered around curiously at all of the hubbub, only sleeping for a couple of hours during the long flight. The other passengers were all new immigrants, like us, so we were all busy exchanging stories and making connections. It felt like we were part of a big happy club that we had never known existed.

When the plane landed, we all clapped and sang. Our longing had been fulfilled, and my husband and I felt complete joy as our flight taxied to a stop at Ben Gurion. Our now two-and-a-half-year-old daughter woke up with the noise and looked around, picking up on the thrill growing inside the plane. She clapped and sang along with the crowd. We were exhausted, but we were finally here, starting our new life. Living our dream.

Of course, at that moment, I had no concept of how my views on living in Israel would grow and develop. I had no foreknowledge of the many challenges or amazing experiences that would come our way just by virtue of the fact that our lives would be lived in Israel.

We disembarked to a meaningful welcoming ceremony. My sister had come to greet us, and she and Tzion stood among the crowd in the airport hangar with their entire family, which now included five small children. It was a beautiful ceremony, only slightly marred by one reporter who questioned us from the sidelines, "Why did you leave America? In America you can make a million dollars!"

Despite knowing full well that he was on the verge of being jobless, Avi replied, "I can make a million dollars in Israel too!" For the time being, he would be continuing his employment at Citigroup remotely, on a week-by-week basis, just until he had completed the knowledge transfer that was required. He was smart, talented, and capable—surely, we thought, he could find some financial success even in this new land of no guarantees. We had both agreed that, should push come to shove, he could get a job flipping burgers at Burger Ranch (not that we really imagined that it would come to that). Somehow, our financial worries took a back seat to our idealism. It helped that we only had two small children, and a bit of money in the bank. Under these circumstances, we figured that we had sufficient resources to get us through a few months of job searching. I guess that was our leap of faith. With very few material needs at that time, our desire to move to Israel seemed more important than financial certainty. And, truly, we weren't thinking very much about making a million dollars.

We stood through the ceremony, listened to speeches, and sang "Hatikva" with overflowing hearts. We were here. We had made it. We were *home*. In the place where we had vowed we would raise our children and live out our future. Then, tired, sweaty, euphoric and worn out, we waved good-bye to Sharon and Tzion and my many nieces and nephews, knowing that this wasn't a real goodbye—we would be see-ing a lot of each other now. Then we boarded our free taxi for the forty-five-minute ride to Ramat Beit Shemesh, and promptly fell asleep.

When we pulled up at our temporary apartment in Ramat Beit Shemesh, generously lent to us by the Wildmans, who were back in America visiting family, we were jerked out of our slumber by the friendly taxi driver. "*Alo, chevre...higanu,*" he said as he shifted the van into park.

We've arrived.

It felt like we were still dreaming. Stumbling out of the taxi with our suitcases and small children, we thanked the driver and made our way down into what was going to be our home for the next few weeks.

As the door opened, I smelled Israel: summer, sunshine, and soap. We scoped out the small apartment: a highchair with a few remnants of Cheerios, American toys filling the toy chests, the cream colored couches we remembered from the Wildmans' old apartment in Teaneck. This was our home, at least for now. We lay our exhausted children down on the beds in the kids' room: one car-shaped toddler bed and one wooden bunkbed. Next, we found the big bedroom, put fresh sheets on the mattresses, and settled in for our first long nap as a family in our new land.

The Transformative Power of Aliyah

AS I CHILD, I remember learning that the Jewish people were special, the "Chosen People." Because of this, Jews are supposed to act as an *Or LaGoyim*, a light unto the nations. Our nation's higher purpose is to demonstrate, by example, the correct way to live and behave. Each and every one of us is supposed to live out our individual lives in *kiddush Hashem* (sanctification of God's name).

But after moving to Israel, I discovered that there is another level to living as the chosen people, something beyond our individual experience and responsibility:

"This *nation* I have formed for myself; they shall declare my praise," (Isaiah 43:21). In other words, part of our job of sanctifying God's name is connected to our existence as a nation.

Rav Tzvi Yehuda HaCohen Kook, son of Rav Avraham Yitzchak Kook, Israel's first chief rabbi and the father of religious Zionism, elaborated on this idea: "The Kuzari explains that our unique essence is as a community, and not as individuals (*Kuzari* 1:95)…Our whole nation is holy, as Isaiah says, 'Your people shall *all* be righteous (Isaiah, 60:21).'"[1]

Rav Kook took these verses from Isaiah to mean that our

---

1   *Torat Eretz Yisrael*, The Teachings of HaRav Tzvi Yehuda HaCohen Kook (Jerusalem: Torat Eretz Yisrael Publications, 1991), pp.106–8.

true purpose and value as Jews is as a nation, a community. He wrote further: "The specifically designated place on this planet for this segment of mankind [the Jews] is here in the Land of Israel. 'And who is like Israel, one nation in the land?' (II Samuel 7:23). The *Zohar* states: 'In Israel, they are one nation' (*Zohar*, Emor, 93). In Israel, and not outside of it."[2]

What I learned later in life is that Judaism is more than a religion—we are a people. One of the things that makes the Jews special is our nationhood; the only place where we can properly fulfill our role as a nation is in our homeland, the Land of Israel. Just as every other nation is connected to their particular land, God's nation belongs to the Land of Israel. And it is only in Israel that we can completely fulfill our mission to sanctify God's name.

Furthermore, according to Rav Kook, this idea doesn't only apply to the Jewish people as a nation; rather, each *individual* Jew can only reach their own personal pinnacle of development by being in Israel. This is particularly true now, thanks to the benefits we enjoy as Jews in our modern-day State of Israel. In other places around the world, we can't benefit as *Jews*, even on an individual level, from our own government, our own army, or a national calendar that is based on the lunar cycle that we follow. Outside of Israel, we don't necessarily live within a system that supports our values, our religion, and ties them into the fabric of our daily lives. Living in Israel makes our lives as Jews complete, enabling us to fully achieve our highest potential and serve our God and nation.

---

2   Ibid.

So, what happens when a Jew moves to Israel? Rav Kook, who was a great student of mysticism, believed that a Jew's soul is transformed when he arrives, and not in a metaphorical sense: "This is an actual occurrence, not always recognized on a cognizant level, but a phenomenon which has a profound internal effect."[3]

As Rav Kook asserted, living in Israel transforms a person. This is true even if they're not aware of it, and even if they aren't *planning* on being transformed. For Jews, being in Israel allows us to fulfill our unique purpose as a people on earth.

3   Ibid.

V.

Enchantment and Sacrifice

"For the Lord has chosen Zion; He has desired it for His habitation. This is My resting place; Here I will dwell." –Psalms 132:13

GRADUALLY WE SETTLED into a routine in our new country. When our rental apartment became available, a few weeks after our aliyah, we moved a block away from the Wildmans into a fourth-floor apartment with a beautiful view out to the mountains. In September, Elie began attending a small English-speaking playgroup across the street. Avi continued working at his American job remotely, which was still being extended on a week-to-week basis so he could finish up his knowledge transfer. He worked from home. I spent my mornings taking care of Eitan, making friends at the park, and learning the ropes of this new life in a familiar foreign land.

I was living my dream. For years, I had idealized the life I was now living. Even as a kid, before my plans included Israel, I had fantasized about being a mom, a prim and perfect caretaker. The reality, I had already discovered, may have been less than prim and perfect (changing dirty diapers at 3 AM, anyone?) But I was so happy now, raising our two little kids in our Israeli apartment with its speckled wall-to-wall tile, outfitted with our own American area rugs and plush bedding. For the first time, I felt like I was truly living my own independent life—away from my husband's family's familiar life in Teaneck, away from the material pressures of the Orthodox world in America. Although we were still renting, this new place somehow felt more our own.

When we ventured forth from our apartment, we would visit the area's many parks and playgrounds. With two little kids, our outings were still quite limited, but even a trip to a quiet park (with stunning views out to the Judean mountains in the distance) made us appreciate the special place we were living in. Since Avi's job was flexible, we had time to go wandering all together, in the land that I had dreamed of living in for years.

At least once a week, I set off to Jerusalem with the kids to visit my sister. Sharon was a stay-at-home mom too, so we had plenty of opportunities to hang out, wander the playgrounds of Ramat Eshkol, have pita-pizza picnics in the park with popsicles for dessert, and take in the magical atmosphere of the Holy City while we checked off her errands. This juxtaposition of the mundane with the wonderful made me feel like I was living in a dream world. There I was, with my amazing older sister, living everyday life in Israel.

Along with my children, I rediscovered shoko-in-a-bag and Bissli. We scouted out colorful wildflowers, which we quickly learned not to pick, a well-known rule in Israel! The world is often novel and exciting for children, but in Israel, that's how I felt too. I felt like a child again, with a child's delight, but all the while, the adult in me was attempting to gain a deeper understanding of the country that was now my home.

Holiday spirit was in the air. Seasonal songs played over the loudspeaker in grocery stores and shopping centers. Crowds filled the streets, shopping for gifts and special food for the holidays. Christmas spirit was everywhere…wait a minute. Did I just say Christmas spirit? What I meant was Rosh Hashana spirit! This kind of pre-Jewish holiday excitement all around us was something completely new to me. Perhaps you're thinking, *Hey, wait, I know what that's all about! I've been in Israel for the High Holidays, and boy is it special!* Well, I'll venture to say that until you experience this time of year as a fulltime resident of Israel, especially a resident of a religious town, you simply can't imagine the extent to which the Jewish holidays so thoroughly take over your everyday activities. Actually, you probably can imagine it. It *is* like Christmas in America. You know the drill: Once Christmas season arrives, candy canes and Santa hats appear everywhere—at the grocery store, at work, in the libraries. Christmas carols play on repeat over the radio. When you go shopping, every cashier wishes you a Happy Holidays… or even a Merry Christmas. The Jewish holidays in Israel are similar. Holiday preparation and merrymaking affects all the minutiae of daily life. The difference is that in Israel, as a Jew, everyone is celebrating *your* holidays. For me, this experience was one of the most thrilling of my aliyah. As Rosh Hashanah drew near, we began to see pre-holiday *shiurim* (classes) advertised all around town. I would start my day hearing the soul-touching call of the shofar echoing through the streets. This continued throughout the morning, as *minyanim* (prayer groups) scheduled at different times would announce the Hebrew month of Elul and the approaching holiday with shofar blasts. I would hear the shofar's call on my morning runs and when taking Elie to pre-school, and while I completed my everyday tasks. They called out to me to focus inward, spiritually.

I was reminded of Rosh Hashanah's approach in more mundane ways as well. Come September, there were rock-bottom sales on honey in the grocery store—the typically pricey product was offered as: "Buy one, get the second for just one shekel!" And most entertaining: when I went to purchase our usual loaf of gefilte fish at the store during the weeks before Rosh Hashana, it came with a frozen fish head attached, a boon for those who include one in their Rosh Hashana seder.

Instead of saying goodbye when I left a store, or parted with friends and acquaintances on the streets, we said "*Shana Tova*,"—Have a Good Year. I really enjoyed taking part in this new way of saying hello and goodbye. In my old life in America, I had struggled to keep track of the Jewish calendar, especially when it came to mentally preparing for the holidays. As a young mom whose life was ruled by sleep schedules and diaper changes, I found it hard to even remember what month it was! In Israel, my new home, I had no trouble remembering that it was Elul—the reminders were *everywhere*. Every interaction throughout the day reminded me that it was time for me to focus on personal refinement and repentance.

Once I finally got used to the flurry of Rosh Hashana preparations, they all stopped. Several hours before the holiday began, the streets quieted down to a solemn silence to welcome the Days of Awe. Rosh Hashana itself was an experience unlike any I had ever had before. In America, the holiday usually fell on a weekday, so car traffic, mail deliveries, and construction noise continued even in the large Jewish community of Teaneck. Not so in our new community in Israel, where the only traffic on Rosh Hashana was the foot traffic of worshippers going to and from synagogue, and families joining one another for the festival meals.

The charged atmosphere continued during the week between Rosh Hashana and Yom Kippur. The daily greeting changed; "*Gmar Chatima Tova*," became the refrain. There was no mistaking the time of year. On the morning of the big day, I witnessed many the mad dash through the streets as my neighbors ran out to give charity and dip in the mikva before the fast. Chickens squawked in the streets where crowds gathered to perform *kaparot*, a ceremony that involves metaphorically 'placing' your sins on a chicken, which is then slaughtered and donated to the needy. All the people around me were completely focused on achieving forgiveness from God with the help of this ritual, giving *tzedakah* (charity), and their contrite prayers.

On Yom Kippur itself, everything shut down. It felt like the whole country prayed together as one. The streets and highways were free from car traffic, once again. Solemnity and hope hung in the air as the majority of the Jews in Israel (even many who don't consider themselves to be observant) fasted and prayed for twenty-five hours.

Once the holiest day of the year had passed, rejoicing over God's forgiveness of the nation commenced—in the form of loud banging. As if everyone had tuned in to a new national rhythm, huts for the festival of Sukkot started to go up everywhere, hammers loudly announcing the change in pace. Sukkot is so important that all religious Israelis consider the size of the "Sukkah *mirpeset*" (balcony) when purchasing or renting an apartment—despite the fact that it's only actually relevant for one week of the entire year. Every resident of our neighborhood built their very own Sukkah, whether they had to squeeze it onto the teeniest apartment balcony or could construct an elaborate home away from home in their sprawling garden.

In our first apartment in Israel, our balcony was located off of our master bedroom. Our sukkah *mirpeset* wasn't tiny—it was miniscule. Still, it was the first time we had had an opportunity to build our own Sukkah in four years of married life—our apartment in New Jersey had had no outdoor space at all for Sukkah building. Before we moved to Israel, Sukkot for us had involved visiting our parents, or searching for public sukkot to eat in. During the week, we would huddle in the cold on folding chairs and share sandwiches near other displaced Jews in Teaneck or Manhattan.

After years of marriage during which we never had a Sukkah at all, our own tiny little Sukkah off our bedroom in Israel was tremendously exciting.

My husband planned it all out down to the last, minute detail. Then he drove to one of the many Sukkah pop up shops around town, consulted his plans, and picked out the requisite wood, cloth, nails, *schach* (roofing made of completely natural material, as required by halacha), and lots of tinsel (his family tradition). He knocked the Sukkah together over the course of a couple of days, only risking his life a few times as he dangled precariously from our fourth-floor balcony. I steered totally clear of this exercise at tempting fate, preferring that our small children not get any wild ideas about what constituted proper balcony-safety protocol. But when the banging stopped, there it was! We had our first little Sukkah in Israel.

I felt an abundance of pride. I was proud that my family could experience the holiday of Sukkot the way that Jews were meant to—with our very own sukkah. My eyes teared up as we put the finishing touches on the Sukkah, stapling my three-year-old's pictures to the wall. Nostalgia washed over me—my mother had performed this same ritual when I was a little girl. Passing down these traditions, I felt that our kids would finally be able experience the essence of our faith.

Once the holiday began, we seized every opportunity to head into the Sukkah, occasionally pulling back the curtains to watch the neighborhood action. There were lots of people to look at on that holiday—not only families walking in the streets, but friends in their sukkot in nearby buildings.

During the days leading up to the holiday, we had paid special attention to our downstairs neighbors as they constructed their Sukkah, looking down on them every morning and night. Their teenage girls had made adorning the Sukkah walls with decorations a daily activity, laughing and talking all the while, a picture-perfect scene of family life. Now they were hosting loud nightly gatherings in their beautiful, temporary outdoor home. We loved to peek down at their fun: Would our family be as cute and cohesive as theirs one day?

Throughout the holiday, we dined outside for breakfast, lunch, and dinner. We sat with our children at our tiny table, eating bakery bread or rugelach, watching the sun's rays filter through our white curtain walls. Sometimes we pulled the curtains back to let in the breeze. We felt like we were living in the lap of luxury: it felt unfairly amazing to be able to eat a meal whenever we wanted to; no crowded communal Sukkahs for us. The gorgeous weather *every single day* made it feel even more like a picture-perfect scene out of a storybook.

Somehow, we even managed to host weeknight dinner guests in our little Sukkah. My husband had an old yeshiva buddy who lived in Israel, married, with a baby son and another on the way. We got along well: they were chilled out and fun to be around. The four of us (adults) squeezed in together, my pregnant friend barely able to fit between the wall and the table. I made Pasta Napolitana and Greek salad. We lit candles and laid the table with our best dishes. And despite the Sukkah's size, the atmosphere was declared quite charming. Which to us, of course, it was.

Beyond our sukkah, the daily holiday scene unfolded around us, the whole town celebrating together. Each night, we would hear music pouring forth from *Simchat Beit HaShoeva* parties. Each day, we went on excursions with friends to explore the country. The Wildmans took us on a trip to Neot Kedumim, a biblical landscape reserve that featured a series of different types of sukkot as described in the Mishna. We went to the beach. We went hiking, my husband and I beginning to discover the beautiful local trails in the Jerusalem mountains.

As we set out each morning, we watched our neighbors pack up their cars for their own days out. We found ourselves completely immersed in Sukkot in a way that we never had been before. Just maybe, we thought, this one small transformation made the process of moving to Israel entirely worth it. Our kids would be growing up in a place where their holidays were the country's holidays! Our kids would be able to celebrate their holy days without having to miss work or school! How was it going to feel for them, to see that their nation's values were the same as their own? Would they truly never experience that awkward moment: when they had to explain their weird hut holiday to co-workers or classmates? I could hardly even imagine a childhood without this strange dissonance. What would life be like for my children, now Israeli, growing up in a land where they totally and completely fit in?

For the first time in my life, there was no cause to feel strange or different as the Jewish holidays rolled around—in fact, just the opposite. Experiencing our first series of chagim in Israel as Israelis we truly felt a part of something greater: our inner and outer lives, for the first time, fit perfectly together.

Of course, it wasn't all easy. In fact, once we got past the high of the chagim, many things began to seem difficult. I frequently found myself reduced to tears. Sometimes this occurred in the park, as I tried to negotiate in Hebrew with a seven-year-old over access to the swing for my daughter. Other times, it was on the phone, as I tried to make myself understood to a sales rep, or the bank teller. That foreign language obstacle again. Tears of frustration seemed to be becoming a standard element of my new life in Israel. And one Wednesday morning, I snapped.

I was driving along towards home, minding my own business, when, out of nowhere, an angry-looking police officer appeared, waving me to the side of the road. "Hey!" he yelled at me when I opened the window, wondering what I did wrong. And then, in Hebrew I just about understood: "Why aren't you looking where you're going? Are you staring at your friend on the side of the road?"

He was right. I hadn't been paying close attention. Routine pull-overs to check for terrorists, or whatever the heck they were checking for, were still something I had to get used to. I wasn't yet attuned to the possibility of police officers waving down cars from the side of a residential road. But give a gal a break, will you?

I began bawling and gulping like a three-year-old in the

middle of a temper tantrum. The police officer just gaped at me through the open window. *Uh-oh, what can of worms did I just open,* was what he was clearly thinking. But what he said was, "*At beseder geveret? Hakol beseder?*" (Are you alright, Ma'am? Is everything alright?)

He awaited my answer as I gulped back the tears. "No!" I snapped, trying to gain control of my emotions "I'm not okay. I don't understand why all you *people*," heave, sigh, "Are *out to get me*!" Sob.

"Okay," the policeman said, in a new, more soothing voice, "Okay. Just be careful. Go home." He waved me away with a look of sympathy which may have included a touch of guilt.

I rolled up the window, attempted a few deep breaths, rubbed my eyes, and slowly pulled away to drive the five minutes home with my car full of groceries.

I'm not quite sure what made me snap at that exact moment. Was it the eight times in the grocery store that it had taken me several minutes to find a basic item like baking soda or yeast? Was it the surly cashiers? Maybe it was the race to bag my own groceries before they got crushed in the monumental pile so unlovingly thrown to the side by said cashier? Perhaps my breaking point had been the fight to get my grocery cart to steer its directionally challenged way toward the car. I don't know how all of those things contributed to my sudden outburst, but I do know that being pulled over by the police had been the very. last. straw.

Picking up and moving to another country, I realized, was not for the faint of heart. From language frustrations to general feelings of ineptitude when dealing with a foreign system,

I was experiencing a lot of bumps along the way. I had spent many evenings since arriving in Israel in a state of shellshock after a long, hard day. I felt like a child much of the time, unable to understand even the most basic phrases spoken by the adults around me. I myself could barely string together a sentence in Hebrew, leaving me unable to express myself (and then unable to express my frustration at this fact). As a stay-at-home mom with a baby, ulpan (free Hebrew class) was going to have to wait a while. Due to these gaps in my communication ability, it sometimes seemed like a simple series of tasks had sucked away my entire morning and afternoon—things like purchasing a new cell phone or opening a bank account. For the first time in my life, I felt like the people around me perceived me as, well, dumb. Even the grocery store checkout lady spoke to me as though I were hard of hearing. Until I made aliyah, there had been a few simple facts that I was sure of in life: I was smart and competent. And I was efficient; able to accomplish many tasks in a short period of time. A machine. In Israel, I felt more like a blubbering sea sponge, floating along in the water, watching the more impressive and sophisticated fish swim about with great ease.

At least my kids still seemed to think that I knew what I was doing. *They* still saw me as a had-it-all-together goddess. To my three-year-old and one-year-old, I was stability and security incarnate, the source of all things right and good. This may have been why negotiating the elementary school crowd at the park was *such* a big challenge for me. I was worried it would affect how my kids saw me. If I couldn't appear all-knowing to them, then what would I have left of my identity?

I wish I could say that I accepted these developments with grace and calm. Deep in my heart, I must have known that this experience could be taken as a useful exercise in humility. But I felt like I was being pounded on, day after day. There were plenty of tears, not only in front of the police officer who pulled me over. Sometimes the only thing that kept me positive and happy was the support of other new immigrants.

Thankfully my community was full of other Americans who were fresh off the boat like us. I found them in my daughter's playgroup, and at shul on Shabbat. They formed Mommy and Me groups and invited me to hang out with them at the park. This support system allowed me to commiserate in my own language. Within our tiny bubble, I didn't feel like a complete idiot, and with daily discussions of aliyah drama with friends in the same situation, I felt like things were probably going to be okay. I wasn't the *only* one who couldn't find onion powder at the grocery store. There were other people just like me who missed the silly, material comforts of home. Getting it all out was cathartic and returned me to my normal optimistic self.

As we pushed kids on the swing or just sat on a park bench, our conversations would turn from our latest aliyah misadventures to what was *wonderful* about moving to Israel. We talked about the view, our latest trips to Jerusalem, a new *shiur* (Torah class) we'd been to, who made the best felafel in town. We did normal people things, exchanging tips and tricks, sharing recipes and parenting advice. These friendships turned what would have been an impossibly difficult experience into a manageable—even a wonderful one. For what was probably the first time in my adult life, I felt like I could really relate to the people around me. They shared my hopes and dreams, *and* my challenges. I felt like I belonged. I was a sea sponge amongst other sea sponges, and we spoke our own secret language.

Years later, most of what I recall about my first years of aliyah is a feeling of sunshine and happiness. There *were* a lot of difficult things to get used to, but there were also a lot of amazing things that I couldn't believe I was going to *get* to get used to. Things that I didn't even know I made aliyah in order to experience, like the wonder of running day-to-day errands in Jerusalem, the holiest city in the world, the magical sunsets from our picture window, the deliciousness of Israeli tomatoes and cucumbers on my kitchen table, the ease of moderate winters, and that special feeling that descended onto our community every Shabbat. Unexpected surprises appeared, like finally finding a community of other people like me—passionate and value-based and willing to pick up and move to another country for the sake of their beliefs. I never anticipated the lasting friendships I would form, or the long, Shabbat evenings I would enjoy spending with these new friends, talking around the table while our toddlers fell asleep on the couch.

During those first few years, there were so many things that surprised and inspired me. Quite unexpectedly, I became enchanted with the natural beauty I saw flourishing beyond our city. Until I made aliyah, I hadn't had a true chance to experience the change of seasons in Israel. My childhood trips to Israel all took place in the summertime, and during my seminary year I had stayed close to Jerusalem, so I didn't get to see the land turning green and flower-filled in the wintertime.

Our first year as a family in Israel was our first year of hiking. As young, city-dwelling parents in America, we had never been out on the trails with our kids. Instead, we mostly stuck to stroller-friendly city parks. But once we moved to Israel, we discovered local trails in the woods near Beit Shemesh. Our first hike was suggested to us by Israeli neighbors over a Rosh Hashana meal. They called it "Shvil HaSchuster" (because of the name on the memorial plaque at the trailhead) and it was an easy circular hike, only twenty minutes away. When we finally made it over, weeks later, we were completely taken by the views, the trees, the scenery, and the cute log benches that dotted the trail, perfect for our pint-sized crew to stop for a Bamba break. We were thrilled to discover that kid-friendly hiking paths were available to us, in the mountainous region near Jerusalem, close to home. Once the rainy season came around, the views changed to green hills and flower patches. I had never known this type of natural beauty existed in Israel. The super mild winter weather in Beit Shemesh meant that we could enjoy the outdoors throughout the rainy season, a sharp and welcome contrast to the long snowy winters of New Jersey.

Still, even after our forays into the great outdoors during our first winter in Israel, we knew next to nothing about what to expect from nature. We could still be surprised. In early March, we were driving along a local highway when out of the corner of my eye I noticed a massive field of flowers, their crimson heads bobbing in the wind. It looked like a scene out of a movie. We pulled over and went off to explore. As we walked and then ran through fields and fields of red anemones, I experienced a moment I can only describe as surreal. We kept moving through the seemingly never-ending fields, as if standing still would make the anemones disappear. When we finally slowed down, I felt a deep happiness coursing through my veins. The land I loved wasn't only spiritually beautiful; it was *physically* beautiful too. Coming across this spot by chance was like stumbling on a buried treasure. It felt like a gift from God.

Our children pranced through the fields with us, also struck by the magical beauty of the place. By some odd chance of fate, they happened to be wearing red shirts that day. We snapped lots of pictures, then basked in the early spring sunshine, feeling incredibly thankful to be able to experience scenery like this. At the time, I had no idea that magical red flower explosions were a yearly occurrence all over Israel, or that the anemone was the national flower of Israel.

Faith and Half Faith

"The opposite of doubt is not certainty, but rather, faith." –Rabbi Lord Jonathan Sacks

IT'S A LIFELONG challenge to have true faith in God, the type of faith that carries us through every challenge and big decision. Just like there are different levels of Torah knowledge, there are different levels of *emunah*, faith. Like anything else, faith is something we must work towards: *emunah sheleima*, complete faith, doesn't just come naturally.

We are not alone in our struggle to put our full trust in God. There are many examples of even very righteous men in the Torah who, despite their righteousness, lacked complete faith. According to Rashi, Noah was "small in faith." He was willing to spend years of his life building an ark, but he wasn't convinced that the floodwaters would actually arrive, and he didn't enter the ark until the water forced him in (Rashi on Genesis 7:7).

Other righteous men in the Torah faced similar internal struggles. After the Exodus from Egypt, Moses chose leaders of the Jewish people, righteous men, to advance into Israel ahead of the people and spy out the land. The Jews of that time had grown up as slaves in Egypt; they had never fought a battle in their lives. Heading into the uncharted territory of the Holy Land was a new and frightening prospect. The spies' fear led them to fail in their divine mission; they brought back a negative report about the Promised Land, which led to forty years of wandering, and the death of their generation in the desert. It says in the Torah, about the spies: "And in this matter, you did not believe in the Lord your God" (Deuteronomy 1:32).

According to Rav Tzvi Yehuda HaCohen Kook,[1] the Torah uses the words "this matter" to highlight the fact that in *other* matters, they *did* believe; the spies were righteous men, good Jews. Yet their faith was incomplete. They didn't trust that Hashem would bring them into the Land of Israel safely.

The Talmud (*Sotah* 48b) describes types of *"tzadikim* (righteous men) who don't believe." These righteous Jews may neglect some of God's commandments, while strictly following others, picking and choosing based on which precepts are pleasant and which ones are less so. In contrast, it is written of Abraham, our first patriarch, who was commanded to leave his home and journey to a new one, that he "had faith in the Lord" (Genesis 15:6). Abraham, who went *"el ha'aretz asher areca"* (to the land that I will show you) is highlighted as an example of someone with true *emunah*, with complete faith.

Living in Israel may not be easy, but according to many of our sages it is one of the mitzvot, something that God

---

1   See *Sichot HaRav Tzvi Yehuda, Emunah,* Section 7 (Yeshivat Ateret Cohanim). Edited by Rav Shlomo Aviner.

desires for us, and of us. One way to come closer to complete faith is to be in Israel, despite the challenges or misgivings we may experience. In this way, we can rectify the sin of the spies by having complete faith in God that His chosen land is the right place for His chosen people.

VI.

DISILLUSIONMENT

"Three good gifts God gave to Israel, and none were given without having to suffer for them. They are Torah, the Land of Israel, and the World to Come." –Brachot 5a.

I T WAS ELIE's first day at her new pre-school. My ever sensitive four year old had only ever been in small play-groups, and even those had been difficult for her; it had taken until the end of the last school year for her to stop bursting into hysterics every morning when I left her, and start enjoying herself. I couldn't imagine how she would manage in a group of thirty-five children, as was typical in the local pre-schools, so before the summer I had signed her up at an ultra-Orthodox pre-school in Ramat Beit Shemesh Bet which boasted only eighteen children per class. Now, back in Israel after six weeks with family in New Jersey and New Orleans, it was time to send Elie off to her new class. Trying to look the part, I pulled on a pair of nude-colored knee highs that I had stowed away in the glove compartment of the car. Then I took Elie's hand, walking her inside.

My daughter's new teacher was bubbly and warm, pleasantly plump with a slightly lopsided wig. She welcomed the children with a smile and a loud "*Boker Tov!*" I liked her already.

My daughter seemed content to be left in her care, along with two of her old friends from last year. I lingered a bit, then gave my daughter a big kiss and left, walking slowly back to the car. I was a little nervous leaving her there. But on the other hand, after an intense summer with the kids… it was finally time to get back into my routine!

It was a beautiful day. The bright blue sky was filled with little white clouds sprinkled about like pieces of popcorn. I began walking across the courtyard back towards the street, daydreaming about how my daughter would spend her day at school. Would she be happy there? Would she make new friends? Someone called my name, snapping me out of my reverie. "Hey, Susannah!"

It was Rachel, someone I just barely knew from my neighborhood.

"Hey, what's up!"

Rachel hurried to catch up with me and then leaned towards me, conspiratorially. "You know," she whispered, "You really shouldn't wear jean skirts here."

I felt my face go red as I looked down at my long denim skirt. "What?" I stammered, "It didn't say anything about that in the rules."

"Yeah, but it's looked down upon," she explained, "I know someone who was told by the staff not to wear jean skirts. You just shouldn't wear it *here*."

I was embarrassed, shocked, and a little bit horrified. Here we were in the Land of Israel, two good Jews in search of a quality Torah education for our children, and in the first moments after drop-off on the very first day of school for my daughter, I had seemingly broken an unwritten rule about the dress code: denim fabric not allowed, even for parents of preschool students. Maybe Rachel was just trying to help me out, to prevent me from having to deal with a reprimand from a staff member, but I was too dismayed to be thankful. This was worse than what I had anticipated. I got back into the car feeling angry and ashamed. What had I gotten myself into? I ripped off my knee highs and drove back home in a grey mood, and a state of extreme confusion.

A year into our aliyah, living in Ramat Beit Shemesh, a mixed community that was becoming predominantly ultra-Orthodox, had become confusing for me. There was a whole new aspect of Judaism which I had not realized that I needed to consider. When we arrived, I had been twenty-three years old and fairly new to the different delineations of Orthodox Judaism. I didn't necessarily understand the differences between the different religious communities in Israel. My sister's family, who were my best model of a deeply observant family in Israel, seemed to fit right into their Ramat Eshkol neighborhood living as "modern Orthodox" Jews, despite the large ultra-Orthodox presence around them. Perhaps things were different for them because Tzion had actually grown up in Ramat Eshkol, before the ultra-Orthodox population moved in. As far as I knew and believed at that point, a religious Jew was a religious Jew.

Judging from my experience growing up in Chabad (also an ultra-Orthodox group), other religious sects were accepting and welcoming, even to those who may dress differently.

We had been welcomed to Ramat Beit Shemesh by other young families who attended an ultra-Orthodox shul for Anglos. It was full of the type of Jew I was used to—English speakers deeply devoted to community, Torah, and halacha. It seemed like a good community to be a part of. As far as I knew, being an ultra-Orthodox Jew simply meant being fully devoted to Torah Judaism, and I valued that. So I had attended *shiurim*, joined shul projects with the other women, and felt that, perhaps, I had found my crowd. But the more time I spent with my new peers, the more I began to realize that, in many ways, I didn't fit in. Over the course of a few casual conversations, I began to see that some of my values were different than those of my chosen community. My perspective on the importance of the connection between the modern state of Israel and Judaism was different than that of many of my neighbors. I believed that Israel, as a state, was a blessing for our people, one that we should support in every way possible. The *majority* ultra-Orthodox perspective was different: while they valued the physical Land of Israel, they did not necessarily support the modern-day state.

One day, I was driving my friend's two daughters home from school in our minivan, around the time of Yom HaAtzmaut, Israel's Independence Day. The girls pointed to the Israeli flag I had attached to my car window. "We have one of those," they said, "but we keep ours inside our car instead of on the outside."

"How come?" I asked, completely oblivious.

"Our parents say they'll tell us when we're older." Translation: "We don't know how to explain the dissonance between what *we* believe—that the State of Israel is our state, and we love it, and what the people around us expect us to believe—that we hold no regard for Israel as a Jewish state.

I couldn't believe it. I knew that their parents were ardent Zionists who had moved to Israel out of great love for the land *and* the state. They were now part of the ultra-Orthodox community in Ramat Beit Shemesh. Did that mean that they could no longer declare their support and love for Israel publicly? And was that *okay* with them? It would never be okay with me.

Another big clue that my values were different than those of the community I lived in was the women's *shiur* I went to one evening. It was a short Torah class on film, given with the support and involvement of a few local rabbis. The premise of the film was as follows: Modesty is the most important religious precept for Jewish women; being modest is what *makes* a Jewish woman a Jewish woman. It is such an important *mitzvah* for women—and here is where they lost me completely—that it's even more important than keeping Shabbat. I had heard some surprising things over the years, but that the necessity of covering one's body sufficiently was more important than keeping one of the Ten Commandments, one of the foundations of our faith? It just didn't make any sense to me.

On the one hand, I had always truly appreciated

ultra-Orthodoxy's attention to halachic detail. Before moving to Israel, this had seemed completely praiseworthy to me. But once I started living in Israel, associating with an ultra-Orthodox community, I began to be confronted by some of the ramifications of that single-minded focus which didn't fit my understanding of what it meant to be a religious Jew.

I'll never forget the admittance interview for my daughter's pre-school. The interviewer had focused intently and exclusively on one question: Did we have a television in our home? We didn't, but she didn't seem to accept my answer. She asked the question over and over again, each time in a different way. My answer didn't change—but my demeanor did. I left the interview feeling mildly annoyed. Although the small class sizes seemed important enough to send my daughter to this institution for pre-school, there was no way I could send her there beyond that. I was also left wondering: how could so many parents in my community be okay with sending their kids to a school where this was the sole focus of the interview? What about the *actual* important stuff, like building humility and kindness, serving God, and learning Torah?

Incidents like this made me feel like, perhaps, I didn't belong in the community I was living in. I was beginning to realize that there were some small but outspoken segments of the ultra-Orthodox community that had an almost cultish worship of rabbinical figures, and some of *them* were focused on certain mitzvot at the expense of others. *Tzniut* (for all women). Learning Torah all day (for all men). With those unwavering priorities, many religious precepts of great significance could be pushed aside. And while many community members (and community leaders) did *not* follow this kind of Torah, the outspokenness of the more radical types penetrated the fabric of my day-to-day existence. It was hard to ignore.

Other aspects of life in ultra-Orthodox Ramat Beit Shemesh were also hard to accept. There was a ban on public images of *all* women, no matter how they were dressed, which even included little girls. When we visited our pediatrician, all of the posters around the clinic featured only men and boys, fathers and sons—not one mother or daughter. In the grocery store, cereal boxes displayed pictures of cute little boys. In the toy store, images of little girls on toy packaging were blacked out! Come Purim time, there were advertisements for little girls' costumes—brides and princesses. Here too, the child models were made into faceless blurs, deemed too provocative to display. I felt torn. The pursuit of modesty and chastity were worthwhile causes, but not at the expense of respect for all human beings. How could a society that viewed the faces of women and girls as an enticement towards sin really respect them?

I believed that devotion to Torah and halacha was of primary importance. I knew that most of the people around me were just aiming for the same focus. But this ideology, within ultra-Orthodoxy, was tainted by extremist elements. To me, being a religious Jew meant being open to *all* of God's commandments and meant putting an emphasis on love and respect for *every* fellow Jew. As much as the ultra-Orthodox would disagree, I felt that a lack of respect for different types of Jews emerged from their otherwise wholesome ideology.

I *did* want to serve God in the best way possible, but to me, that meant embracing the land *and* the State of Israel with all of its complexity and diversity. It meant doing everything we could to strengthen the nation. To me, the people and the state were an integral part of what it meant to be a modern Jew. I couldn't ignore that, no matter how much I wished for the simplicity of a life of total religious insulation, especially when it came to raising kids. And Avi was going through the exact same sort of thought process that I was, in his own way.

So, after jumping on board at first, after our second year in Israel, we slowly extricated ourselves from the ultra-Orthodox community. First, we switched shuls. Then, after one year in the ultra-Orthodox pre-school, we moved Elie somewhere else. There *were* other families like us in town, and we found our place in a Carlebach shul up the block where other modern Orthodox American-Israelis gathered. Still, despite finding a better community for our family, we spent the next couple of years in Ramat Beit Shemesh with one foot out the door.

Time moved along. With Eitan starting pre-school, I was finally able to attend ulpan, which improved my Hebrew a bit. I became pregnant with our third child. Avi settled into his technology job at a new finance company in Jerusalem, which he'd found just a month after finishing up at Citigroup. I began venturing out on weekly shopping trips into the adjacent mixed secular-religious city of Beit Shemesh rather than shopping closer to home because of the new signs displayed on every store in Ramat Beit Shemesh, requiring modest dress for women, began to disturb me—regardless of the fact that I was always modestly dressed. I still enjoyed some amazing classes given in the community we had left, but felt the pinch of exclusion—like when I wasn't allowed to return to a particular class because the teacher decided that I didn't fit in ideologically. Ouch.

Eventually, despite the good friends we had made in Ramat Beit Shemesh, we decided to look for a larger and more permanent home elsewhere and move our expanding family to an entirely new place. Ultimately, I couldn't raise my children in a community where females were hidden from public view. Although our new community in Ramat Beit Shemesh didn't support this filtering of all things female, I didn't want my children to grow up in a place where the majority rule meant that images of girls would be outlawed. The time had come. I was happy with the decision. Living with the constant clash of ultra-Orthodox vs. non-ultra-Orthodox was too hard. It was not a fight I wanted to be a part of. We had moved to Israel so that our children's experience of religion would be authentic. For us, that meant that we needed to get them away from the friction and exclusion we were experiencing, that was being espoused in the name of God.

We were on the search for a different type of society, a new community to be a part of. A community where we could feel at home; a place where Torah and Israel were *both* recognized as essential elements in the life of a religious Jew. A community that more accurately reflected our values and would encourage us to impart them to our children.

VII.

Pioneering Lite

"Ani baniti bayit b'Eretz Yisrael." –Nira Rabinovitz, Israeli singer

Near Jerusalem, on a little hilltop in the mountains of Gush Etzion, the small religious *yishuv* (settlement) of Neve Daniel was building a new neighborhood. And there were plots for sale! We were interested in finding out more, so we arranged to spend Shabbat there with friends we had met in Ramat Beit Shemesh who had already made the move into one of the first completed homes in the new development in Neve Daniel.

Over Shabbat, we got to know some of the local residents. They weren't that different from many of the people we had become close to in Ramat Beit Shemesh, the ones at the Carlebach shul and the other parents at Elie's new pre-school. We also spent time in Neve Daniel just walking around town and hanging out in the park, trying to get a feel for what life was like in this modern Orthodox and Zionist community. We had visited lots of places in our quest to find a new home, and so far, none of them were quite right. Ma'aleh Adumim was nice, but real estate was hard to come by. Modi'in was way too big of a city. But Neve Daniel felt different than those places. It seemed to be a town with a rich community life, where neighbors knew each other by name, and cared for one another. Most of the people there considered themselves to be religious Zionists, those for whom Torah and the State of Israel were irrevocably intertwined. And after visiting Neve Daniel for just twenty-four hours, we knew that this was a place we could call home. It felt like suburbia, but an Israeli, religious version. Jerusalem was a short drive away, only fifteen minutes by car—this was a major upgrade from our longer commute from Beit Shemesh. Most importantly, lots of young people like us were building homes there. We looked forward to being part of a growing community where the values around us would support our own. We pictured our family here as it grew; that one day when our kids were older, they would attend the weekly parsha classes given by the rabbi of the *yishuv*. Our life would run at the slower, quieter pace of suburbia, in a town whose front gate closed on Shabbat, with no cars entering or departing. I imagined taking Elie and Eitan to the sprawling park in the older part of Neve Daniel, filled with painted wooden playground equipment and surrounded by tall trees. It felt like we would fit here, in this place where we could proudly display a huge Israeli flag in our front yard, taking its place among many others on the street.

The next step we took was to purchase a lot and begin our building project. In this new community, there were no move-in-ready houses. Every residence was being built from scratch. The process of building our house in Neve Daniel was long and arduous; the thought that we would one day get to actually live in it seemed almost unbelievable. The entire process took about eighteen months, and was all-encompassing. After choosing the plot, we had to choose an architect, a *kablan* (contractor), and an engineer. We spoke to friends and future neighbors to gather recommendations, then interviewed all the top candidates, going on home tours around Efrat and Gush Etzion to help us make our decision. After selecting our team, we finalized our plans (and when I say finalized, I mean designed from scratch and agonized over every small detail, from the exact measurements of each and every room to where our outlets would be placed) and set the project in motion.

The Friday after they broke ground on our plot, we went to visit. Pictures from that day show me, nine months pregnant and showing it on every inch of my swollen body, perched on a rock within a huge hole that would one day house our basement. Back in Ramat Beit Shemesh that evening, I lit Shabbat candles, then took Elie and Eitan out to the park near the shul. I felt a little off, but at nine months pregnant, I blamed it on indigestion, perhaps from the croissant I had eaten for breakfast in Neve Daniel that morning. However, what started out as a minor stomachache quickly turned into serious labor pangs. I barely made it to the hospital to give birth to our daughter, Dalya, a few short hours later.

Every night during Dalya's newborn no-sleep phase, thoughts of floor plans, tiles, light fixtures, and paint colors filled my brain. While cradling her in the rocking chair, I would picture our new living room, dining room, and kitchen. I began to miss the times when my mind had been able to focus on loftier, less materialistic things.

Every Friday we would drive the half hour from Ramat Beit Shemesh to Neve Daniel with Dalya to inspect our construction site (stopping at the local bakery for cheese Danishes first). As the months passed, I began to feel like our construction project had taken over my life. I remember reaching the point when I was sure that I had begun to attach an unhealthy importance to our future home—I would lie in bed night after night, awake, irrational fears racing through my head: What if we died before we moved into the house? What if it burned down before we got to live in it?

None of that happened. Slowly, as we lived out our last year in Ramat Beit Shemesh, the house progressed. The foundation was completed, and walls went up, along with floors, windows, electricity, and plumbing. Once summer came along the house was almost finished—and yet what remained seemed to drag on slower than ever.

When the new school year started in September 2006, our built-from-scratch home *still* wasn't finished. Our kids were registered for pre-k and elementary school in Neve Daniel. We had started thinking about leaving Ramat Beit Shemesh ages earlier, when Elie was only four. Now, she was entering first grade, and we still hadn't made the move.

We took up temporary residence at my in-laws' apartment in Beit Shemesh (they had purchased a second home there to be close to us on their visits). Every morning I would embark on the long drive from Beit Shemesh to Neve Daniel with my three children so that Eitan and Elie could start the year in their new educational frameworks. Our old friends from Teaneck, Mendel and Chaya Gottesman, had made aliyah and moved to Neve Daniel over the summer, and were renting a temporary home while they built their new permanent home right next door to ours. I would put Dalya down for her nap at their house, drinking an iced coffee from the bakery while she slept. Then I would spend the rest of my morning keeping an eye on the progress of our new house across the street, running errands in nearby Efrat, and going for walks around the neighborhood with Dalya. At the end of the school day, I would schlepp all three kids back to Beit Shemesh once more, where we would spend a few hours playing in the yard before Avi returned home for dinner. In the evening, Avi and I would review our construction progress and make a to-do list. And then, the next day, we would wake up and do it all again

Although Elie and Eitan were new in town, they quickly made friends at school. They were ready to be in Neve Daniel, and so was I, even if our home wasn't ready for us. So right before Rosh Hashana, we finally bit the bullet and moved into a beautiful shell of a home with no kitchen, no sinks and no showers, missing paint and every type of finishing touch, and full of lots and lots of dust (we did have two bathtubs and an outdoor spigot). But it was *our* home, *our* walls, *our* floors…and *our* dust. We were thrilled and felt like kings in a large and beautiful palace.

This was the first time I had lived in my own house—until

then, Avi and I had always rented apartments. Some of them had been really crummy. Over the course of our first six years of marriage, choosing an apartment to rent had been more about its location than its style. We had lived in three different apartments over those years, all of varying degrees of unattractiveness. My personal favorite had been the one which boasted the bathroom opening immediately off the "dining room" (truthfully just part of our kitchen). On the bright side, it had been very convenient to be able to access the fridge from our dining room table. All we'd had to do was lean back and swing open the door if one of the kids asked for the ketchup.

We had become accustomed to squeezing our growing family into tight spaces, so a little bit of dust and no kitchen appliances in our brand-new two-story house didn't faze us. We were living in a happy fantasy; all the difficulties we encountered seemed minor when we remembered that we were living in our own spacious home, planned and design to exactly suit our family's needs. We had fun coming up with creative solutions to our unfinished home's small deficiencies. Our "kitchen" was made up of a borrowed travel stove, a microwave, a water urn, and a waffle maker. We temporarily gave up daily showers in favor of "luxurious" baths. And what child really *needs* a bedroom door?

In addition to its temporary shortcomings, we had no budget left for finishing touches after sinking all of our funds into the building of a new house—if you consider things like closets for the kids to be finishing touches. We sprung for our own closet, and one to keep all of the many toys organized in the new playroom, but our kids had no storage for their small wardrobes. When my sprightly mother-in-law came to visit, she helped us fix up a disassembled, old, cabinet to store Eitan's clothes. For Elie, we put an old pop-up canvas closet to use. We found ways to make things work, even if our solutions were quirky. We couldn't buy curtains or blinds, so we arranged a series of framed pictures side by side to block out the open view into our master bedroom. And who really needed front steps? A hill of rock and gravel served just fine as our entryway for the first year of our residence. Besides, it was fun to slide down.

Our back yard was nothing but bedrock and boulders. After Yom Kippur, we tried to put up a little pop-up Sukkah, fighting the famous Neve Daniel wind, which was even more intense with no plants or trees to cushion us from its blasts. We fought desperately, battling to get our Sukkah into standing position, but to no avail. Eventually, we came up with a solution. We attached four buckets full of rocks (items readily available in our yard) to each corner of the Sukkah. This worked perfectly, and our Sukkah finally stayed put. That Sukkah may have been a step down from our beautiful balcony in Beit Shemesh, but the novelty made up for it.

Until about Hanukkah time (when the construction was finally finished), we would cloister ourselves in our little home office every day after school—the only room that was finished and construction-worker free. This room was about the size of a large bathroom, but we managed to have good times in it nevertheless, sharing bags of pretzels, tackling Elie's homework, and attempting to build jumbo Lego towers in a space so small that we had to step over each other to reach all the pieces. Dalya would often nap in the stroller for much of that time (removing a large part of our play area), but she would awaken to join us in our miniature play world during the last half hour or so. We would count down the minutes to 4:00 p.m.; that was when the workers cleared out and we were free to roam the open dusty spaces of our new home. I would sweep and mop the floor once again while the kids drew pictures in the thick dust on the windows. Then we had dinner, took baths, and read stories snuggled in bed.

I couldn't wait for the day when loud banging, shouting, and dust would no longer be a necessary part of my daily routine, but we were making good memories even as we were. At the end of the day, it was wonderful to be home, in our *own* home in Israel. Minor or even major inconveniences couldn't impact our deep feeling of gratitude. As I closed my "curtain" of picture frames each night before I went to bed, I couldn't help but be thankful that we were finally in the place where we would raise our children, within a community that we loved.

We weren't the only ones on the block living in a construction zone. Outside of our four walls, there was a whole street of unfinishedness to marvel at. More than what *was*, I remember what *wasn't*. There were houses without roofs, no sidewalks, and no green spaces or playgrounds whatsoever.

Our new neighborhood was one big construction site,

complete with yellow trucks to watch, and progress to witness, along with the musical accompaniment of loud Arabic music and drilling. Every so often, we would see the local workers pull out their prayer mats for a midday supplication to Allah. This part of life in Neve Daniel took some getting used to.

When we decided to move to Neve Daniel, I didn't consider myself to be a pioneer, settling important Israeli land. In fact, up until moving to the community, I had remained largely ignorant of the cause I had now become a part of. As far as I was concerned, I was looking for a nice place to live near Jerusalem with my family. The schools were great. There were plenty of kids around. And housing prices were reasonable. But the reality was that we were moving to a whole new world: a community in Judea and Samaria, otherwise known as the *shtachim*, or settlements. We were officially over the Green Line.

This terrain was shared by Israelis and non-Israelis, Jews and Arabs. Palestinian-Arab locals lived nearby, worked nearby, and drove down the same streets as we did every day. When we made the decision to move to Neve Daniel, back in 2005, just after the Second Intifada had ended, we had considered the safety (or lack thereof) of the area. Ultimately, we made the determination that there was an equal likelihood of terrorist attacks occurring in Jerusalem as in Neve Daniel—and we would have moved to the Holy City in a heartbeat if funds, housing, and community had all matched up. So, it seemed to us that there was no unacceptable risk to our family in moving them to Gush Etzion.

Even now, a decade and a half later, I still think that's mostly true. But over time I began to see that there is a huge difference between what daily life feels like in Neve Daniel, and what it feels like in some other parts of Israel. In Gush Etzion, we feel real strain in times of trouble. There is no escape from the harsh realities of the Israeli-Palestinian conflict that surround us. Here, we live in close contact with Palestinians, most of whom just want to live good lives and support their families. Many of them are genuinely friendly and kind to their Jewish neighbors. We are friendly and kind in return. We meet them when we walk outside of the gate. Some of them offer a smile and a bushel of freshly picked grapes. We exchange greetings with these local farmers. These are good people.

But we also know that an extremist element exists within the Palestinian leadership—there are those who have learned a deep animosity towards their Jewish Israeli neighbors and feel idealistically compelled to liberate what they see as their land from the clutches of Zionist usurpers. This element is impossible to ignore, especially during times of terror, all too frequently aimed at settlers waiting for a bus at the Gush Etzion Junction. Many Palestinians support Hamas—a terrorist organization that calls for the complete destruction of the State of Israel—and teach their children that Jews are essentially bad. Some of these more extremist individuals live in the hills and farm the valleys that surround our community, a reminder every single day of our tenuous grip on our homeland. This issue, considered at depth, seems to have no easy solution. Every possible fix, from giving Israeli citizenship to Palestinian Arabs, to giving them their own state, comes with a host of new problems. And while "Land for Peace" could theoretically be a realistic solution, is there any evidence that this would work? As former prime minister Golda Meir wrote in her book, *My Life*: "In June, 1967, the Sinai, the Gaza Strip, the West Bank, the Golan Heights, and East Jerusalem were all in Arab possession, so it is ludicrous to argue today that Israel's presence in those territories since 1967 is the cause of tension in the Middle East, or was the cause of the Yom Kippur War. When Arab statesmen insist that Israel withdraw to the pre-June 1967 lines, one can only ask: If those lines are so sacred to Arabs, why was the Six-Day war launched to destroy them?"[1]

Golda Meir's words are still very relevant today, especially for those of us living in the "territories." A problem exists, and there is no easy solution. Unfortunately, it's all too common to tune into the news and hear a report of an attack on soldiers at the *tzomet* (the local intersection), by a Palestinian Arab. This is the place where we shop for groceries, get eyeglasses, and pick up bakery goods. It's where we go out for coffee. Right outside of the (relatively safe) main shopping center on the highway, teens have been kidnapped, cars have been stoned, and pedestrians mowed down. Thank God, most of these attacks fail. But the knowledge that they could happen at any time can change the way it feels to run errands.

We develop an unusual relationship with some of the Palestinian Arabs we come to know—part friendliness and

---

1   Golda Meir, *My Life*, (New York: G.P. Putnam and Sons, 1975), p 364.

part caution. These details of day-to-day existence in Gush Etzion keep us all acutely aware of this fact: we are engaged in a struggle to hold onto our land. Too many would like to take away our freedom to live as Jews in our homeland. After the events of the Holocaust, when six million Jews were murdered, having no means of escape or homeland to flee to (these facts often dismissed as fabrication by more extremist Arab elements), this is no small consideration.

The struggles of our predecessors have given us what we have today: a country where we can simply *be* Jewish, a right we have had to fight for throughout our centuries in exile. In modern-day Israel we are allowed to *exist*, despite (and because) of the fact that we are Jews. Having our own country, our own land, is a privilege that we can't take for granted.

Living in this part of the country has helped me better understand what life must have been like for early pioneers, who came to Israel before the state was a done deal. Over a century ago, idealistic Jews arrived here to find the land barren, filled with disease and environmental destruction after centuries of war and neglect. These settlers worked the earth and began the fight, both politically and militarily, to give the Jewish people a state. Without those early pioneers, Israel would never have become our very own country.

Strangely enough, this was something I had never given much thought to at all before making aliyah. In the back of my mind somewhere, I knew that Jews had sacrificed to secure our country, but I didn't relate to their experiences at all. I had no idea that moving to Gush Etzion would teach me a new respect and understanding for those early pioneers who made Israel possible.

Their experience was my experience—times a hundred thousand. I was living with modern-day comforts. Our family had the ability to cloister ourselves in our safe, gated community and drive from place to place in big cars with shatter-proof windows. We installed an alarm system, adopted a dog for protection, put into place safety rules for our children. I was spoiled with my modern-day solutions. How could I possibly imagine what the early pioneers gave up to chase after their nation's dream? Early settlers raised families in a land where there was no escape from the harsh realities of daily existence—be they human threats or environmental ones. They walked away from their communities in pursuit of a dream that religious Jews around the world pray for every day. This type of idealism has *always* been what makes our people great.

For some religious people, paying tribute to the early secular Zionists seems anti-religious. They do not consider themselves Zionists at all, and do not consider the role of the pioneers as significant; they see the miraculous return of our people to the Land of Israel as a gift bestowed *only* by God, without acknowledging the human effort and sacrifice that was involved. But Religious Zionist thought suggests that it was God who inspired those early pioneers to return to our nation's homeland. In the early days of the yishuv in Palestine, and then in the newly declared State of Israel, religious and non-religious Jews fought side by side in the struggle for the country we had longed to return to for thousands of years.

During our first years in Neve Daniel, I had the chance to learn the book of Ezra. The stories of the Second Temple make it clear that Jews of all colors played a part in the return to the Holy Land after the first exile, and in the rebuilding of the Temple. To me, the fact that modern Zionism was a largely secular movement doesn't change the fact that it turned a religious prophecy into a reality.

So, as days and months and years passed living in Gush Etzion, my understanding of what it meant to be a Jew in modern day Israel changed once again. For the first time, I deeply related to the stories of the book of Joshua, and of Ezra and Nehemiah, the Second Temple religious leaders. Like the Jews of those times, I found myself staking a claim to the land. The longer we lived there, the more our identity changed. I never set out to be a pioneer, but somehow, I became one.

As I spent more time in a Religious Zionist community, I learned more Torah *and* more about the early struggles of those first *olim* who started building the first independent state for Jews in two thousand years, who arrived when the land was held by the Ottoman Empire and then by the British until eventually, we achieved independence and declared the State of Israel. I recognized the devotion of the early settlers as something akin to a religious act. Without their idealism, our dreams of redemption would still be far away. And I wouldn't be here in Israel to tell my story.

Rebuilding Israel is a Religious Act

I USED TO BELIEVE that ancient times were completely different than modern times. I always imagined, when thinking
about the building of the Second Temple, that it was constructed during a time of nationwide holiness and revealed
miracles. Surely, I thought, during a time when books of the
Tanach were still being written, the Jews were on a higher
spiritual level than they are today.

But as I learned more about the Second Temple period, I discovered a jarring truth: when King Cyrus sent out a proclama-
tion that the Jews of Persia could go back to their homeland and
rebuild the Temple, only about ten percent of the Jewish people returned from exile. That's a miniscule amount. One might
imagine that the exiled Jews would have been eagerly waiting
for this moment; after years of being exiled from their homeland,
it would stand to reason that they would all return as soon as it
was possible. Why didn't the Jews immigrate en masse to Israel,
after just seventy years of being away? It's confounding.

The most likely explanation is that these Jews had made a
home in their new lands. Their lives were different now; they
had achieved some level of comfort in their foreign homes.
Living in the Holy Land was no longer a priority for them
(although many did send money to assist with the Second
Temple building process).

Anyone reading the book of Ezra can see that the time of the rebuilding of the Second Temple was no religious utopia. As the leader of the Jews in Israel, Ezra had to contend with all sorts of issues, one of them being that many of the people who *had* returned had brought along their non-Jewish wives (Ezra 9:2). These Jews were not very religious. If they had married non-Jewish women, they must not have fully understood or observed the laws of the Torah. But they were still ready to pick up their lives and come back to rebuild their homeland.

A similarity can be seen in modern times when many of Israel's early pioneers were non-religious Jews. These Zionists played an integral role in re-establishing our nation. As Rav Tzvi Yehuda HaCohen Kook said: "It is important to understand that every Jew who comes to live in Israel is fulfilling a Torah commandment. This is true whether he is an observer of Torah or not, whether he knows it is a mitzvah (commandment), or not; whether he comes with the intention to do the mitzvah, or not."[1]

Sometimes, history can give us a deeper understanding of the present. Just like in the times of the Second Temple, secular Jews came back to Israel in the last century, fulfilling a divine precept even if that wasn't their intention.

Perhaps our own secular pioneers were performing a religious act after all.

---

1   *Torat Eretz Yisrael,* The Teachings of HaRav Tzvi Yehuda HaCohen Kook (Jerusalem: Torat Eretz Yisrael Publications, 1991), p.221.

VIII.

From the Mouths of Babes

"When the Land of Israel will give fruit bountifully, this is an indication of the impending redemption, and there is no greater indication than this." –Rashi on Sanhedrin 98a

I T was a year of firsts. Our first daughter was completing her study of the first book of the Torah, *Sefer Bereishit* (Genesis), during our first year in our new home, during her first year of elementary school.

Elie's graduation from first grade was my first time ever at Ma'arat HaMachpela, the Cave of the Patriarchs—the ancient, holy gravesite of our forefathers and foremothers. Ma'arat HaMachpela is in Hebron, an important biblical city that is now predominantly Palestinian. Some parents simply drove in their cars, but back then there was no chance I would have gone to Hebron without the protection of an armored bus, so Avi and I boarded the bus along with Elie and baby Dalya (Eitan was in pre-school that Friday morning). And we set off on the half hour ride to Ma'arat HaMachpela.

For the duration of the bus ride, I was on edge. We wove our way through what look liked abandoned buildings, defaced with graffiti in Arabic. I held my baby close, anticipating an imminent attack by some mystery gunman emerging from a nearby hiding place. My fears ruled my imagination.

After a half hour ride, we reached the heart of the city. We saw groups of men in kaffiyehs, signs in Arabic, and green and white license plates. I felt slightly scared, and way out of my comfort zone. But perhaps the most unnerving part of the journey was at its end, when we finally reached Ma'arat HaMachpela itself and disembarked from the bus. Local children crowded around us, their definition of personal space different than my own. They were too close for my comfort.

"Give me a shekel," they clamored at us, in accented Hebrew.

These kids must have been used to collecting change from tourists. Maybe they used it to purchase popsicles and treats. Or maybe they really needed it. But we didn't dare stop to find out; we were too nervous to take out our wallets. Instead, we shuffled away, clutching our babies close. It was strange to feel fearful of little children, but we were overwhelmed by our desire to keep our own kids safe.

As I headed towards the gates of Ma'arat HaMachpela, I thought about how complex life could be. In Israel, even the most beautiful moments aren't necessarily neat or simple. Even a Chumash party can have a tough side.

Despite all this, the stress and agitation that had built up inside of us dissipated completely as we approached the

Jewish section of Ma'arat HaMachpela, housing a synagogue adjacent to the mosque on the other side. We were
now walking into a Jewish bubble within the predominantly
Muslim city. It was as if we were ascending into an entirely
different world, a holy place untarnished by the struggles
outside of its walls. We climbed the steps towards a grassy
hill and a large, square building with walls of Jerusalem
stone. Speakers dotted the grass, protruding from the tops
of poles, blasting music by well-known Israel religious
singers—Aharon Razel, Udi Davidi, and Yosef Karduner.
Parents settled down strategically on the lawn, positioning
themselves at vantage points to best see their first graders
perform. We had arrived for first grade graduation and their
Siyum Chumash Bereishit at Ma'arat HaMachpela. Our six-
and seven-year-olds were about to finish the first book of
our beloved Torah, after a year of reading the lines out loud
and learning the stories contained within. It was an important milestone in our children's lives.

A hush settled upon us as the principal walked up to
the podium to begin the ceremony. He stood in front of
the crowd, turning to speak directly to the kids, a playful
smile on his face and a familiar twinkle in his eye. He began by presenting them with a series of questions on the
chapters they had learned. The parents laughed at their children's cute responses. Afterwards, we looked on as the classes performed themed dances connected to stories from the
book of *Bereishit*. First, we watched the dance of Creation,
then the dance of Yaakov's sheep. Elie starred in the dance
of the Twelve Tribes. Then we reached the highlight of the

morning, the recital of the final few lines of the book of *Bereishit*. Our children lined up in order like little soldiers. The principal gave the cue, and words of Torah poured forth from their mouths in a beautiful, sing-song recitation, following the melody of the *ta'amim*, the musical cantillation used for Torah recitation that they had learned in kindergarten. Little Elie stood there, her green eyes shining, singing with the rest of her class, the words pouring out from deep in her heart, as if they were lyrics to her favorite song.

And then just as quickly as it had begun, it was over. "*Chazak, chazak, venitchazaik!*" they chanted together, three times aloud. These words are recited by all congregations when they reach the end of a book of Torah. And today it was the turn of these wonderful first graders.

It was so beautiful. Thoughts and emotions flooded through me, my eyes moist with tears that I wiped away with the back of my hand. I couldn't help but feel like we had done something right. That moment at Ma'arat HaMachpela was confirmation that we were doing okay as parents. Eight years earlier, when we had made the decision to raise our children in Israel, it was scenes like this that we had hoped for. Most of all, I was filled with wonder and gratitude—I couldn't believe that my daughter's first grade graduation was happening here, in one of the holiest sites of the Torah. And it actually existed under an hour away from our home in Israel.

Moreover, I knew that this was only the *beginning* of my daughter's Torah study career. At her school, the kids worked their way through all five books of Torah by fifth grade. They would read all of it out loud, learning its stories at an impressionable age, tucking the words away in their hearts like those from a favorite book, to return to again and again. Then they move on to the Prophets, reading about Joshua conquering the Land of Israel—a part of their national history. And it doesn't stop there.

When the performance ended, Elie ran to us. I gathered her up in a big hug and showered her with kisses. "We are so proud of you!" I whispered in her ear. We asked another dad to take a picture of us all together. My daughter held up her new certificate of completion with a big semi-toothless smile. Ma'arat HaMachpela was our impressive backdrop.

After the ceremony, we walked towards the synagogue, where we visited the presumed gravesites of Sarah, Abraham, Isaac, and our other matriarchs and patriarchs (only Rachel is not buried there). As we strolled through the halls, I remembered learning about Ma'arat HaMachpela myself as a fourth grader, never truly picturing it as a real place I could still visit. We peeked behind each curtain, into the ornamental tombs beyond. Was there a spot for Esau's head, I wondered, recalling a midrash that it had rolled into the cave.

The morning ended with Torah games for the children and a proper feast of rugelach and cheese danishes fresh from our local bakery. The parents chatted, easy and relaxed. The children wandered through the crowds. Although Shabbat was approaching, nobody ran off to do their Friday morning chores. It seemed that the importance of the day was as evident to everyone else as it was to me: we were imparting the message to our children that Torah was exciting and alive. The cleaning and cooking could wait.

We've repeated that same outing five more times since that day. Whenever one of my children begins first grade, I get excited all over again. The Ma'arat HaMachpela graduation is the highlight of my year. Having learned about the burial place of our forefathers and foremothers as a child—then perceived as a mystical cave described in a barely understandable book of my heritage—seeing it before me, so real, so simply *there*, and so available for appreciation by a six-year-old…it gets me every time. The living Torah is here for all to experience, especially our children. This is what it's really like to live as a religious Jew in our homeland.

As we approached summer, almost a year had passed since our move to Neve Daniel. The kitchen and bathrooms were now complete, we had steps to the front door, and had even invested in paper shades. The kids were thriving in their new classrooms and playgroups, and we had made many new friends. However, our garden remained unchanged.

Our yard was nothing like the green, overgrown paradise for plants that I had grown up with in New Orleans. Instead, a thirty-centimeter-deep depression in the ground extended from our patio all the way to the walls that surrounded the lot. It was white bedrock: chalky stone, without an ounce of brown earth. I had always dreamed of having a yard for my kids to play in. I envisioned birds chirping outside our windows in the early morning hours, and lazy summer afternoons lying around on the grass. I wanted to see my own childhood memories relived by my children. I dreamed that they would pick dandelions, turn over rocks to find earthworms and doodle bugs, and climb our trees. But our "backyard" was nowhere near that idyllic vision. Instead of grass, we had fields of boulders. Instead of dirt, there was the white bedrock. One might have thought that nothing could grow in terrain like that but, somehow, spiky thorns still managed to sprout everywhere, pricking our heels whenever we dared walk outside barefoot, as if to lay claim to their turf.

So, we formulated a plan: We were going to transform this yard from a barren wasteland into a Garden of Eden, step by slow step. Phase one in our grand garden plan was to haul in dirt. We ordered two truckloads, and we all watched through the windows as dump trucks poured the smelly, rock-studded earth into our hole in the ground. We were now ready for phase two.

In my head, I imagined our future yard as a lush tropical garden with exotic fruit and shade trees, maybe with giant magnolias and banana plants like we'd had in New Orleans. My kids couldn't stop talking about the berries we would grow, along with apples, peaches, and corn. But the reality was that we lived on top of a foggy, windy mountain. I wasn't positive, but I was pretty sure that exotic fruit trees would shrivel up and die in a climate like ours. And the truth of it was that I had never so much as planted a seed before. So, we called in the experts for help.

We met with four gardeners to hear their ideas and get their price quotes. As each one walked into our yard, notebook in hand, we felt a sense of nervous excitement. Their dreams for our yard were awesome—even better than ours. But as they sketched and scribbled on their notepads, we couldn't help but wonder if their proposed yard transformations could possibly fit within our small budget. Could we afford rockeries? And climbing rose arches?

Days passed and the quotes finally came in, all of them completely out of our price range. After hanging up the phone with the last gardener, we made a decision: we would not be hiring anyone to plant this yard. Instead, we asked the most chilled out (i.e. cheapest) candidate to help us figure out the basics. We would have to do the rest of it ourselves.

This was going to be an adventure.

Two days later, Dov the gardener pulled up in his pickup truck and walked into our dirt pile, his sandal-clad feet making impressions in the fresh mud. He walked back and forth, inspecting our pile of mud from every angle. As he reached one end of the property, he crouched down low to the ground, his head at an angle. He repeated these movements at every corner of our yard. Then he offered his opinion: "I'll flatten this earth out for you. You won't be able to do anything until the lot is even."

That made sense to us—and how much could that possibly cost?

"And unless you want a lot of back-breaking work, I should probably put in the irrigation system and sprinklers. Then you can plant everything on your own. I recommend you start with trees around the perimeter."

"Trees?" we asked, a little confused. Trees were nice, but we weren't going to be able to cover this giant pile of dirt with a few saplings along the wall. And besides, we wanted grass for the kids to play on!

"Yes," he confirmed, "first the trees, *then* the grass. The trees need time to grow and develop. Once you have shade trees, it will change the way your garden feels. The grass and plants grow fast—they come later."

I guess what he said made sense. For just about forever, I had entertained visions of birds chirping outside my window, in a yard buzzing with life. To get birds, we needed tall trees, so the sooner we got started the better. We agreed on a price and hired Dov to take over the professional work right away.

Over the next few days, Dov worked hard with his pickaxe and shovel. Our children looked on once again, enthralled with the messy but exacting process. He installed a sprinkler system for the grass and used string and levelers to level our soil until, eventually, it sort of looked like a respectable yard. When he was all finished, we paid him, thanked him for his help, and got ready to get to work.

Sitting around on the patio with the kids, we surveyed our newly-level lot of earth. It was time to discuss the first thing we were supposed to plant: the trees. "Let's plant at least one tree with colorful autumn leaves," I suggested, thinking back on the yellow and red maple trees we had left behind in New Jersey. I had loved autumn in the New York area.

Avi looked toward the corner of our property, where two houses towered over ours. "We need to get a big shade tree right there, to block off the corner," he pointed out. His eye was focused on the practical side of our planning.

"What about fruit trees?" I asked the kids. "What kind of fruit trees should we put in?"

"Apples!" said Eitan, now four and a half.

"Cherries?" I suggested.

And that's when it happened. "Okay," agreed six-and-a-half-year-old Elie, "but we have to have one of the trees from the *Shivat HaMinim*."

"That's nice," I agreed. Of course, it made sense to plant one of the seven species native to Israel discussed in the Torah. "But how come?"

"Because, Ima," she explained, "when Mashiach comes we can only bring *bikurim* from our fruit trees if they are from the *Shivat HaMinim*."

I was floored. My sweet little girl knew that the offerings of the first fruits in the Temple could only be made from fruits of the seven species, something I had not known. But not just that. She also had complete confidence in the imminent arrival of Mashiach and was planning our backyard accordingly.

This was more than a surprise; it was a sort of epiphany—another unexpected benefit to making aliyah that I couldn't have predicted when we moved to Israel. The realization hit me—my children were growing up with an understanding of Torah that I had never anticipated. They *felt* it as part of their lives. When I thought about it, this actually made a lot of sense. Thanks to Elie's daily immersion in the words of the Chumash at school, the Torah wasn't some ancient book. It was alive and relevant. The land that she was learning about in the Torah was the land that she was living in, her backyard, in fact. To her unjaded mind, the Torah had an application in *all* facets of our life, even planning a garden. For my six-year-old daughter, words she learned that had been handed down to us through thousands of years of transmission were as pertinent as if they had been given from the heavens just yesterday. And this may have made perfect sense, but it also amazed me. For religious children in Israel, Tanach is more than an ancient tome. They grow up seeing it as a practical guidebook for our everyday actions.

We put together a very non-professional garden plan, including a pomegranate tree, our representative of the seven species. Then, rather than follow Dov's advice exactly (we were really ready to cover that patch of dirt!), we opted for grass first, then trees, with the rest of the planting to be left for later. We rushed off to the garden center and, after consulting with the owner, we purchased several packages of grass seeds, fertilizer, and a seed spreader. Then back at home, we dove deep into manual labor, hoping our physical efforts would turn our desolate wasteland into a blossoming paradise. We took turns using the seed spreader. We filled it up, turned the handle to spin the wheel and—pop, pop, pop!—green seeds and blue fertilizer balls went flying all over our large patch of dirt.

Then we dragged over heavy bags of compost and, one at a time, punched a hole in each bag and walked back and forth over our "lawn." It was comical to watch Avi shuffling back and forth, shaking the bag's stinky, black contents over our mountain of dirt and multi-colored pellets. We had absolutely no idea what we were doing. Could this process possibly result in green grass?

After that, we set up the computerized sprinkler system to kick into motion four times a day—that's how much water was required for new seedlings, according to the man at the garden center—and warned our children not to set foot on the "grass." Then we waited, full of anticipation for the lush green lawn which would soon appear.

The very first morning after the seeds were planted, Eitan woke us up at the crack of dawn. "Is there any grass yet?" he asked.

"No, buddy," my husband replied as he smushed his head back on the pillow, "it'll take a while."

But that didn't stop us from heading outdoors and crouching over the ground as soon as we were up and out of bed. Maybe something had changed out there under the compost?

Day one. Day two. Day three. The sprinklers went on religiously four times a day, soaking the stinky compost with no visible results. Day four. Day five. Everything looked exactly the same. We began to despair. Perhaps we weren't just novice gardeners, we were incompetent gardeners.

And then suddenly, on day six...was it our imagination? Or did our future lawn have a very faint greenish hue to it?

Elie put her head down close to the dirt. "Yes, Ima! I see grass here!"

All of us got down on our knees to look. And there it was! Teeny tiny sprouts were everywhere, like a green five o' clock shadow. We were thrilled with this proof that our first effort at gardening had been successful.

Days, weeks passed, keeping off the lawn. We watched

the grass growing in deeply enough to capture in a photo. Then we watched the five o' clock shadow turn into a thick green lawn, like the full beard of a burly Irishman. And finally, we watched as weeds grew all over it. But we still weren't allowed to step on the grass.

Sloooowly…four weeks passed. It was finally time.

Avi broke the news. "Ok, kids. We can step on it now."

I looked on from the side, more than a little nervous that our wild kids would ruin our beautiful new grass.

"Just take your shoes off. Be careful!" I pleaded.

Everyone (including me) stripped down to bare feet and tiptoed across the long, luscious grass. It felt like the softest carpet in the world to our (totally non-biased!) feet. One careful step, two steps, three…and then we all ran around.

I plopped myself down in the grass by a clump of weeds and started pulling. Avi joined me. The kids ran free, lay down in the grass, did cartwheels. It was our own piece of the Land of Israel, actually growing vegetation that we had planted. Even if it was just, well, grass. It was the best grass ever. Perhaps it was just the best *feeling* ever: to cause something to grow on our thorny, barren wasteland. To produce a place to play for our children and fulfill prophecies about the time of redemption at the same time. I had never experienced that feeling before.

Our new, green, yard was a head-turning novelty amidst the thick dust of construction that characterized our side of Neve Daniel. Friends and neighbors walked past and oohed and aahed over the carpet of green. It was a conversation piece. But more than that, our sprawling lawn was our first taste of what it felt like to plant the land, to have the capacity to turn something lifeless into something green and thriving. After reading about the desolation of the Land of Israel following the destruction of the Second Temple, we didn't take this new life for granted. Before our very eyes, thorn bushes were replaced with myrtle (or grass in our case), stinging nettle with cypress trees[1].

But I wanted more.

So just a few days later, we began to plant fruit trees. First, two cherry trees. We dug holes with a big shovel and a small spade, pulling out giant rocks as we went. I placed each tree in its hole, then set aside the pots—these became very useful in the coming months: we used them to gather rocks, weeds, and all sorts of refuse from our garden while we prepared the earth for more planting. Next, we turned on the hose and let it run for one full day—a requirement to prevent these tender saplings from going into shock.

Then came the peach tree, then the apple. Last and most importantly, we planted the pomegranate tree, as instructed by Elie.

That summer (of 2007), I ran a backyard camp for my children. Between the singing, baking, and arts and crafts, we added gardening to our repertoire of camp activities. The four of us spent many fifteen-minute intervals in the yard each day. We hauled rocks in buckets (this was a surprisingly successful activity for little kids, as long as they got a treat for each bucket they filled). We made trips to the garden

---

1   Isaiah 65:13

center for stepping-stones and fill-in plants. My kids picked up their own packets of vegetable seeds. We felt like real farmers.

Finally, we chose the last of the shade trees for our yard at the garden center, then squeezed them into the van between children, branches popping out of the windows. I'll never forget that trip. Eighteen-month-old Dalya laughed hysterically, caught as she was in a mini-forest, the highway wind blowing soft leaves in her face.

After digging the rest of the holes and planting the last of our trees, phase one of paradise was complete. Maybe it wasn't perfect, but in our eyes, it was pretty darn close.

By the time we were done, summer had ended. The kids went back to school and kindergarten. The long, carefree days in our new backyard would have to wait for the next vacation.

We continued to care for our little piece of land. Over the months and years, we planted rose bushes, lantanas, irises, geraniums, sunflowers...even corn, cucumbers, and tomatoes. We collected rocks from nearby construction sites, turning them into raised beds. A cluster of stepping stones and river pebbles became a miniature front patio. We loved seeing the fruits of our labor, and for a long time, spent every single Friday morning working in that yard.

Eventually our yard became exactly the paradise that I had imagined, filled with chirping birds, doodle bugs, ladybugs, and all sorts of other surprises. The kids had trees to climb, flowers to pick, and cherries to savor in June. As the seasons changed, we were blessed with colorful leaves in autumn, irises in winter, roses in spring, and pomegranates at Rosh Hashana. We were constantly drawn outdoors by the exciting things going on in our yard.

I learned a lot in the process of creating our dream garden. Being immersed in the struggles of our small piece of the Land of Israel changed me as a person. It is hard to convey how planting our garden created in us all such a deep love for the land. The backbreaking labor we took on had evolved into a real relationship with the earth. My hands regularly found their way into the grass and groundcover, to feel its softness and dislocate any invasive weeds. Like a newborn child, we had given the land our all, and it had given us back a thousand times more. The process had been challenging, and at times it had seemed like it might never pay off, but gradually the fruits of our labor had appeared. I guess the garden project was reminiscent of the way we had uprooted our family and replanted them in a new country; kind of like our cherry trees, our kids grew and flourished, little sabras in the Land of Israel.

All that time we spent digging, weeding, and planting, we were fulfilling the mitzvah of *yishuv ha'aretz*, building and beautifying the Land of Israel, doing our part to make it green and flourishing. Being part of the process of redemption. Our yard became a source of pride, happiness, pleasure, and even holiness. Pretty good for a little patch of rock-filled dirt.

The Land of True Holiness

"From Zion shall go forth the Torah, and the word of God from Jerusalem." –Isaiah 2:3.

BACK WHEN I was in seminary, I remember learning that the true place for the performance of all *mitzvot* (religious commandments) is in Israel. Having grown up in religious communities in America, this idea seemed kind of strange. As long as one kept the laws of Kashrut, Shabbat, and all the rest, what difference did it make whether the *mitzvot* were being performed inside of Israel or outside of the land?

Rav Abraham Yitzhak Hacohen Kook, a great student of mysticism, thought about this idea in an atypical way. *Lights on Orot* is a commentary by David Samson and Tzvi Fishman on Rav HaCohen Kook's esoteric book, *Orot*. In it, the authors explain that "blessing comes to the world in all its fullness *only* when the Jewish nation is situated in its homeland. Concurrently, as Jewish sovereignty spreads over all parts of the Land of Israel, greater and greater Divine blessing flows into the world."[1]

---

1   *Lights on Orot: The Teachings of HaRav Avraham Yitzchak HaKohen Kook*, Commentary by Rabbi David Samson and Tzvi Fishman (Jerusalem: Ktav Publishing House, Torat Eretz

At first glance, this statement is incomprehensible. Why would Jewish sovereignty in Israel cause the whole world's holiness factor to increase?

As Rav Kook explains, God divided the earth between all of the nations of the world and then gave each nation its own, perfectly-suited land. The Land of Israel was created by God for the people of Israel, a nation particularly suited to holiness. When God himself looks for an earthly expression of holiness, he first seeks it in the Land of Israel: "For the Lord has chosen Zion; He has desired it for His habitation. This is My resting place; here I will dwell" (Psalms 132:13–14).

It's a difficult concept to digest, but Rav Kook seems to be saying that God's holiness is manifested in the world through Israel and the Jewish people. For this reason, Jews need to be *in* the Land of Israel in order to gain complete access to God's holiness. When Jews have sovereignty over and fill the Land of Israel, more holiness flows onto earth through their performance of *mitzvot*, and the effects of this blessing can then spread throughout the world.

There's a less metaphysical reason that Jews need to be in Israel to perform *mitzvot*, too. According to many Rabbinical sources, the Land of Israel is the *only* place on earth where the Torah can be observed completely (as many of the commandments pertain only in the land), and also the most ideal place for the performance of all of its *mitzvot*. The Ramban wrote explicitly that the *mitzvot* were given to be observed in Israel (commenting on Leviticus 18:25). He goes on to say

Yisrael Publications, 1996), pp.12–15.

that we only perform the commandments in other parts of the world as *practice* ("so that they shall not be novelties") until we can return to the Land of Israel to observe them correctly.

According to this perspective, performing *mitzvot* outside of Israel definitely has value (we are still required to keep Shabbat, Kashrut, and all the rest when living elsewhere in the world), but our Holy Land is the true place for their performance. Taking this thought process to the next level, our sages have said[2] that living in Israel is equal in value to all of the commandments in the entire Torah.

---

2   *Sifrei, Reah,* 80.

IX.

It's All About that *Beis*...
HaMikdash

"It is a positive commandment to construct a House for God...as it states: 'And you shall make Me a sanctuary.'" Rambam, Mishneh Torah on Exodus 25:8

As the first anniversary of our move to Neve Daniel approached, it felt like we were finally settled in. Our garden was planted, our house was mostly finished, and we had picked up the routine of life in our small town. Shabbatot were spent with new friends, each with their own set of small children like ours. For the first several months after moving, we had enjoyed an endless string of invitations...and then we spent the next several months returning the favors. Avi hopped back and forth between two nearby shuls—he appreciated the homey atmosphere at one, and the rabbi's speeches at the other. On long Shabbat afternoons, we joined our new friends in the park at the center of Neve Daniel, socializing while we watched our kids play. It had been easy to make good friends in Neve Daniel. Aside from the fact that many of our neighbors were in the same life stage as we were, we also shared common ideals, which we loved to discuss in lengthy conversations whenever the opportunity arose. Sometimes we would bring a *seuda shlishit* meal with us and sit around the playground talking until the sun went down.

That fall, I signed Elie up for her first art *chug* (after-school class). She was quite comfortable with her school and her new friends—she didn't need any help in that area. Since she had exhibited some artistic talent, I decided that weekly lessons with a local artist would be a good addition to her schedule. The *chug* was just down the block; she could even walk there on her own, although she didn't always agree to! Eitan was in kindergarten, where he was learning to read Hebrew. At home, we began English reading too, in the afternoons, between play dates with friends. Dalya, a delightful toddler, still stayed home with me all day. She was not yet two, and I loved to hang out with her, run errands together, and play with her on the new wooden swing set in our yard (just built by Avi that summer). Along with enjoying our daily life in Neve Daniel, we were experiencing the benefits of our new closer proximity to Jerusalem. The zoo was only fifteen minutes from home now, so we purchased a family membership. We began to take occasional outings with our three small children, to the shuk and to the Old City.

On one of those outings, I discovered Machon HaMikdash, by accident. It happened one Friday morning just before Sukkot. We were wandering around the Old City with our three children, exploring its twisty cobblestone streets lined with Jerusalem stone homes. Turning a bend, we walked past an old building on our right that had a big sign hanging on the wall. My husband backtracked to take a closer look.

"Oh look, here's Machon HaMikdash," he said.

"What's that?" I asked, rolling the stroller backwards.

"The Temple Institute. It's where they study the *Beit HaMikdash*," he explained. He had heard about it at someone's Shabbat table. "Want to go in?"

We took a peek through the doorway into a small room full of artwork, books, games, and other assorted paraphernalia. In the back, a curtained-off area concealed what seemed to be a small museum. We would have to descend a steep set of stairs to get inside, an obstacle for our bulky stroller.

Rather than commit to a family entrance, Avi went in to check it out while I waited outside with the kids. We sat there for few minutes, waiting on the street in the hot sun, and then Avi reappeared, a grin on his face. "You should come in," he said, "I want to show you something. You're gonna want to see this."

So, we carried the stroller down the steps, Dalya and all, and went inside. With my three young kids, I felt extremely out of place, worried that they would upset the delicate balance of books and artwork in the small shop with just a few of their wild jumps. My husband approached one of the displays and pulled open a large, flat drawer.

"Look at these," he said, leafing through the posters inside. He pulled out a laminated page for me to examine: it was a beautifully depicted scene of the water drawing ceremony in the *Beit HaMikdash* on Sukkot. "Wouldn't these be great for our Sukkah?" he asked.

"Yes!" I had long been frustrated with my husband's idea of Sukkah decorating, which always featured his childhood favorites: lots of tinsel and tacky artwork. "This is beautiful! Let's get a few."

I held Eitan's hand and encouraged Elie to entertain Dalya in the stroller. Avi and I sorted through the posters one by one and picked out three of the best—the water drawing ceremony, a depiction of a High Priest offering incense, and one of the *Aliyah leRegel* (pilgrimage to Jerusalem). These posters were something new to us: I had never seen artwork that reproduced actual scenes from the *Beit HaMikdash*. To me, the Temple had always been an unimaginable concept. But these paintings brought that ancient holy place to life.

We headed to the register to pay and then dragged our children up and out of the store.

A few days later, when the Sukkah was all ready for us to use for our fifth Sukkot in Israel, Avi attached those posters to the walls with great ceremony. It was a small act, but for us it was memorable. Over our years in Israel, our awareness of the deep importance of the Temple had grown, so we took great pleasure in spending a bit of extra money on Temple-themed Sukkah decorations and hanging them to share with our guests. With those pictures, our Sukkah felt complete.

That was our first experience with Machon HaMikdash, but it wasn't our last. Our interest in the place had been piqued. What was this magical little place in the Old City all about? And how could we make it more a part of our lives? Months later, we planned a second trip to Machon HaMikdash. This time, we were going in deeper, to visit that small room in the back, where a tour would be given. And not only were we taking our kids, but we were taking my in-laws, who were visiting Israel on one of their regular trips from America. We packed a bag full of diapers, toys, and snacks, and set off.

We parked near the Old City and walked through its tiny alleyways in search of the museum. Twenty minutes later, we headed back down those narrow steps, and this time we paid for access to the small back section of the institute. We filed in, sat down, and waited for the tour to begin.

I looked around the room, at the small and large vessels, exact replicas of those used in the Temple, at the artwork, and the priestly clothing in glass cases. I felt lucky to be able to bring my husband's parents here, to show them this beautiful aspect of Judaism they had never seen before. As religious Jews, they had always valued Torah observance and *chesed* (lovingkindness) first and foremost. As Zionists, they had encouraged their children to move to Israel, and visited themselves. But here, these two great values were coming together in one small room. Machon HaMikdash was following the laws of the Torah to prepare for actual Temple service in a way that could only happen in Israel, at a time when the rebuilding of the Temple was no longer a distant dream. I hoped that they would love this idea as much as I did.

Eventually the guide appeared. The tour began with a short film, describing Machon HaMikdash and explaining what the institute was all about. To put it simply, they existed to raise awareness and prepare for the building of the Third Temple. Our guide showed us actual vessels they had crafted for the Temple service—trumpets, garments of the High Priest, a breast plate—recreated exactingly from biblical descriptions and protected for future use. He told us the story of the giant golden menorah they had crafted out of one piece of solid gold, just as was described in the Torah. They had thought long and hard about its design, basing it—of course—on the biblical description. It stood right behind the Western Wall Plaza (today it stands in the Hurva Square). We had passed the menorah dozens of times but had never really known what it was.

My in-laws were fascinated with the level of detail, and the attention to the words of the Torah, used to create each item. Of course, they had read the descriptions of the vessels of the Temple every year during Shabbat Torah readings in shul, but that had all been theoretical. They had never imagined being able to *see* the Temple vessels with their own eyes. Their eyes were aglow with wonder. We pored over the beautiful pictures and intricately crafted pieces at the museum for as long as we could. Eventually, the kids lost their patience, so we left the museum in search of felafel.

As we sat around the Hurva Square in the Jewish Quarter with our overflowing pitas in hand, full of felafel and salad and French fries and dripping tahini, life seemed less lofty. We ate with relish. The kids ate copious amounts of French fries, and then we sent them to buy popsicles from the nearby *makolet*. Still, throughout our meal, everything I had seen that day at Machon HaMikdash remained at the forefront of my mind.

The more I thought about it, the more I became convinced that Machon HaMikdash was on a holy mission—one that all those whose focus is on serving God get to be a part of. As religious Jews, we ask for God to bring our redemption every single day, during our Shacharit, Mincha, and Ma'ariv prayers. We yearn for Mashiach and the time of the Third Temple…or at least that's what we *say* in our prayers. But what do we actually do to *achieve* this goal *besides* pray?

Machon HaMikdash was the first organization I had come across that seemed to have truly internalized the meaning of imminent redemption. Rather than wait and see, they were taking action beyond praying. They were attempting to prepare the Jewish people for a time when God will *answer* our collective prayers. They were spreading hope. From their modest quarters in the Old City, Machon HaMikdash had created the vessels of the Temple, piece by piece, all completely ready for use. Using the Torah as a guide, they had even drawn up the blueprints of the building, specifying exactly how the Third Temple should be constructed when the time came. To me, this was true passion.

It reminded me of the level of thought I had put into a far more mundane project: the building of our home in Neve Daniel. If all of us had that level of passion for the rebuilding of the Temple, could things be different for the Jews?

On our next visit to the institute, we discovered a new coffee table book: A compilation of artwork depicting daily life in the Holy Temple, from the different services and ceremonies to the priestly garments. It was divided according to holiday and Temple service, along with thorough explanations of all aspects of Jewish life connected to the Temple. We purchased the book and brought it home, setting it in a prime spot on our living room side table for our children to look at whenever they wanted. It was also placed in the hands of every guest who entered our home.

My brain became infected by an idea. If Machon HaMikdash had their way, imminent redemption could become part of our national consciousness. If more people cared, if more people knew, if we all just focused *more*, then could we possibly build the Third Temple together and bring about the final redemption?

Eventually, the topic of the Third Temple morphed from a novel passion into a part of our everyday conversation. At random intervals, my kids would express their wish for a rebuilt Temple in the near future. At holidays, they would fantasize about what it would be like if we were celebrating at the *Beit HaMikdash*. It was a part of our life.

Many years after our first visit to Machon HaMikdash we were sitting around the table eating our pre-fast meal before Yom Kippur. My mind was on the next twenty-five hours of fasting and prayer. I was concerned about making sure my kids had enough to eat, and about drinking enough water to get me through the fast. Then Elie piped up from the other end of the table. "Ugh," she burst out, "I wish were having Yom Kippur at the *Beit HaMikdash* this year."

Her words made me stop and think. Sure, holiday prep was nice—and important! But my daughter's perspective was the correct one. As Jews, we should be wishing for the rebuilt *Beit HaMikdash* from the core of our beings, especially around the holidays. If we really understood what we were lacking, we would be thinking about the missing Temple, rather than the long fast ahead.

Elie was completely familiar with the Yom Kippur service as outlined in the Torah. With her knowledge and sensitivity, it was hard for her to separate the rituals of the High Priest that had once been performed from the meaning of the holiday today. A day of intense prayer was, of course, meaningful, but it was not a real replacement for the holy service in the Temple.

The vision of the rebuilt Temple had become incorporated into the symphony of our daily life, something that my children naturally shared with family and guests. Countless times over the years, they would ask: "Why can't we just build it already?"

Putting politics and the existence of the Dome of the Rock aside, some devout Jews would answer them this way: Wouldn't it be a sin to build the Temple without explicit word from God?

Maybe. But it's a reasonable question. Is our return to Israel, the establishment of a Jewish state, and dominion over the Temple Mount not enough of a divine sign that redemption is on its way? Maybe it's up to us to bring divine plans to fruition through our actions. Machon HaMikdash is preparing for that redemption in a way that every Jew should be able to agree on: by crafting what they can for the building of the *Beit HaMikdash* and showing what it means to have true hope.

Preparing a Nation for the Divine

THE RELIGIOUS JEWISH world is divided about the building of the Third Temple; should we take steps to prepare for its construction or are we required to wait until commanded to do so? Our visits to Machon HaMikdash had me wondering: was there any precedent for preparing to build the *Beit HaMikdash* before it was time to actually build it?

In chapter seven of Samuel II, King David asked Nathan the prophet if God would permit him to build the *Beit HaMikdash*: "See now, I dwell in a house of cedar," said the king, "but the ark of God dwells within curtains" (II Samuel 7:2). King David was not happy to be living in a king's home while God's earthly palace was yet to be built.

God told Nathan that King David must wait—there was too much blood on his hands for him to build such a holy place. The building of the *Beit HaMikdash* would fall instead to David's son, Solomon.

According to the Ramban[3], there was another reason for the delay in the building of the Temple: "Had Israel...really wanted to build the sanctuary, and had they bestirred themselves to action from the start, it would have been done already." The *Beit HaMikdash* was not being built because

---

3   See his commentary on Numbers, 16:21

the people were disinterested: they didn't truly desire the Temple.

But King David, ever a passionate leader, took a creative approach to his problem. Although God had given him explicit instructions *not* to build the Temple, King David did not give up. Instead, he set to work *preparing* for the building of the Holy Temple by his son Solomon.

There are, in fact, seven chapters (I Chronicles 22–28) devoted to these preparations. Chapter twenty-eight describes the king's drafting of architectural plans for the Temple. King David gathered gold and lumber for the project, along with silver, copper, iron, and precious stones. And it wasn't just the physical materials that the king prepared. He also divided the priests into groups for their future service.

After donating his private hoard of silver and gold, the king encouraged his people to volunteer their own possessions, which they did; this expression of devotion brought the nation great excitement. With this act, the people, too, were being prepared for the upcoming building of the *Beit HaMikdash*. They were finally interested.

When he had finished the prep work, King David held a *Tefila Chagigit* (a celebratory service). The king had accomplished something massive; the plans and materials for the Temple were ready and waiting. All that was left was for David's son, Solomon, to implement the construction.

Before King David's death, he gave the people one final speech full of encouragement: "Set your minds and hearts on worshiping the Lord…build the Sanctuary" (I Chronicles 22:19). Although he didn't merit to build the *Beit HaMikdash* himself, the king's excitement and solicitude were what got the project off the ground.

So many modern Jews believe that our hands are completely tied when it comes to the *Beit HaMikdah*. We believe that any practical steps towards this process are contingent upon divine instruction. But that's *not* how the First Temple was built. There is a clear, historical precedent, written in the chapters of our very own Torah, for starting the preparatory work of our own volition. In fact, these very preparations are part of what brought the Jews to a place of merit and readiness in ancient times.

King David was a man of action, a leader who made what seemed impossible, possible. His devotion to the cause helped make the building of the First Holy Temple a reality.

X.

TURNING POINT

"Though I walk through the valley of the shadow of death, I fear no evil, for You are with me." –Psalms 23:4

No, no, no, no!" I dropped the phone, pain and anguish coursing through my body, my voice suddenly choked in tears. Clutching my pregnant midsection, my heart filled with despair. A sob escaped.

I picked up the phone again, holding it at a distance from my ear. "Susannah? Susannah?" I could hear my mother's worry in her voice, her own pain evident. But I couldn't speak. Elie, who had watched all of this happen from the kitchen table, had taken off in a panic upstairs. Dalya was clutching me around the knees, worried in her two-and-a-half-year-old innocence. What was happening to Ima?

My brother had died.

It had been a horrible accident, an unexpected tragedy. I was in complete shock, along with everyone else. Avi came running down the stairs, put his arms around me, and took the phone out of my hand. My mother explained everything to him. I collapsed onto the floor in a puddle of tears, unable to function with the pain I was now feeling. Aaron and I had grown somewhat distant in recent years, as our life circumstances separated us. He was a young and successful bachelor, living in New York City. I was a soon-to-be mother of four, living in Israel. In addition to the physical distance that separated us, our lives were completely different. And now I would never see him again.

Despite the separation, I loved my brother deeply. Memories raced through my brain—our childhood, our inside jokes, our swim meets, our teenage escapades. Now all of that was gone. Aaron was gone.

I can't even remember what happened that morning. Somehow the kids were dressed, lunches packed, and they were whisked away to school. All I remember is the horrible pain that washed over me, obscuring my ability to think straight.

The rav of Neve Daniel came by. He spoke to me gently, with compassion, while I sat huddled in a ball on the couch, unable to control my tears. Somehow it was decided for me—I would fly to New Orleans that evening, in order to make it to my brother's funeral. My sister, Sharon, couldn't join me. At eight months months pregnant, she was in an even more precarious state than I was, at six months. It wouldn't be safe for her to fly at this stage in her pregnancy. I would have to travel alone.

I remember leaving Avi in the airport, tears shaking me to the core when we parted at security. He gave me one last hug.

As I walked away, I looked back over my shoulder and saw him standing there, his very presence offering support. "You can do this," he seemed to be saying with his loving look.

It was all horrible: the two plane rides, the luggage pick-up, the taxi ride to our big yellow house in Uptown New Orleans. I couldn't process the fact that I was flying home under these circumstances—to say goodbye to my brother. The reality just wouldn't sink in. I saw my mother, my father, and my brother Jesse, all looking completely shell shocked. It was only during the haze of the funeral that I finally absorbed the situation fully. It was the worst day of my life.

Shiva (seven days of mourning) followed the funeral. During that time, it seemed that everyone who had ever been part of our lives in New Orleans came to visit. And despite the shock and pain, over the course of the week, I found comfort in the presence of others. Still, each night, as I curled up in my old bunk bed, I found that I couldn't fall asleep for hours. When I finally did sleep, it was like a blissful dream— the new facts of my life still hadn't sunk into my subconscious. Upon waking, I would remember the horror of it all over again.

We talked about Aaron a lot, remembering his infectious laugh, his quirky personality, his friendly smile. When we were little, he had been nicknamed "Mouth of the South"— he never stopped talking, and he had the ability to connect to almost anyone. That was Aaron. Reviewing these memories helped us process his death. It was good to speak about him. As if we could bring his presence back into our living room with stories about his life.

I missed Avi and the children's hugs that week. I missed the comfort of my friends back home. And there was one topic of conversation which I found myself drifting back to again and again—our life in Israel. Between stories about Aaron, the visitors from New Orleans wanted to hear about the place where I lived. And for some reason, talking about Israel was one of the few things that gave me comfort during that time. I remember feeling actually happy, despite the horrible pain in my heart, as I waxed rhapsodic about the beauty of life in the Holy Land. I remember noticing that. And then eagerly seizing up that topic of conversation again and again, whenever I was asked to. It was one of the only things that chased away the pain, however temporarily.

A dark cloud hung over my life for weeks after I returned to Israel. My friends back home had their own chance to comfort me. And then my niece was born. Sharon named her new baby Hadas, in memory of our brother. After Sharon had sat *shiva* for Aaron in Israel, her Iranian mother-in-law had brought her *hadas* (myrtle) branches. Sharon had breathed in the fresh scent and felt some sort of comfort. So, too, her new baby was a comfort. So Hadas she became.

That summer was not easy. Of course, life went on, and I returned to my regular tasks of motherhood, caring for my three small children. I began to smile and laugh again, as the waves of grief grew further and further apart. Since I was nine months pregnant during August, we couldn't fly to America for our traditional summer visit, so Avi's youngest sister, Sara, flew to Israel instead. Together, we entertained the children—at the zoo with our new membership, at the park, and in the yard with the hose and sprinklers, creating a "water park" out of our swing set and slide.

Despite the resumption of regular life, a part of me was still reeling from the blow of my lost brother. I gave birth to our new baby daughter at the end of August. After a long and difficult labor, our new baby brought me a pure joy that I had almost forgotten I could feel.

We named her Noa Hallel. Noa, after one of the righteous daughters of Zelofachad in the Torah. His five daughters had loved the Land of Israel. When their father died, they turned to Moshe with a request that his estate remain in their hands. Since speaking of Israel was the one thing that comforted me during the mourning period, the name seemed fitting. Hallel, too, was to be a gentle reminder of my brother. After his death, I had to learn how to praise God once again, despite all of the difficulty and confusion that is a necessary part of life. We offer Hallel, praise, to the one true Judge.

XI.

EVERYDAY INSPIRATION

"Appoint for yourself a teacher." –Pirkei Avot (Chapters of the Fathers) 1:6

T*HE SECRET* TOLD me to do it. *The Secret* is a popular self-help book about accomplishing goals which was a *New York Times* bestseller in 2006. One Shabbat lunch, our neighbor, Jeremy Gimpel, lent me the book, telling me that it was life changing.

The Secret suggested that I write down a list of my goals, but that instead of writing, for example, "I want x," I was to write "I am so happy that x is happening," as though my goal had already been accomplished. According to the author of *The Secret*, this simple formula would make all of your dreams come true.

I figured that after spending time reading the book, the least I could do was give it a shot. Jeremy *had* said it was life changing. Even if it didn't work out exactly as the author suggested, at the very least I would be thinking about what it was that I wanted to accomplish. Perhaps that, in and of itself, would help me achieve my goals. So, one night after the kids were in bed I got out my journal and made a list. It felt good to get it all down on paper, especially since all I had to do was write them down—no other action required! I did this again the next night, and then the next night. I wrote about all the things I wanted to happen in my life, in present tense, as though they had already happened. I tore the pages out as I constructed newer and better lists of my hopes and dreams. Then I filed those lists away in a drawer of my bedside table. Eventually, I forgot about them.

Years later, I was rifling through old papers when I happened upon one of my lists. At first, I didn't remember what it was, but when I saw the date, it all came back to me. *The Secret*! There were some pretty amazing goals on that list. I had no memory of ever expressing them as intentions, but many of them *had* actually become a part of my life. My favorite "wish prophecy" was this one: "I am so happy that I have found inspirational people and mentors and have made them a part of my life. I have started attending a regular *shiur* given by someone I admire."

I knew why I had written that. I was a young and overwhelmed mother in a new community, and I had found myself missing the days of seminary, when I had had a full staff of rabbis and teachers available to aid me in my spiritual development. My days were full of things like surprise lice checks and finding ways to convince my small kids to clean up their toys. It was hard to even attend a class regularly while parenting little kids, let alone find the perfect mentor to really inspire me. For a lot of people, this may not sound like a "big goal." But it was a big one for me. I'll never know if it was *The Secret* that helped me accomplish my goal, but accomplish it I did. And that allowed me to access a whole new perspective on the Torah, and specifically, Israel.

I took my first steps towards achieving this goal three years after we moved to Neve Daniel, when my husband left his job in Jerusalem to embark on a new career that allowed him to work from home, all online and over the phone. This was an ideal setup for him; by conducting business from our home office, he was able to avoid lengthy commutes and spend more time with the family.

This happened in April 2009, about eight months after Noa was born. By that time, I had my baby daughter on a pretty tight schedule. I knew when she would nap and when she would wake up, when she would eat and when she would go to bed for the night. After the terror that was Elie's new-bornhood, I had learned that babies actually craved routine; it seemed to make them happier. And in my case, this applied equally to their mother.

With the other kids off at school in the morning, I had some time to myself during Noa's naps. I often used part of this time to practice music, write, listen to Spanish language podcasts, or try to improve myself in other ways. It didn't seem like it would be too difficult to leave my sleeping baby in Avi's capable hands while I left home, at least once a week. So, it seemed only natural that I take my first steps towards finding mentors with a Wednesday morning Torah class in Efrat.

Rabbanit Shani Taragin is an educator who lives in Alon

Shvut. She's beautiful and always dresses elegantly, her hair neatly tucked into a hat, accessories perfectly matching her clothes. She's mother to six children and teaches at several educational institutions. One of them is the Women's Beit Midrash of Efrat.

Every Wednesday, religious women gather there to listen to her speak. She speaks about typical Torah topics. A year-long class may work through one specific book in Tanach (usually one of the Prophets) from beginning to end. Sometimes she will cover several shorter books. We've learned Jeremiah and Ezekiel, Samuel and Kings. The most fascinating to me were the books from the Second Temple period, Ezra and Nehemiah. Whatever subject she teaches, Rabbanit Taragin is an engaging speaker who provides incredible insight into the Tanach, transforming often confusing and difficult passages into stories that we can relate to. She does this all with the help of the commentators and rabbinic authorities. She brings ancient texts to life with drama and insight.

Sometimes the lessons she teaches demonstrate that the whole way you look at life can be completely changed through your study of Tanach. She shows us that the Tanach is alive, a vibrant text that we should be able to connect to, not an impenetrable history book filled with facts that have no bearing on our lives except from a halachic perspective.

One Wednesday morning, while Noa was napping back at home, I was sitting in class with my Tanach open and pen in hand, listening to Rabbanit Taragin going through the verses.

"Do you ever wonder," she asked with a smile, casting her eyes up to the ceiling, "whether when the *chachamim* (sages) wrote about *kanfei nesharim* (wings of eagles), they were imagining a little El Al logo on the eagle's wings?"

The women laughed.

"No, really," she insisted, nodding her head vigorously, completely serious, "Don't you think that if Isaiah saw thousands of Jews flying back from *Galut* on an El Al plane in his prophecy he would have described that as flying on *kanfei nesharim* (wings of eagles)?"[1]

Cries of delight exploded around the room. We had heard stuff like this before from Rabbanit Taragin. But her perspective on the Torah never got old, and this was a particularly tickling notion to the newcomers. Could it be that we don't have to wait for giant eagles to swoop down from the sky and wait in Brooklyn for the Jews to alight on their wings before we take the *Geula* seriously? If the prophets had had to use their words to describe something that didn't exist (airplanes), wouldn't "returning on the wings of eagles" have been an excellent metaphor to describe a big white El Al plane full of new Olim?

I sat at the side of the classroom, reveling in Rabbanit Taragin's words, for I found far more to appreciate than a creative metaphor. Her class again brought home to me how

---

1   When it was time for the Jews to leave Egypt, they gathered in Ramses and traveled to Sukkot at near-miraculous speed (see Rashi on Exodus 19:4). The Torah describes their departure as having been "on eagles wings" (Exodus 19:4). This phrase has come to be used as a metaphor for the prophesied return of the Jews from their exile, which will also be at a miraculous pace. See also Isaiah 40:31, which discusses the future redemption, and states that those who place their hope in God will grow wings like eagles and have renewed strength.

happy I was to be living in a place where people took Torah and halacha so seriously and are able to see it, all of it, in the context of their lives and the current realities of the Jewish people.

I also loved to listen to Rabbanit Taragin's occasional musings on prophecy. One Wednesday, in a class on Jeremiah, she stopped right in the middle of a particularly dry verse, putting down her Tanach, and said: "Can you imagine the difference between the way people viewed prophecy back then and the way they would view it today?"

Eyebrows went up. There were puzzled looks all around the classroom.

"No, really! Back then there was no such thing as seeing anything unless it was right there before you. That's why the mass prophecy at *Matan Torah* (when the Jews received the Torah) was so incredible. But today we have virtual reality! I'm convinced that this is God's way of preparing us for mass prophecy! We are already used to experiencing and seeing things that aren't physically in front of us; that means it will be one short and easy step to mass prophecy when Mashiach comes."

Smiles and murmurs of agreement were heard around the room.

With Rabbanit Taragin, any topic can be fodder for an inspirational message. Once, she told us: "Women today are one step closer to the undoing of the curse of Eve. Have you ever really thought about the epidural?" A pause and a nod of her head. "I really believe this...the epidural has essentially removed the pain and suffering of childbirth! God is slowly preparing us for the times of Mashiach."

I love this. I think it's because this is how many people real-ly *want* to approach the Torah. We want to deeply relate to it. We want it to make sense to us, in our own lives. But when we see God returning the land to the Jewish people and bringing us home, our human nature doesn't always make it easy for us to acknowledge that we are witnessing a miracle. We look at the Tanach and conclude that this phenomenon we are expe-riencing can't be divine: "Since we aren't experiencing obvious miracles like being carried on eagle's wings," we say, "it can't really be redemption." But when we look through Rabbanit Taragin's eyes, and through the eyes of most Religious Zionist rabbis, we learn that the Torah was written in the language that existed at the time. It's up to us to see how the words of the Torah are expressed in today's terms. And when we are able to do that, it all becomes clear: our experiences over the past century have been the fulfillment of the prophecies we were given. Leaders like Shani Taragin helped me understand that we Jews are here in Israel living the next chapter in this holy book we call the Torah.

I checked my watch: 8:25 AM. The sun shone through the trees that Sunday morning as I walked down the steps to my neighbor's house, hurrying a little since I was late. I opened the door, and I heard the familiar chorus of female voices gen-tly debating and discussing. I found a seat—as usual there was only one left—and put down my phone, getting ready to de-vote the next twenty-five minutes to learning about Jephthah (Yiftach in Hebrew) and his ill-fated daughter.

Yiftach was one of the leaders of Israel in the time before King David's reign, called to lead Israel in war. Before going to battle, he delivered a brilliant diplomatic speech to the enemy nations. The content of his speech would have been equally relevant to our enemy nations of today: Yiftach eloquently refuted the Amonites claim that Israel stole their land. In doing so, he tried to avoid a military confrontation between the two nations. Sound familiar? His political plea was ineffective; a war was waged. And just to be sure that God would help Israel win the battle, Yiftach made a vow: Whatever emerged from his house first, upon his victorious return from war, would be offered as a sacrifice to God.

Israel did win the war, but unfortunately for him, Yiftach's only daughter was the first to run out to greet him upon his return. He was devastated. One might have expected Yiftach, a victorious general, to seek out a high priest to annul his vow after it went so horribly wrong, yet instead he and his daughter decide that the vow must be fulfilled. She was offered as a sacrifice to God, just as Jephthah had promised.

It's a sad story, strange and incomprehensible. One of many strange and incomprehensible stories that we had studied in this class over the years. As we finished up the chapter, I glanced around the table at the ten or fifteen women sitting around, books open, some with babies on their laps. I had this little group to thank for most of my understanding of the Tanach. For so many years I was a stranger to its pages, except for the very little I had learned in high school and seminary. Around this table, that had all changed.

Here we gathered to study *Tanach Yomi*, one chapter of

Tanach a day. I can say with confidence that my knowledge of Tanach had already improved since joining the group, and I was hoping for many more years of learning ahead. The words and verses were finally becoming familiar to me. I had begun to recognize the main characters of each book and was starting to be able to identify a verse based on the style of its language.

This had been another door for me, opened into the wisdom of our holy texts. I didn't take it for granted, especially as an adult with most of my opportunities for higher learning behind me.

I now knew enough to know that this story about Yiftach was going to give rise to some controversy. The questions began:

"How could he make a vow like that?"

"He could *not* have intended for the sacrifice to be one of his animals—just look at the wording! What animal comes out of a door of your house?"

"Well, there are sources that say he intended a human sacrifice," our teacher explained, "which shows that he was likely corrupted by the surrounding Canaanite culture, which endorsed child sacrifice to appease their gods."

Each day of the week, a different teacher volunteered their time to the group. Our lineup of five included three men and two women, with guest teachers who stood in as substitutes on occasion.

That day's teacher was Sally Mayer, a friend and neighbor, seminary teacher, and *yoetzet halacha*. Sally has always explained our daily chapter with a hint of real-life humor and an abundance of rabbinic sources all ready and waiting on the tip of her tongue.

Mondays, our neighbor taught the class. A rabbi who had led a large congregation back in New York, in Israel, he worked teaching in seminaries and yeshivot, but always shared free Torah in our community on the side. On Tuesdays, we were guided through the verses by the rabbi of Neve Daniel, Rav Matanya Ben Shahar, who devoted his time to teaching and leading his congregants, as well as the members of a nearby mixed (secular and religious) community, Har Gilo. Wednesday's teacher was a recent immigrant, also a successful psychologist. She always presented a unique perspective on whatever she taught to our small class. And then, on Thursdays, we had Rabbi Yitzchak Twersky, an important writer and teacher. His classes were brilliant dissections of the day's chapter, which he always tied into a larger theme in Tanach. Any one of his classes could stand entirely on its own. It was a solid line-up: that's part of what made this class so incredible. Yet this class was only a tiny fraction of all that was available in Gush Etzion every day. Our Tanach *shiur* was best suited for women who worked from home or didn't work at all (beyond the challenging job of motherhood). But there were many other classes available in Neve Daniel alone throughout the week, days, and evenings. These classes were all free, given by rabbis and teachers offering Torah wisdom simply to enhance people's lives.

In our community, pursuit of Torah knowledge was a highly valued part of life. I loved this aspect of life here. Leaving Ramat Beit Shemesh, I had definitely worried that

I was leaving a strong emphasis on this value behind. But I had been wrong to worry. Although the philosophy of life was different here in Neve Daniel, the passion for Torah was exactly the same. Easily accessible learning is what I dreamed of before I moved to Israel. Here in Gush Etzion, it's kind of taken for granted.

That day, as we discussed Yiftach and his failings, we got caught up in the questions.

"Was it wrong of him to make a vow in the first place, or just wrong to leave his vow so open ended?"

"Why on earth didn't he just nullify the vow?"

"It doesn't say explicitly that he sacrificed his daughter in those exact words. The text says that he did to her as he had vowed—are we sure that's what happened?"

What came out of that day's discussion (with more always to come the next day) was that Yiftach was clearly a product of his times, during which the Israelites had once again fallen into sin, and were being punished for their iniquities with war. Yiftach's good actions were so tainted by bad values that he couldn't differentiate between a sign of worship to the pagan gods around him (human sacrifice) and a sign of worship to God. And perhaps pride played a part in his inability to go to the high priest to have his vow nullified.

His story was a lesson to us—to always keep our eyes open and be aware of moral laxity in our world so that we can avoid getting swept up in it. To never be too full of pride to admit that we've made a mistake. And at the most basic level, to be careful what we say—words are important and can be dangerous. And they are out of our hands once they leave our mouths.

When it was time to stop, we knew that tomorrow's teacher would pick up where we left off. There was a lot more to the story. We closed our books and let out a communal sigh before starting the day. Many of my classmates set off to work. I climbed the steps to meet Avi, who was waiting for me with little Noa in the stroller. Since Avi had started working from home, we had adjusted his work schedule to include playground time with Noa in the park along with a morning walk together.

On these walks, we often spoke about what I had learned in the class that day. Avi had studied almost all of Tanach in his grade school and yeshiva days; I, on the other hand, had not covered much over the course of my sparse Jewish education in the South. Since it was basically all new to me, I liked to hear his perspective on what I had learned. That day I was tickled by some synchronicity I had discovered.

"Guess what?" I asked him as we walked. "We are learning about Yiftach this week in *Nach Yomi*, and on Wednesday, Yael Ziegler is giving a class at Matan and the topic is 'Yiftach: The Power of Words.' Isn't that neat?"

Avi liked the synchronicity too, and he agreed that I would definitely have to attend the class. We continued our walk, discussing Yiftach some more while Noa leafed through the pages of her board books in the stroller, and then moving on to more mundane topics of conversation.

My day had been blessed from the outset. It was such a small investment—only thirty minutes of a day largely filled by childcare and home responsibilities. But studying like this had a huge impact on my life as a whole. Not every class left me feeling warm and fuzzy—in fact, many difficult chapters had the opposite effect—but adding a new dimension of knowledge to my understanding of the Torah was always awesome.

Miracle or Natural Occurrence?

G ROWING UP, I always thought that miracles were completely…well, miraculous. I imagined rays of golden light, background music playing, a voice speaking from the heavens, and the laws of nature being bent in a way that was absolutely impossible. But, as I later learned, there were many times in our history that God performed miracles in ways that, on the surface, seemed completely natural.

This type of miraculous intervention is sometimes indicated in the Torah by the use of the word "*vayahem*," which translates into some kind of confusion (see Rashi on Exodus 14:24). This word is used in a few different places. The first is within the verses that describe the Egyptians' pursuit of the Jews after their exodus from Egypt.

As the Jews crossed the sea, the Egyptian army followed in chariots. They got closer and closer, while the Israelites looked on in fear, and then suddenly, "…God looked down on the Egyptian encampment in the pillar of fire and cloud and brought *confusion* into the camp of Egypt. And he took off their chariot wheels, that they drove heavily, so that Egypt said: Let us flee from Israel, for the Lord fights against Egypt" (Exodus 14:24–25).

The commentators had different ideas about what kind of confusion God brought upon the Egyptians. Rashi suggested that use of the word *vayahem* indicated a loud noise. The Kli Yakar wrote that God brought moisture into the air through the Pillar of Cloud, wetting the ground, which caused the Egyptian's chariot wheels to stick in the mud and break off. Together, these ideas form a picture, of a storm emerging from the Pillar of Cloud. One can just imagine the scene: The Egyptians looking on as a fierce storm gathers, thunder and lightning crashing down, the weather destroying their implements of war. As fear penetrates their hearts, they become convinced that God has arrived once again to save the Jews—so they flee.

Similarly, in the story of the prophetess Deborah with Barak, in their battle with Sisera at Mount Tavor, it says that "God *confounded* Sisera, and all his chariots, and all his host." (Judges 4:15). This caused Sisera and his army to retreat, even though they had many more warriors than the Israelites and could have won the battle.

In the subsequent chapter, Deborah uses poetic imagery to describe the kind of confusion that caused Sisera's army to fall. She describes the Kishon river, at the foot of Mount Tavor, sweeping his army away. Applying the same idea to this passage, it could be that God's confusion descended on Sisera and his army in the form of a great storm. This storm may have filled the river and caused Sisera's unwieldy chariots to stick in the mud, allowing Deborah and Barak to decimate his army.

To anyone looking on, this event would have seemed completely natural. But the words of the Torah tell a story of divine intervention.

We've heard similar tales of inexplicable confusion as recently as the Six Day War. During this fight for our national survival in 1967, the surrounding Arab countries attacked Israel. One of the battlefronts was in Sinai, close to Kusseima. This heavily fortified position was controlled by the Egyptians, and although the Israelis had significant forces, their numbers were far less than those generally considered necessary to defeat a fortified post such as that of the Egyptian army.[1]

When the Israeli battalion approached the battlefield in the morning, they discovered that the Egyptians had abandoned their base and fled, leaving behind valuable equipment and territory: "In the early hours of the 7th of June, the Israelis occupied Kusseima, which the Egyptians had deserted."[2] More disorder and flight occurred on the frontlines in Sinai throughout the course of the day, as a general panic seemed to be setting in among the Egyptian forces. The Egyptians were abandoning their posts all along the defensive line. The Israelis didn't understand it—why would the Egyptians flee when they were still at a technical advantage?

After an Israeli attack on their air bases the night before, the Egyptian army commander, Field Marshal Abdel Hakim Amer had become convinced that the Israelis had the upper hand, despite the fact that the Egyptian forces were mostly intact, and a resupply of fighter jets was on its way. In his panic, he instructed his army to abandon their posts, causing greater casualties and a total defeat for the Egyptians.

---

1   As noted by Ariel Sharon in *Warrior, an Autobiography*, (New York: Simon and Schuster, 1989), p.188.
2   *A Survey of Quick Wins in Modern War*, prepared for the Office of Secretary of Defense, October 1975, p.6.

The unexpected triumph of the Israelis over the Egyptians at Kusseima was one of several "miraculous events" that lead to their ultimate victory in the Six Day War.

Surprising events can always be explained in natural ways. Was the Israeli victory in the Six Day War a miracle or a natural occurrence? No one will ever know for sure. But for those who believe that God controls the world, perhaps there isn't much of a difference.

Just as He intervened with Sisera and the Egyptians at the Red Sea, God brought salvation to the Jews in modern day Israel through hidden miracles. This wouldn't be the first time that God disguised divine intervention under a cloak of confusion.

XII.

SOLVING MYSTERIES IN THE LAND

"And now we have only white, for the tekhelet has been hidden." –Bamidbar Raba 17:5

IT WAS LATE August 2010 and we had just begun one of our last summer adventures before the start of the school year. We were near the Dead Sea, in Ein Gedi National Park, at the beginning of the Nahal David waterfall hike. We had returned a week earlier from a summer in New Jersey, where Avi's family still lived. Since his family had now grown to include other spouses and little cousins, we tried to visit every August, and we spent our days with family, entertaining the kids at swimming pools, museums, mini-golf, and water parks. Of course, we also flew down to New Orleans to visit my parents too.

Now, still jet lagged, my kids had begun complaining about the burning intensity of the unreasonable desert heat at Ein Gedi, since what they were really here for was the waterfalls. Decked out in bathing suits and water shoes, they were eager to start swimming—what was with this hot, dry, rocky place? And they weren't shy about complaining (especially Dalya, who at almost five years old, did not enjoy delayed gratification.) But luckily, just in time to distract the kids from their discomfort, we came face to face with a pack of cute, horned ibexes.

"You know, when I was little, I don't think I ever realized what these looked like," I said, watching as one of them munched leaves on the side of the trail. "They're not really mountain goats."

Avi took a good look at the ibex before replying. "Really? I don't think I ever thought about what they looked like!"

"Yeah," I continued, still watching the ibex munch in front of me, "Growing up, I always pictured a *yael* as a fluffy white goat, kinda' like a Billy Goat Gruff." The animals perched on the side of the desert canyon looked nothing like the goats from my childhood story books. Instead, the *yael*, or ibex, was a majestic deer-like creature, two horns protruding above its shining eyes, its glossy tan coat shimmering in the desert sun.

After watching the herd stare back at us for a minute more, we told our kids to say goodbye to the animal pack, and we proceeded along the trail. Ein Gedi was beautiful as usual—the stream trickled along between the rocks of the red canyon, creating a happy abundance of plants and reeds. Birds flew overhead, chirping merrily in the late summer sun. When we reached the first glimmering waterfall, my husband and the big kids ran in to cool off, leaving me to daydream on a boulder with my feet in a shallow pool. Noa, preferring the safety of my arms to a waterfall pool, remained on my lap.

My middle name was Yael. Growing up, I had always been confused about its meaning. I liked the *sound* of my name, but when I was eight, I had learned that it meant 'mountain goat' in Hebrew, and I thought that seemed a very strange name to give a child. Why would anyone want to be named after a mountain goat?

Later, I learned the story of the Yael we meet in the Tanach. The battle with Sisera during the time of Deborah and Barak had ended definitively only because of Yael. The wife of one of his allies, she had welcomed Sisera into her tent, lulled him into a false sense of security by feeding him and taking care of him, and then, when he was asleep, she had driven a tent peg through his head, killing him.

I realized that my name was pretty cool, after all.

But I still couldn't wrap my mind around the mountain goat part. It was only on that hike, decades later, that I began to understand that a *yael* was a majestic creature whose nimble feet and shiny coat make it perfectly suited to Israel's rocky desert terrain. An expert at climbing and hiding, its sand-colored fur serves as the perfect camouflage. An ibex is like an incognito adventurer. Not bad, as namesakes go. Particularly for someone who loved hiking as much as I did.

I thought back to a conversation we had had several years earlier with Rabbi Natan Slifkin, affectionately known as the Zoo Rabbi, back in Ramat Beit Shemesh (Rabbi Slifkin would later go on to found the Biblical Museum of Natural History, a center built to teach about the animals of the Torah, which nowadays houses locusts, snakes, stuffed wolves, foxes, and much more.) During a conversation over a Shabbat meal, Rabbi Slifkin, had mentioned that some of the animals written about in the Torah were of unknown identity until recently, when the Jews returned to the Land of Israel.

Rabbi Slifkin even published an article on the topic on his Zoo Torah blog, "Regarding the Identity of the *Shafan*." The *shafan* is one of the four non-kosher animals that is explicitly listed in the Torah, animals which have one kosher sign but not the other (all kosher animals must have split hooves and chew their cuds). The identities of three of the animals are agreed upon—the pig, the camel, and the hare—with *shafan* often having been translated as rabbit. According to Rabbi Slifkin, however, the *shafan* was, actually, not a rabbit at all. Rather, it was the rock hyrax, a badger-like creature native to Israel (they're all over Ein Gedi, too). So why did some of our holy sages conjecture that the *shafan* was a rabbit when it was a completely different animal?

Rabbi Slifkin explained that it was because *there were no rock hyraxes in Europe*. Most of our sages wrote their commentaries on the Torah centuries after the Second Temple was destroyed. Once the Jews had been expelled from the Land of Israel, it wasn't long before their memories of its native animal life faded, leaving only mystery behind. To determine the possible identity of the last non-kosher animal, they chose the closest local equivalent (the rabbit) having no direct knowledge of the rock hyraxes that lived in the Land of Israel, far away.

Rabbi Slifkin's idea made so much sense, but I had still found it incredible. Had I somehow accessed a hidden layer of the Torah just by moving to the Land of Israel? I felt privileged and blessed to be able to understand these Torah mysteries by doing something as simple as going for a nature walk. Here in Ein Gedi, I could see a *shafan* with my very own eyes (they love hanging out on rocks and boulders just like the one I was sitting on). Putting together these little pieces of the puzzle made the picture of the Torah so much clearer. Now, it was almost hard to recall that for thousands of years Jews had been almost entirely cut off from the land and its natural world. How lucky I was to be living here.

I let out a contented sigh and watched as Noa splashed in the shallow pool at my feet in her little bikini and sun hat, having squiggled out of my arms while I was ruminating. The rest of the kids ran over, breaking me out of my reverie. They were soaked and happy.

"How was that?!" I asked.

Elie began chattering about how freezing cold the water- fall was. Eitan was ready to go jump into the next one. Even Dalya was now wet and happy, eager to participate in our adrenaline-filled adventure through Ein Gedi—although, from the looks of it, she would have been happy to stay in this first "swimming pool" all morning.

To our children, growing up in the Land of Israel in the twenty-first century, this nature reserve in the Judean Desert was basically just a really cool water park, but for me, be- tween the biblical animal life and the historical significance of the place (King David had hidden from his enemies in Nahal Arugot, a stream just a few hundred meters away), it was so much more.

We set out on our way again, past a group of rock hyraxes and on to more incredible waterfalls. This was Ein Gedi: just a typical Israeli hiking trail, bringing our Torah to life.

Autumn came and went, and we settled into our long winter routine. Between Hanukkah in November/December and Purim in February/March, the days seemed to sort of bleed together, as school day after school day followed, one after another, without any real break (other than Shabbat). While the kids were at school, I stayed at home, keeping busy with the many tasks that constantly occupied my life as a mother of four (grocery shopping, laundry, making dinner, doctor's appointments, etc., etc.) and trying to make time for various forms of self-improvement. I was, of course, still really enjoying my daily and weekly *shiurim*—Wednesdays with Rabbanit Taragin, and *Tanach Yomi* every morning. But I needed a break, a breath of fresh air. One of the few drawbacks of living in Neve Daniel was the pillar of cloud that seemed to encircle our little mountaintop for months at a time during the winter season. Come late winter, things began to feel kind of dreary. I was starting to dream of spring flowers and sunshine, still just out of reach.

One February morning, I woke up earlier than usual, ready to start the day. I was eagerly awaiting an escape from my daily routine: today was *tiyul* day at the Women's Beit Midrash. Rabbanit Taragin was going to be leading our class on an adventure into the story of Jeremiah the prophet. That day's excursion was taking place at one of my favorite hiking trails: Nahal Prat. Avi had promised to be available to pick up Noa from her little playgroup in the early afternoon, and watch her and the other kids until I returned from hiking.

I loved Nahal Prat because of its cooling streams and beautiful desert oasis scenery. I couldn't imagine I would learn anything revolutionary about Jeremiah there—we had already been studying the book for months—but I was looking forward to visiting one of my favorite places with one of my favorite teachers on a beautiful day. I hopped out of bed and began tackling the minutiae of our morning routine.

An hour or two later, the kids had boarded the bus safely to school, I had my homemade cup of coffee in hand, and I was ready to go. Away I drove to our meeting point in Efrat, where the minibus was waiting. The (mostly older) ladies from my class were decked out in hiking hats and sneakers. They were chatting excitedly, like school kids on a field trip.

After piling into the minibus, we drove for an hour, through Jerusalem, and then east towards Jericho. I watched through the window as the terrain became dry and desert-like. Towards the end of our drive, we pulled through the gates of the small community of Almon and continued down a treacherous road to the Ein Prat Nature Reserve parking lot.

As I stepped out of the bus and onto the dusty earth, I took a deep breath of blissfully fresh air. It was a gorgeous mid-winter day, warm and sunny at Nahal Prat, a welcome break from the rainy winter blues typical for February in Neve Daniel.

My friend Anita and I walked together, catching up as we

climbed along a rocky pathway and down towards the rushing riverbed. We passed under a cluster of almond trees, covered in little white-pink blossoms. Rabbanit Taragin stopped next to the almond trees and waited for us to gather around. "This is where Jeremiah lived," she began, "Right above the stream in the community of Anatot, a city of Kohanim." She pulled out her Tanach and began to read, in Hebrew: "The word of God came to me saying: What do you see, Jeremiah? And I said: I see a branch of an almond tree [*makel shaked*]. Then God said to me: You have seen well, for I will hasten [*shoked*] my word to perform it" (Jeremiah 1:11–12).

She went on to relate the whole of Jeremiah's backstory; he had grown up right here, with the Prat Stream in his backyard. Rabbanit Taragin explained how his familiarity with the nearby terrain made him capable of identifying a branch of wood, a simple stick with no flowers or leaves, as having come from a specific type of tree—the almond tree. There was a reason that God had used this tree as a metaphor for the punishment he would mete out on his people. Like an almond, the first fruit of the season to blossom, God was going to bring destruction on the Jews with haste, sooner rather than later.

The breeze picked up a bit. I stood near the Prat River as a shower of almond blossoms drifted down in a gust of wind. My soul was inspired—by the falling flowers, the beautiful stream, and Rabbanit Taragin's words. I wasn't sure how I would have understood these prophetic verses in another time or place, before Israel and its plentiful almond trees were returned to the Jewish people. But I knew that my experience of Jeremiah's prophecy wouldn't have been the same.

We made our way down the path, closer to the rocky riverbed, watching rivulets of water rushing past over miniature waterfalls. Rabbanit Taragin opened her Tanach one more time and read to us again, this time verses three and four of chapter thirteen: "And the word of God came to me a second time: Take your belt that you bought that sits around your waist and get up and go to Prat!" She paused, lifting up her hand as if holding a linen belt. "And hide it there in the hole of the rock."

Rabbanit Taragin explained that some commentators had suggested that Prat might be the Euphrates River, the mighty river that runs far to the north and west of modern-day Israel. "Doesn't it make so much more sense now when you know that Jeremiah lived in Anatot and Prat wasn't the Euphrates River, but a stream right in his backyard?!"

We had driven through the modern-day town of Almon-Anatot on the way down to this stream. As Rabbanit Taragin explained, the *yishuv* had been named after the ancient cities that once stood in the exact same place. Jeremiah hadn't traveled hundreds of miles north or west to bury a linen belt. Instead, he had performed this task assigned to him by God near his home.

Growing up, the historical landmarks I visited were never more than a few hundred years old. The historical figures I learned about as a child were John James Audubon, a renowned nineteenth-century ornithologist, and Jean Lafitte, a pirate-turned-war hero during the Battle of New Orleans. On school field trips, I had visited Audubon Park and Jean Lafitte Reserve.

Nahal Prat is a popular hiking spot today. Visitors can see and experience the terrain described in the Torah for themselves. That day it struck me deeply: living in our homeland, a local field trip brought our own history to life as it hadn't been for thousands of years.

We slogged through the rest of the mostly cold and rainy winter, eagerly awaiting spring. In mid-March, warmer weather finally arrived, just in time for Pesach. I was so ready for it (and the kids were too). In honor of the holiday, I planned a week full of warm-weather family activities. We were all aching to get out and enjoy the outdoors.

Early one morning, we got the kids into bathing suits, packed up towels and food for the day, and piled into the car. It was beach day, a family favorite. My kids were all geared up for a day full of sand and surf, but this wasn't going to be a typical morning at the beach. We were headed up to Dor Beach, just past Caesarea, to search for snails with representatives from Ptil Tekhelet, the leading experts in Israel on the distinctive blue dye necessary in the production of tzitzit, as commanded by God: "Speak to the people of Israel and instruct them to make for themselves fringes on the corners of their garments throughout the ages; let them attach a cord of blue to the fringe at each corner" (Numbers 15:38).

After a long and challenging drive, broken up by bathroom stops, fights, and lots of snack breaks, we pulled up to the meeting point. Avi and I slathered the kids with sunscreen and approached the small group that had already gathered on the shore. Our guide from Ptil Tekhelet distributed snorkel masks and gave us a lesson in snail hunting.

"*These* snails," he said, holding up a large mollusk with a brown and white striped shell, "are *chilazon*—the ones with *tekhelet* inside. That's the blue liquid we once used to dye our tzitzit. Their shells look striped once they are cleaned, but underwater they blend into their surroundings on the sea floor."

"And these," he said, holding up a more typical-looking shell, "are just regular snails. We don't want those." He tossed the unwanted snail into the water with a ker-plunk.

With that simple lesson, he sent us off into the Mediterranean Sea, armed with blue plastic beach pails. Our mission for the day: to gather as many *tekhelet*-producing snails as we could find. When we were all done, we would return to the beach to watch a demonstration of the *tekhelet* production process.

We searched and searched for snails. My kids picked up random seashells, certain each time that they had unearthed a *chilazon*. As the minutes ticked away, it seemed like we weren't going to find anything important at all, but then Eitan, now almost nine years old, pulled something out of the water, "I found one!" he shouted, "A *chilazon*!!" And it was.

We studied our discovery closely, training our eyes to recognize more *chilazon* in the murky water. After that first find, it was smooth sailing. We started to spot striped snail after striped snail, filling our bucket to the top with them. Eventually the kids got distracted by the fact that they were in the sea; they went off to splash and play in the gentle waves, but my husband and I kept collecting snails in the shallow water until the guide blew his whistle to call us back to the shore.

Back at the beach, our guide told us the tale of the lost *chilazon:* After the Romans took control of Israel, Emperors Caesar and Augustus issued edicts outlawing the use and production of the royal-looking dye by commoners. Production went underground. But then, in 639 CE, with the Arab conquest of the Middle East, the remaining dye houses were destroyed, and their methods were completely lost. The *Midrash Tanhuma* laments, "and now we have only white, because the blue has been hidden."[1]

Once the Jews were exiled from the Holy Land, to which the *chilazon* was native, the knowledge of which exact creature produced the correct blue dye was lost. They were forced to leave the blue strings of *tekhelet* out.

The only clues that remained were some passages in the Talmud that described the *chilazon*. According to the description, the marine creature had a shell and could be found along the northern coast of Israel. The snail itself had to blend in with the sea. And when the dye was properly extracted from the live snail, it was deep indigo in color, "like the sky and sea."[2]

Interest in the *chilazon* was piqued during the nineteenth century, when a few pharmacologists, zoologists, and rabbis from Europe began searching for the correct snail and process to produce the dye. The famous Radzyner Rabbi eventually began producing a form of *tekhelet* from squid, in the

---

1   *Midrash Tanhuma, Shelach,* 15.
2   *Sotah* 17a.

late 1800s, after extensive research and travels. Many of his chasidim wore his form of *tekhelet* on their fringes. Then, before World War I, Rabbi Isaac HaLevi Herzog (who would later become the chief rabbi of Palestine), did further research on the *chilazon*, selecting two candidates for the correct snail based on the Talmudic passages.

Years after our nation's return to Israel, in 1969, scientists and scholars embarked on intensive research once again, to correctly identify the *chilazon*, once and for all. For years, they only managed to produce purple and black dyes from the various marine animals they investigated, rather than the coveted blue. But then a remarkable discovery was made with one particular snail, by Professors Otto Elsner and Ehud Spanier. If the snail's dye was extracted as its shell was crushed, and then exposed to harsh Israeli sunlight, a chemical process occurred that produced a deep blue color. The *chilazon* had been found. In 1985, Rabbi Eliyahu Tavger wrote his book, *K'lil Tekhelet*, and became the first person since its loss to use the authentic dye for ritual purpose of tzitzit.

Finally, in 1993, the Tekhelet Institute was founded with Rav Tavger, to research, educate the public, and produce *tekhelet*. This happened just a decade before the time that I, myself, had made Aliyah with my small family. And here we all were, less than a decade later, sharing this unbelievable historical and religious experience on a morning out at the beach.

We were shown how to extract the liquid from the snails, then how to soak wool fibers in the dye and leave them to dry in the sun. The kids (especially Eitan) enjoyed these experiments with slimy snails, although I can't say the same for myself! As the day slipped away, and morning turned to late afternoon, they remained completely absorbed in the process. The only one who didn't seem particularly intrigued was Noa, who at two and a half was more interested in the pretzels we had in our diaper bag than the slimy dye coming out of the snails. When the workshop was over, we took one last dip in the water and set out for home. It had been a perfect day at the beach—a day that took us far beyond sea, sand, and surf.

Once we were in the car, all the kids passed out from exhaustion, leaving only me and Avi awake to discuss our coastal adventure. We had done so much more than build sand castles and jump waves. We had learned how to process *tekhelet*, something that had been lost to history for over a thousand years. Free to live our lives in the Land of Israel, Jews had painstakingly researched and reclaimed this lost commandment. And because we had chosen to live our lives in Israel, we were able to have days like these. Living in America, we could have ordered *tekhelet* strings from the institute and had them shipped to us. But we could never have hopped in the car and had an experience like this. In Israel, hikes and excursions were so much more than a way to enjoy the nice weather and nature. They were more than family entertainment, an opportunity for togetherness. They were an opportunity to really get to know Israel, the physical land of our forefathers, and to understand its hidden messages. For thousands of years, it had been the missing piece in the puzzle of our ancient texts. With our adventures here in Israel, we were gaining a deeper understanding of our Torah, our most precious treasure.

The First Fruits of Redemption

AS A CHILD raised within the *Mashiach* (Messiah)- focused world of Chabad, I often wondered what the
coming of the *Mashiach* was supposed to look like. My
imaginative scenarios were many, but I always thought that
the changes would occur all at once, in one great flurry of
miracles, beginning with the arrival of *Mashiach*.

But as Rav Tzvi Yehuda HaCohen Kook wrote in *Torat
Eretz* Yisrael, the period of *"Yemot Hamashiach"* (Days of the
Messiah) doesn't begin when *Mashiach* actually physically
appears and is acknowledged; instead, it is a process that
includes several steps. These include: "A returning of the
Kingdom of Israel to its former sovereignty, emancipation
from foreign rule; and the shattering of the gentile yoke
from around us."[1] He goes on to elaborate: "The first days
of *Mashiach* see the blessing return to the nation and to the
land, in place of the curse of *Galut."*

According to many of our sages, these stages are supposed to take quite a while; perhaps many, many years. The
coming of the *Mashiach* doesn't begin with him riding in on
his white donkey and bringing the Jews into Israel in one
great day of drama; rather, redemption is a slow process that

---

1   *Torat Eretz Yisrael*, The Teachings of HaRav Tzvi Yehuda HaCohen Kook (Jerusalem: Torat
    Eretz Yisrael Publications, 1991), p.279.

begins with the return of God's *blessing* upon the people and the land. As it says in Jeremiah: "And the children will return to their borders" (31:17). As the curse is lifted and God's blessing is returned to the land, the Jewish people will slowly flow back into their homeland.

Still, the question remains: what does it mean to see the curse lifted and God's blessing returned to the land? What does this look like, practically speaking? We can find an answer to this question in the book of Ezekiel: "But you, mountains of Israel, you shall shoot forth your branches and yield your fruits to My people Israel, for they will soon be coming" (Ezekiel 36:8). According to Rashi (commenting on this verse when quoted in *Sanhedrin* 98a), this means that when the Land of Israel gives forth fruit abundantly, the end of exile is near: "and there is no surer sign of the Final End than this."

Today, in Israel, we can see this very reality. The land is bursting forth with fruit: grapes, olives, pomegranates, figs, and so many others. You can see them along the roads in agricultural fields, on hiking trails, and in home gardens (like the plentiful pomegranates, limes, and cherries in our own backyard). Our grocery store shelves and farmer's markets are filled with locally grown fruits and vegetables. To some, this bounty may seem like a simple physical manifestation of people's hard work, but according to Rav Kook, it is our job as religious Jews to see all of this fruitfulness as *God's* doing, as part of the redemptive process.

This is especially true when you consider what Israel used to look like in recent history, before the Jews returned.

For thousands of years, the Land of Israel remained almost completely barren no matter how hard its inhabitants tried to bring it to life. As Mark Twain famously wrote after his visit to the Holy Land in 1867: "Palestine is desolate and unlovely. And why should it be otherwise? Can the *curse* of the Deity beautify a land?"[2]

But now, all of that has changed. Through our wheat fields, date palms, orange orchards, avocado groves, vineyards and more, the blessing of abundance has returned, giving us a real picture of the days of the final redemption.

---

2   Mark Twain, *The Innocents Abroad*, (American Publishing Company, 1879) p.608.

XIII.

Becoming an Influencer

"Rectify the sin of the spies who slandered the land. Measure for measure, we must tell and proclaim, across the entire world, its splendor and magnificence, its holiness and glory."
–Rav Abraham Isaac Kook, Eretz Cheifetz

OUR FIFTH WAS born on Pesach 2012, and he was a sweet, beautiful, bundle of joy. We lucked out with this one; after an easy transition into life in the world, Gabi started sleeping through the night at only seven weeks. (Shhh! Don't tell anyone!) Even so, it took me a good few months to get through the addled newborn phase, even with an angel baby. I rocked and held and fed him all day. It was impossible to get anything of substance accomplished.

But that wouldn't do, because I had two very important tasks on my to-do list. First, Elie would be turning twelve in August—I had to plan her bat mitzvah. And second, in honor of the occasion, my husband's entire family would be coming to spend the month with us in our home in Israel.

That meant his parents, brother, three sisters, one brother-in-law, and five nieces and nephews. Luckily, we had just (finally!) finished our basement floor, so we had two complete guest rooms in addition to a new office space for Avi. With the addition of a few mattresses on the floors of my kids oversized bedrooms, we had plenty of space. So even if I did have a newborn, I was going to have to plan the most amazing summer vacation ever.

It was my dream come true: lots of family coming to Israel. At that point, I was already used to the regular visits from my in-laws and parents (who would also be coming for the bat mitzvah in August). And we often spent Shabbat and holidays with my sister's family (which now included eight nieces and nephews!) in nearby Ramat Eshkol. But having my husband's *whole* family, especially all the nieces and nephews, who were about the same ages as my own children, was a novelty. We finally had enough space to hold the whole *chamula* comfortably. I just had to make sure that they left Israel with a favorable impression. Of course, they had all been to Israel many times before. But spending a month here—in our home, getting to know what day to day life was really like—that was a different story. I would have to try to give them a little taste of what I got to experience living in Israel year-round (the good stuff, of course. We try to focus on the positive here—a lesson reinforced by what happened with the spies who were sent by Moses to check out the land). Could I possibly succeed in presenting to them the beauty of Israel, the inspiration, the camaraderie of the Jewish people, and the feeling of being at home, all bound up together and served on a silver platter?

I set to work as soon as I escaped from post-natal fog, working to create an itinerary for the summer of our dreams. With all of my kids home for the summer, we would be on this adventure together. And although Avi wouldn't be able to join us every day, his night hours and flexible work schedule would allow him to join us at least part of the time. So I planned out almost every day in detail—a biblical experience here, a trip to the beach there—and on days that I left freer, with no official event scheduled, I offered a few options to choose from. At the same time, I set my daughter's bat mitzvah into motion, working to create an event that would feel familiar to family members but also have that unique Israeli flair. As the month of July approached, I thanked God for Gabi's new nap schedule, and cleaned the house from top to bottom. I stocked the pantry and spent days cooking, making pots of meatballs and soups, baking lasagnas and cakes, and freezing it all for later. Who wants to stay home and cook when you could be sharing the beauty of Israel with family?

The big month finally arrived. Relatives would be flying in from New Jersey in family groups, requiring trips to Ben Gurion every couple of days. The very first to arrive were my brother-in-law and sister-in-law, Ari and Ilana Erdfarb, with their five children. Of all of my husband's four siblings, our kids were probably most eager to spend quality time with them—three of the Erdfarb children had been born within days or weeks of ours, and despite the geographical distance, the cousins were very close. We were looking forward to hosting them for the summer.

Not surprisingly, they were exhausted after their flight, and they all crashed as soon as they walked through the door, promising that they would be up for any activity we had planned the next day.

As I put Gabi to bed that night, I held him close for a few extra minutes in the rocking chair, saying a silent prayer to God. I prayed that all of my hard work would pay off, and that the summer I had planned for our guests would help inspire their love for Israel, something that had grown to a fiery intensity in my own heart in the nine years since our aliyah.

The sun rose on the next morning, and I popped out of bed. For the first day of our summer adventure, we had decided to share our favorite desert oasis, Nahal Prat, with our visitors. We'd be hiking the same trail that I walked that cool February morning a year and half earlier, but this time, our group would include ten small children rather than twenty adult women. After watching my nieces and nephews crawl out of bed one by one, we lingered a while over coffee out in the yard, under the shade of our now two-story-high trees. The Erdfarb kids seemed to be in good spirits and recovered from their long journey. So, after breakfast, we packed our backpacks, got into bathing suits, and piled into the cars.

A half hour later, we had reached our destination. At the top of the park, the National Parks entryway made the place seem deceptively formal. We exchanged our parks card for a map, and waved goodbye to the ranger, with wishes for a pleasant day. Then, the descent began—a heart-pumping drive down a steep, narrow road that is, somehow, two-way. We drove in a caravan, hearts beating wildly while we tried to suppress the familiar fear that we might tumble into the rocky crevice far below. But we didn't. After a few minutes, we arrived safely at the big rocky area that served as Nahal Prat's parking lot.

It was late July. As expected, the scenery at Nahal Prat was very different than it had been last February. Gone was the gentle green groundcover and spattering of winter wildflowers. There were no almond blossoms blowing in the wind. Instead, the view from the parking lot was of dry, golden hills, contrasting sharply with bright green growth that only snaked along the sides of the river. On summer days, Nahal Prat is pretty much always packed. Being a water oasis, (and one located in Judea and Samaria, at that) it's a welcome escape from the summer heat, full of both Israelis and Palestinian Arabs looking for a cheap and easy way to get wet. That day was no exception.

We parked in the closest spot we could find to the trailhead (which was pretty darned far) and got out. It was hot. Middle eastern kind of hot. Desert sun beating down upon you hot. My family was used to this: dry heat like this was fairly typical, and it's not like we were jetlagged or anything. But Ari and Ilana and their children appeared to be melting.

The solution to this problem, of course, was a desert oasis—and luckily, we were in one! The pools were only a few hundred meters away. I kicked into high gear and led the way, starting us all towards the park. But after only a minute, I heard a loud cry of pain and a yowl. I turned around, afraid of what I would see.

Ilana, still a few steps from the van, was carrying a huge

bag (towels, I think?) and her eighteen month old, Akiva. Ari held baby Ezra and the hand of their third son, Elisha. And six-year-old Koby (child number two!) was on the ground, crying—he had fallen down, and had a bloody knee. He was the source of the yowling. I'll never forget all their miserable-looking faces at that moment. At least eight-year-old Gaby looked okay.

I ran back to help, grabbing the bag and baby so Ilana could soothe Koby. He stopped crying, stood up, and then we continued the trek toward the first part of the park.

"We're not in Kansas anymore, are we?" Ilana observed in an unhappy tone as she looked around at the throngs of adults and children, some in swimsuits but others just stripped down to underwear. There was quite a scene at the main pools: barbecue pits were perched near every available picnic table, emitting wafts of thick smoke and scents that seemed out of place at eleven o'clock in the morning. Between the picnic tables, children were splashing, running about, and shouting wildly in both Hebrew and Arabic. Ilana looked nervous about the thought of joining this crowd for a day out.

"Let's just stop and go to the bathroom," I offered. "We can wash Koby's knee here. And it's less crowded up ahead."

We stopped at the bathroom, restored the peace, and got ready to move on. Ilana and Ari clearly weren't too happy about my choice for the day's outing, but rather than complain, they had decided to be troopers. Despite the jet lag, injuries, and underwear-clad swimmers, they were ready to embrace the challenge. I really wanted to turn this trip around for them, and fast.

The main trail was the quieter part of the stream, reserved for those who don't mind walking a bit. It was still sunny and hot, but no longer rocky. Just up ahead, we could hear water rushing and the promise of cool pools.

When the first pool appeared, we stopped for a quick dip. The kids popped their feet in the water, then, after getting used to the cold, jumped in completely, splashing each other playfully. Now that the intense heat was behind us, and it was a little quieter and less crowded, everyone's nerves were calmed. I was relieved to see our troops smiling again.

"Let's keep going," Avi suggested. "There are even quieter pools up ahead."

After a few more minutes we reached our breakaway trail. The sound of rushing water filled our ears as we made a turn towards a densely thicketed area. Holding on to our children tightly, we crept through the trees, climbing over roots, branches, and river rocks toward our final destination. Then, we stepped through a dark opening in the trees, into paradise. A gentle mist rose through the air from the crystal pools at our feet. All around this little hideout there were smooth, flat rocks. And best of all, we were all alone.

We had arrived. We threw down our backpacks and got comfortable on the grey stones.

While the adults sat with their feet in the water, the older children set to the task of exploring our private oasis. Shielded from the sun, we took a collective deep breath of cool, misty air. I watched as our guests from America absorbed this Eden-like hideout.

Surrounded by birdsong and rushing water, pure

tranquility was ours. We sat and caught up on the latest family news, enjoying the tickling feeling of tiny fish nibbling on our toes. Eitan and Elie showed the rest of the kids how to catch frogs and fish, and they all splashed and explored with endless energy. As a sense of deep relaxation set in, my exhausted brother-in-law and sister-in-law stretched out on the smooth stones and fell asleep.

Thank the Lord! Our guests had experienced a complete turnaround in less than an hour. This part of Nahal Prat—concealed by rocky paths, accessed only through heat, raucous crowds, and a forbidding descent—did, indeed, make a great outing. True, we had gotten off to a rocky start, quite literally, but for their first day in Israel we had succeeded in giving our family a small taste of the beauty of our land.

My husband and I exchanged a knowing glance, congratulating ourselves on a job well done.

But of course, our work (vacation?) was not yet done. That evening, Avi's parents and remaining three siblings arrived, completing our group for the next day's outing to the Beit Guvrin National Park, which contains the ruins of Maresha, an important town during the time of the First Temple, and Beit Guvrin, an important town during the Roman era. This trip was a major success. There's nothing more quintessentially Israeli than digging for fragments of pottery from the Second Temple period in a cool, dark cave in the summertime.

We spent a long-awaited family Shabbat together in

Neve Daniel. This wasn't the first time any of Avi's family members had spent Shabbat in our community, but it was the first Shabbat that they were all there *together*. Ari and Ilana stayed in one basement room, moving their kids into the playroom and the girls' room. Elie, Dalya, Noa, and Gaby all shared the big pink room upstairs. Eitan vacated his room (sleeping on a mattress on the floor of the baby room) so that Avi's sisters Leah (my ex-roommate) and Sara, could stay there. Yehuda, Avi's twenty-four-year-old brother, dragged a mattress into our home office. And my in-laws used the pull-out couch in the second basement room. Needless to say, it was not a quiet Shabbat, but it was a fun one. And I was very thankful that I had made sure to cook and stock up in advance—I didn't have to bake a thing.

The next day, we helped Leah and Sara prepare for a three-day, seventy-one kilometer trek from the Kinneret to the Mediterranean, otherwise known as *Yam el Yam* (sea to sea). With backpacks and sleeping bags borrowed from our neighbors, and a big jar of peanut butter, they set off up north, leaving the rest of us parents and kids to explore the more local terrain. And that's what we did: from Ein Gedi to Ein Yael, we tackled every activity we could reasonably reach in the Jerusalem area.

Some of our adventures were amazing…and some were mediocre. We spent a hot day at the zoo, enjoying the cooling water fans more than the actual animals. At Neot Kedumim, the biblical landscape reserve, the kids tried their hand at pita baking on a Taboun, making pottery out of heavy clay, and sheep herding. I just hoped that our relatives were absorbing all of the beauty of Israel as I saw it. After many years of living in the Holy Land, I saw past the less-than-sanitary conditions of Israeli ball pits and the lack of mini bagels and caramel iced coffee. Would they be able to overlook these deficiencies too?

Once my sisters-in-law returned from completing their *Yam el Yam* trek, we set off on the "Schild Family Vacation." For years, my in-laws had made a point out of taking the entire family away for one week every summer in the United States. Traditionally, we spent the entire time at an oversized house with a huge pool, usually in the Hamptons, or upstate New York. My kids already had fond memories of years of Schild Family Vacations, their best time with their cousins, aunts, uncles, and grandparents on my husband's side. Costco-sized boxes of treats and snacks were always part of the drill, along with too much television, and lots and lots of swimming.

For this year's week-long getaway, I had scouted out a big vacation rental in Caesarea, with a large, beautiful pool and a spacious garden area. It wasn't quite as huge as those mansions in the Hamptons, but it was pretty luxurious. And there was no stocking up at Costco required—thanks to the easy availability of kosher food just about everywhere in Israel, we had no trouble restocking with delicious snacks and kosher meat for our many evening barbecues throughout the week.

Deep calm set in as we spent our days swimming, snacking, and sleeping. We took breaks from doing absolutely nothing to explore the wealthy beachside town of Caesarea, where bougainvillea blossom in abundance in the sea air. As our week by the pool drew to a close, we got ready to head home for the second big event of the summer: Elie's bat mitzvah.

Every event has its own personality. For Elie's bat mitz-vah, I wanted our guests to experience the beauty and his-tory of the Land of Israel while enjoying simple comforts like good food and plentiful wine. To facilitate this experi-ence, we had chosen a unique event hall for our venue—The Bedouin Tent in nearby Kfar Etzion.

The big day arrived, and family and friends assembled in Kfar Etzion as the sun began to set. The burlap walls of the tent were raised to let in the gentle breeze, revealing roll-ing mountains, vineyards, and a sky painted in hues of pink. Inside, the tables were covered with satin in shades of lav-ender and white, decorated with candles, and vases of deep purple and white flowers. The dance floor was right outside the tent, in the blessedly cool open air of Gush Etzion.

After warm greetings, everyone began to feast on chick-en with prunes and olives, rice with meat and almonds, and schwarma. We danced for hours, stopping at intervals for toasts and speeches. The kids oohed and ahhed over the elaborate dessert buffet created with the help of my closest friends. In addition to the usual—decorated cookies, layer cakes, fruit platters, and trifles—there were multi-colored cake pops, artistically and individually decorated by my good friend Anita.

Most importantly, our friends, the members of our com-munity, were all there celebrating with us. A supportive community full of wonderful people—the type of warm community that anyone would be glad to be a part of.

As we took a second round of family pictures together on the grass, walls built of Jerusalem stone as our backdrop, I felt content. Hopefully, all of my efforts had succeeded in giving our family a true experience of the land I so deeply loved. Perhaps this summer would ignite a spark. Perhaps, one day, our family would join us in our ancient Jewish homeland, where reminders of God's connection to the Jewish people are all around us.

The following summer we attended the second Nefesh b'Nefesh Aliyah ceremony of our lives. We all set our alarms for five in the morning in order to arrive on time. Our children were so eager to go that they were up and dressed before we even went in to wake them. We drove the distance to Ben Gurion in sleepy silence, Avi and I sipping our coffee while the kids munched on cereal.

It was quiet when we arrived. Apparently, not everyone was as punctual as we were. Tired but excited looking friends and relatives of the new *olim* about to arrive trickled into the terminal until it was completely full. Then we were ushered into a large auditorium, with a stage, and an enticing breakfast buffet. The guests started to mingle. "Do you know when the plane is getting here?" someone asked. It felt like it was taking forever.

Then, the word went around…the plane was landing! Time to go outside.

Our kids picked up the big sign we had made, and we dashed outside. There were so many people crowded into that space behind the fence that we were just barely able to squeeze in near the back. We weren't the only ones who were excited about greeting the new immigrants. We found a place to prop our welcoming sign and then waited.

One bus pulled up and passengers began to disembark. We scanned the arrivals, wishing them all mazal tov as they passed by, but saw no familiar faces.

My kids started to get antsy. "When will they get here?" asked Noa, "Where *are* they?!"

We watched another bus arrive. More new *olim* climbed off. "Mazal tov, mazal tov!" We greeted each one as they passed. Still not the ones we were waiting for. And then in the distance…was that them?

Avi exclaimed, pointing into the distance. "Look, guys, there they are!!"

"I see them!" shouted Eitan.

"*Erdfarbs!!!!!*" We all yelled in unison.

Tired but happy, the family made their way through the throngs of people. When they finally reached our spot in the long procession of people, we showered them with hugs and kisses.

"You're here!"

"Mazal tov!"

"We made it!"

"How was the flight?"

Totally exhilarated and completely exhausted, our first family *olim* entered the waiting auditorium. My kids escorted their newly Israeli cousins to the buffet table, and everyone helped themselves to slushies, muffins and other treats. After picking up a round of coffee, we sat with Ari and Ilana to review the last twelve hours.

The flight had been amazing. It was loud the whole time, and no one slept. They were barfed on by two different children. No, they hadn't changed their shirts since then. They couldn't wait to bring their twenty-one bags home to our house and settle in for another summer of fun.

I still smile at the memory as I write these words. After ten years of living in Israel, ten years of going back to visit almost every summer, someone had finally come to join us. The happiness we felt as we unloaded those twenty-one bags into random corners of our house (which was now under construction once again, as we completed the final few bedrooms in our previously unfinished attic floor) was incomparable. In our hearts, we couldn't help but believe that maybe we had some influence, even a small one, on our family's decision to make aliyah. And now we were going to get to be Israelis together! We were thrilled. Thrilled that people we loved had understood something that we ourselves hadn't even fully understood when we first came to Israel, despite knowing that we wanted to raise our own family here: the future of the Jewish people is in this land. My brother-in-law and sister-in-law wanted to be part of that future. No matter how much they loved their community back home. No matter how hard it was to leave the rest of their families. The dream they were pursuing was worth this sacrifice.

It was an inspiring experience to watch the Erdfarbs leave behind their old dreams, the home they had invested in, and their close-knit community with happy anticipation for the future. They were going to be living out of their twenty-one bags for several weeks now, while they waited for their lift to arrive. Then they would unpack into their imperfect rental house in Efrat, just across the road from Neve Daniel, and set out to make new friends in a new community. It wasn't going to be easy. But just as they had been at Nahal Prat, they were completely ready to embrace the challenge.

That summer we went on our first *really* Israeli vacation together, to a small moshav the kids nicknamed "Sirachona"—a play on the moshav's name, Sarona, and the fact that it was "*masriach*" (in plain English, it was smelly). We enjoyed a peaceful first half of Shabbat in our cabins, and then, after our air conditioner broke, suffered through stifling heat for the rest of it. We watched the cows graze (this was the source of the bad smell) and had a post-Shabbat diving contest in the above ground pool. During the rest of our week away, we hiked the Banias, biked around the Hula valley, visited a bee farm and made artsy paper at a small workshop in Zichron Ya'akov. Ilana even got a horrible eye infection during the vacation and had to make her first foray into the Israeli medical system in the middle of nowhere in northern Israel.

We did it all together. And the Erdfarbs didn't bat an eyelash at all of the less-than-perfect "Israeli" experiences they had never imagined they would have. We were partners in crime, willing to live in this sometimes-difficult country and give it our best. Seeing everything through the eyes of new *olim* even refreshed our own enthusiasm. All of the good, the unity, the inspiration, *and* the unexpected made our choice to pick up and move to Israel entirely worth every sacrifice that was required. We were living the Jewish dream, quite literally. A people united as a family and a nation in the Holy Land.

Deep Love for the Land

WHAT'S SO GREAT about the Land of Israel? According to our tradition, one of Israel's names is: "Land of the Living" (Psalms 116:9). Radak, commenting on that verse, explains that Israel is: "the most desirous of lands, those who settle there are alive and healthy."

For those of us who were raised elsewhere, however, it can be hard to see the Land of Israel as deserving of *such* deep love and appreciation. As a Jew growing up outside of Israel, I couldn't imagine how the dry heat and dust storms of the Holy Land were more desirable than the comforting humidity and daily rain showers of my hometown in New Orleans. When I moved here, I missed the United States. Attached to my place of birth, my feelings certainly didn't reflect the deep love I should have felt for what was, to me, a strange land.

Rav Tzvi Yehuda HaCohen Kook believed that one of the biggest tragedies of the exile is the fact that the Jews forget their homeland and become attached to foreign lands. Any immigrant is familiar with this feeling. It's hard to move to what is, after all, a foreign country, without retaining some sort of desire and longing for our place of birth, the place we once loved and called home. We like what's familiar. "This," says Rav Kook, "is a catastrophe. It is a tragedy when we fall in love with the *Galut* [exile]."[1]

Continuing, Rav Kook likens this situation to a slave who falls in love with his master. In the Torah, we learn that after six years of slavery a slave must go free. If he refuses, he is marked; a nail is driven through his ear into a door post (see Exodus 21:5–6). Why such a harsh punishment? The Talmud explains, in *Kiddushin* 22b: "Why are the door and a doorpost different from all other objects in the house? The Holy One, Blessed be He, said: The door and the doorpost were witnesses in Egypt when I passed over the lintel and over the two doorposts and I said: 'For to Me the children of Israel are slaves,' and not slaves to slaves. And I delivered them from slavery to freedom, and this man went and acquired a master for himself. Let him be pierced before them."

In other words, we are *God's* servants, not Man's. The doorposts serve as a reminder of the fact that God chose us to be His own when He rescued us from slavery in Egypt. A Jewish slave who chooses to remain under the rule of his human master forgets who he truly serves—God. "This is an awful thing," says Rav Kook. Rav Kook goes on to use this as a metaphor for Jews in *Galut*: "Likewise, when we fall in love with the *Galut*, saying, 'I loved my master, the foreign nation,' this is a tragic mistake."[2]

Fostering a deep love for the Land of Israel, and even coming to see it as our home, is possible. I should know. It just takes time. After a while, even immigrants can feel

1   *Torat Eretz Yisrael*, The Teachings of HaRav Tzvi Yehuda HaCohen Kook (Jerusalem: Torat Eretz Yisrael Publications, 1991), p119.
2   Ibid.

completely at home in their Jewish homeland. Eventually, we come to truly love Israel: its nature and character, traditions, and customs. When we travel abroad to our places of birth, we cherish the Hebrew chatter we hear in the airport upon our return to Israel. After a while, those communities we once called home seem a lot less appealing.

"This must be clear before anything else—no matter where a Jew is, he belongs only to Eretz Yisrael. This is his permanent home. Outside the land, we have the status of guests."[3]

Recognizing this fact can help us see *chutz la'aretz* for what it really is: the house of a master, where we are slaves to the culture, customs, and beliefs of a foreign people.

---

3   Ibid. p.120.

XIV.

LISTEN TO THE MUSIC

"He who sings in this world will merit to sing in the next." – Rabbi Akiva, Midrash Tanhuma

I GLANCED AT MY watch: 10:30 AM. It was now or never. I knocked a couple of times, guitar slung over one shoulder, and then backed up a few steps. Footsteps echoed from beyond the wooden door. Then it opened, revealing a woman of about forty-five, a knitted hat pulled down over short brown hair. "*Shalom, brucha haba'a,*" she said with a welcoming smile as she opened the door wide for me to enter her home. "Michal," she added, pointing to herself.

"*Shalom, ma nishma?*" I responded in my American-accented Hebrew. This was my first time studying one-on-one with an Israeli who didn't speak a word of English. With baby Gabi still at home, my options for musical instruction were limited. I needed a local teacher, one whose proximity to my home meant that I could pop in and out of class in under an hour and a half, just enough time to squeeze in a lesson during Gabi's naptime, while Avi worked back at home.

199

Linda, a woman from my daily *shiur*, had recommended Michal, an Israeli neighbor of ours in Neve Daniel. English or no English, we were going to have to make it work. Besides, it would be good for me to work on my Hebrew.

I followed Michal into a small back room with my guitar. She rearranged some books and papers, moving a pile off of the day bed and instructing me to sit down so we could begin our lesson.

Michal was going to be teaching me how to play the guitar. I had felt like a wannabe musician for what seemed like my entire life. I had always loved to sing and had even been part of a band with my best friend, Peggy, as a teenager. We had played shows at our local coffee house and even sold our "album" in a fanzine. Once I left New Orleans, I continued to sing all the time—one of the things I was best known for as a teenager. But I still felt like an imposter. I may have been a skilled vocalist, but I had only a rudimentary knowledge of piano, and my guitar skills were limited to a few basic chords. In my band, I had played the tambourine, a useful accompaniment for a lead singer. But what I really wanted now was to be able to easily strum a song on the guitar and sing along to the music. My voice wanted musical accompaniment. Learning to play the guitar *well* was the best way to achieve this goal.

We got started with our lesson. In broken fragments of conversation, we worked through the basics: notes on the guitar; simple songs; how to strum. Michal sent me home with a notebook full of music and instructions to practice daily, which I did. I felt kind of silly, struggling with new and tricky finger placements and banging out less than beautiful chords. But I plugged away, a diligent student. And my kids tolerated the cacophonous music—for the most part.

The next time I returned to my guitar teacher, I felt ready to move on to something more sophisticated. If I could just hear myself strum a real song, I would have a lot more motivation and desire to practice and improve. So, I asked Michal, in my imperfect Hebrew, "Can we learn real songs I can play? Like 'Blackbird' by the Beatles? Or 'Sitting on the Dock of the Bay'?"

Michal looked a bit confused. "I'm not sure I know any of those songs—do you have sheet music for them?"

I didn't, and neither did she, so she ran off to a bookshelf in her house and came back with a thin, blue book. "Here," she said, thrusting the book into my hands, "You have little kids. You must know some of the songs in here. You can play those!"

Before opening up the book I took a look at the title on the cover: *Shir HaShavua* (song of the week). I recognized it—it was one of my kids' books from school. All over Israel, first and second graders learn one song each week from this book and sing it together in class. By the end of second grade, the children can sing along with all of the classics and are ready for life as good citizens of Israel.

I flipped through the book, hoping to find a title or two that I recognized. This was nothing like the Beatles, and I was kind of skeptical of the value of learning these old-fashioned Hebrew songs that I didn't understand, but with Michal as my teacher, I realized that this book was my path to becoming a more proficient guitar player.

It took a few minutes of searching, but I found one song I recognized: '*Todah*,' a song of thanks to God. Michal wrote down the chords for me. We played the song together a few times, and then she sent me home to practice.

Weeks and months passed. Every week, Michal taught me a new song from *Shir HaShavua*. I was diligent during my lessons and practicing in between. At first, I wished that she would teach me some other songs, something that I knew from *my* childhood or teen years. But then I discovered an unexpected side benefit to learning these old songs; my kids *loved* listening to me play. They were thrilled to be able to sing and dance along with me while I practiced. To them, this music was way better than anything else I had worked on up until that point—what the heck was 'The Sound of Silence' anyway?

By the end of the year, I was fairly proficient in the basics of classic Israeli folk music. I even began to really love a few of the songs, finding meaning in the poetic words: *"I still live, live, live. The Nation of Israel lives. This is the song that grandfather sang yesterday to father, and today it is I…."* And: *"My Land of Israel is beautiful and blooming! Who built it and planted it? All of us, together!"*

Over a decade after moving to Israel, I could finally play Israeli songs on my guitar. I was fully equipped to be a model citizen.

Yom HaAtzmaut: Israel's Independence Day. As an American religious Jew growing up in Chabad, I had never deeply connected to this holiday. Through my time in Israel, however, that had changed dramatically. Yom HaAtzmaut was one of the highlights of the year, a day when our nationhood was celebrated all around the country. This was especially true in Neve Daniel, where blue and white flags lined the streets, hung from houses, and stuck out of every car window during the days leading up to the holiday. This year my oldest daughter was going to be part of the flag dance in Neve Daniel's big Independence Day ceremony. I was looking forward to watching her perform.

Elie practiced for at least a month, grabbing a broom stick every afternoon on her way out the door to serve as a stand in for a flag. As the big day got closer, we prepared by borrowing a white Bnei Akiva shirt (as American Olim, we never seemed to have the items of clothing which every Israeli had at home), the required uniform for everyone in the performance.

The night of Yom HaAtzmaut arrived. It was a chilly evening in May. Our whole family piled into the car and we drove off to the basketball court where the ceremony would take place. We found seats in the top level of the stone bleachers and cuddled close to each other for warmth, ready to watch my daughter perform.

The whole community was there. The ceremony began as they do all over Israel—with the commemoration of the fallen soldiers of Israel. The day before Independence Day is Memorial Day—Yom HaZikaron. Israel rightly remembers and honors those who sacrificed their lives in order to give us the freedom to live our lives. For the residents of Neve Daniel, this was no abstract ceremony. Just about everyone knows a soldier killed in combat. Just about everyone prays daily for their own children who, at the age of eighteen, become soldiers. Yom HaZikaron is nothing like U.S. Veteran's Day or Memorial Day, not a government or a mail holiday. The pain is real and deep.

We listened carefully, trying to decipher every word; my Hebrew was not yet completely fluent. The somber music set the tone. Candles were lit. Night fell. And then, with just as much feeling, the big flag at the back of the court was raised to full mast. Over the loudspeaker, happier music blared, breaking the solemn silence, and then we heard: "*Bruchim Haba'im l'tekes Yom HaAtzmaut!!!!*" Welcome to the Independence Day ceremony! The day had officially arrived. Our tears morphed from those of choked sadness to joy, in celebration of what our brave soldiers had fought for.

The ceremony began with organized dances according to age—first the kindergarteners performed, and then third graders. The moderator called up a dozen members of Neve Daniel to honor their service to the community in a traditional torch lighting ceremony. There were short speeches.

Eventually it was time for Elie's big flag dance, the main event of the evening. Elie marched out to the tune of a popular Israeli song, one girl in a sea of many. I watched as she swung her blue and white flag in the air in perfect synchronization with the other girls. My heart swelled with familiar pride: I loved seeing my kids in their element, totally at ease within Israeli culture—to outsiders, indistinguishable from the other members of the youth group.

When the song ended, the girls ran together, their flags in

the air, jumping up and down and cheering in a great mass. Afterwards, Elie came to join us on the bleachers, smiling and proud.

I hugged her. "That was awesome!" Cuddled together close, we watched the rest of the ceremony, which ended with "Hatikva," the national anthem. Then we turned our eyes to the sky with great anticipation, awaiting the next attraction of the evening,

"Ima, when are the fireworks gonna start?" asked Dalya (now seven), excited.

"Here they come!" said Avi, who held Gabi in his arms.

One single rocket shot up into the air, leaving a trail of red and white dust behind, then—crash, pop, fireworks exploded! I felt my breath catch in my throat and tears spring into my eyes once again as music played over the loudspeakers, "*Chai, chai, chai, Am Yisrael Chai!*" Alive, alive, alive—The Nation of Israel Lives!

Noa was only four years old, and she was petrified of the noise. She hid behind my knees. As I hugged her close in the cool evening breeze, I let the words and music of the song penetrate my soul. My mind drifted back thirteen years, to a very different fireworks display. It had been the fourth of July, American's Independence Day, and my in-laws had taken us to Six Flags amusement park in New Jersey to celebrate. I had been seven months pregnant with our Elie, who had danced so joyously tonight, and due to my delicate condition, I had to sit on the sidelines while my husband and his siblings enjoyed the roller coaster rides. It was still a supremely memorable day, however, because when evening fell, we headed off to the park's bleachers to see the Beach Boys perform live in concert.

It was incredible. *They* were incredible. I had never seen a band as big and famous as the Beach Boys perform in all my life. We bopped along to the oldies: "California Girls," "Surfin' Safari," "Good Vibrations." My mother-in-law handed out turkey and pastrami sandwiches on onion rolls. At midnight, the massive Fourth of July fireworks display began. In the heat of the summer, in the dark of the night, it had been the most amazing Independence Day I had experienced in all of my twenty years.

But it had just been topped—easily—by a much more modest, but a much more inspiring and meaningful Independence Day celebration. Neve Daniel had no amusement park or world-famous musicians. But listening to *my* nation's music played over loudspeaker in our small town while watching our own sky light up with fireworks touched my heart in a way that no Fourth of July celebration ever had, or could. As a town and community, we were celebrating our nationhood together. We were celebrating what Jews had fought and died for, not with songs about surfing or partying in the U.S.A, but with music that spoke of our purpose as a people:

A hymn passes from generation to generation,
Like a spring that flows eternally,
I ask and I pray,
It's good that hope was not lost.
Alive, alive, alive,

Yes, I'm still alive.
This is the song that grandfather,
Sang yesterday to father,
And today I sing…
The people of Israel live.

I felt my heart swell as the reality sank in. I was now a part of this people, in a country where we composed our own music to reflect our own values and celebrate our own national purpose: To be a unified people in our land, God's land. A land that our ancestors dreamed of returning to for thousands of years.

I was no longer an imposter: not on the music scene nor in any other way. This music *belonged* to me now. It belonged to me in sadness and in happiness, in hope and in celebration.

These were songs that I could sing along to.

XV.

LEARNING TO CELEBRATE THE UNEXPECTED

"Many are the plans in a person's heart, but it is the Lord's purpose that prevails." –Proverbs 19:21

"Man plans, God laughs." –Old Yiddish Saying

AFTER THE ERDFARBS arrived, we fell into the comfortable rhythm of life with more family in Israel. My sister, Sharon, and her husband Tzion, who had managed to squeeze eight children into that tiny apartment in Jerusalem's Ramat Eshkol neighborhood for many years, finally moved into a bigger home in Kochav HaShahar, an hour away. On the other hand, the Erdfarbs lived only a short drive away; they had chosen to establish themselves in the nearby community of Efrat. Now, in addition to holidays spent with my sister's family (easier now in their larger home), we spent holidays with the Erdfarbs, too. Since they lived minutes away, we became a regular part of each other's lives, even eating breakfast together on random mornings in the middle of the week. About a year after they moved, Ilana and I became pregnant in quick succession, and then had our babies within the same few months. Benzion, born just after Pesach 2015, was our sixth child.

That July, Avi's youngest sister, Sara, made aliyah with her husband, Ron. Since we had moved to Israel twelve years earlier, Sara had flown in to visit us for many a summer, first as a thirteen-year-old kid and then as an older teenager, and then she had studied for a year in Israel at a Jerusalem seminary (spending every Shabbat at our house). Now, a year after their marriage, she and Ron were ready to make Israel their home, the place where they would begin their lives together and raise their own family. They moved into my in-laws vacant Jerusalem apartment (my in-laws had long since traded in their Beit Shemesh home away from home for new digs in the Holy City) to find their footing.

We re-experienced the beauty of aliyah through Avi's siblings' eyes. Sara and Ron enjoyed the life of young, newly married Orthodox Jews, living in the heart of Rehavia, Sara spending her days at ulpan and Ron at his new job in hi-tech. Ron's parents had made aliyah to Modi'in just two weeks before them, so they were blessed right away with an abundance of family nearby. The Erdfarbs had already made good friends in their own community. While their older children focused on transitioning into studies in Hebrew, we watched as the younger ones began *Chamisha Chumshei Torah*, and completed *Sefer Bereishit* (The book of Genesis), just like ours. We would frequently receive pictures of pink and orange sunsets above peaceful mountains that they'd snapped from their living room window. Ari, who had worked for Avi's father's company back in New Jersey, continued in the very same position from the comfort of his attic office. Ilana had decided to give up her part-time career as a speech therapist, at least temporarily, while she threw herself into raising her six children and adjusting to life in Israel. With baby Adira in tow, she began making regular trips to Kever Rachel (the tomb of our matriarch, Rachel), a short drive away. The Erdfarbs entered a new routine as they became fully absorbed into Israeli society. Their life path had completely changed direction with their move to Israel.

In the fall of 2015 we reached another important milestone—our first family bar mitzvah would take place in November. Because of his Shabbat Torah reading, Eitan's bar mitzvah celebration would involve more planning than my Elie's bat mitzvah had. Now that two of Avi's siblings were living in Israel too, it would be a family effort to host and entertain incoming guests from America—at least until the actual bar mitzvah. We were all looking forward to making our time together great.

My husband's whole extended family was coming to town. This time, that meant his grandparents, parents, siblings, and even some aunts, uncles, and cousins—we would have sixty guests in all for the bar mitzvah Shabbat, including ten Botesazans (my sister Sharon's family) and eight Erdfarbs. My parents were flying in from New Orleans—they would be there too. I really wanted to make everyone's big Shabbat in Neve Daniel as comfortable and pleasant as possible. As always, it was important to me that they have a positive experience. After running through the different possibilities for hosting, we decided to splurge and put up a giant tent in our backyard. Families with little kids would stay at our house, like the Erdfarbs, and Avi's cousins from Jerusalem—that way, all the babies could sleep in their beds during long and late meals. My sister would stay next door, taking over the attic floor of the Gottesmans house with her husband and eight kids. Everyone else would either squeeze in with my kids or stay with neighbors, except for Avi's elderly grandparents, who would be most comfortable in the ground floor playroom on the queen sized pull out couch.

The Thursday night party would be catered, but Shabbat would be home-cooked (read: delicious and familiar). We were going to make all the food in advance—from individual homemade challah rolls to trays of double decker brownies. My angelic sister and sister-in-law, along with my closest friends, volunteered to do all of the last-minute cooking that I couldn't prepare in advance—salads, grilled vegetables, corned beef, and more.

Weeks and days of preparation passed. Eitan studied his Torah portion diligently, while I scurried about booking a photo magnet guy, renting tables and chairs, and putting the finishing touches on Eitan's *matzeget* (a cute slideshow of photos from birth to present day featured at every good Israeli bar and bat mitzvah). We ramped up our level of activity as soon as the first family members started to arrive. We went on a four-generation family hike on Sunday. On Monday, as a practice run, and with cameras available, Eitan read the first *aliyah* of his bar mitzvah *parsha*, in front of a crowd of family who got up early to be there. Afterwards, everyone returned to our house for a festive bagel brunch. Finally, Thursday arrived, the day of the big party—this would take place at the Bedouin Tent in Kfar Etzion, just like my daughter's had.

The day began as planned. We looked over our to-do list and were satisfied, as usual, with our high levels of organization. The relatives had all arrived? Check. Photographer confirmed and scheduled to arrive in a few hours? Check. Clothes washed and ironed? Check. As we got dressed and ready for the party, I congratulated myself on a job well done.

Then, at about three in the afternoon, our luck started to change. I watched through the window with dread as forbidding dark grey rain clouds gathered in the sky. Just as the last child had been dressed in their best clothes, ready for photos, the heavens opened, and rain started pouring down. Gushing, gusting, torrents of rain, in a howling tempest.

My heart sank. November is an almost spring-like month in Israel, still relatively warm and sunny, but not as hot as the summer. It rarely rains, and when it does, it's usually just a short drizzle, not a downpour. Until that point in the month, we had enjoyed nice days and sunny skies, with only a bit of drizzle here and there. Unfortunately for us, today was the day that God had put together a perfect storm. Usually, we pray for rain in Israel, but that day I prayed for it to stop. How were we going to manage a party in an outdoor tent now? Especially with outdoor bathrooms...and elderly great-grandparents of the bar mitzvah boy on their way.

Moreover, I had planned out the bar mitzvah schedule in great detail, and I hadn't factored in a torrential downpour.

At four o'clock, we were scheduled for pictures in the yard. The photographer was scheduled to be with us before the party so that we could have a family photo shoot framed by green grass and flowers before sunset.

As the rain spattered off of our living room window, our visions of a garden photo shoot faded. Instead, we pivoted: with just a tiny bit of disappointment and a small furniture rearrangement, we put together an indoor photo shoot instead. Once that was over with, we dashed to the store to buy a bunch of colorful umbrellas for the party. We hoped they would help with trips between the big tent and the bathrooms.

As we set out to the venue, we received more bad news. There had been an attempted terrorist attack—a car ramming—at Tzomet HaGush (the Gush Etzion interchange). Thank God, no one had been hurt. But, of course, our hearts still hurt—what if they *had* managed to injure or even kill someone? Thoughts of violence and hatred invaded the atmosphere of excitement in our car. After a silent prayer, I tried to put the attack out of my head, but as we inched along toward the site of the attack, which was on the route to our venue, our mood was dampened. We were on our way, but we were now behind schedule. We were going to have to recalibrate into party mode.

Fortunately for us, everyone *else* was stuck in traffic too, so we arrived at the Tent with plenty of time to get into the party spirit. The place was so empty that we decided to take more photos. There was no one to socialize with except the photographer, who had driven along with us! Everyone else, even the caterer, was held up. Between the torrential rain (which was now, thankfully, slowing to a drizzle) and the attempted terrorist attack, this party was off to a slow start.

We took lots and lots of pictures. It was dark, but the rain finally stopped, so we could finally get that outdoor photo shoot we had wanted. The photographer brought in big floodlights, and our kids posed with the colorful umbrellas in a thousand different ways. At least we would get good family pictures out of this series of unfortunate events. I was relieved to see that our luck was changing. With all of the last-minute stress, I had thought that I wouldn't be able to truly enjoy our first ever bar mitzvah, but as I watched my cute kids ham it up for the photographer, I realized that everything would be fine, even if it was slightly off-schedule.

An hour or so later, our barbecue bar mitzvah event was officially underway. All of our family had arrived, Israeli and American, along with lots of friends. No one seemed to mind the delay—things were just happening at their own pace. The caterer apologized profusely for his lateness. The unexpected downpour hadn't made it easy for him to transfer trays of food from one place to the next. But the guests helping themselves to miniature hamburgers, corn on the cob, schwarma, and potato salad didn't seem to mind. We had fun despite our delayed start. Between the speeches and video reels, food and wine, music and, most importantly, our family and friends, it was a great party.

When Eitan finished his speech, I breathed a sigh of relief. Everything was under control. (I should have known better—when is everything *actually* under control?) When the party ended, we packed up our umbrellas and drove home, watching faint drizzle run down our car windows. Tomorrow was Shabbat. In honor of Eitan's bar mitzvah, we would be hosting sixty relatives in an outdoor, supposedly weather-proof, tent.

I'm a super planner so, as usual, I had Shabbat figured out down to the last detail. When we woke up Friday morning, I was pretty sure that the tough part was behind us. We would glide through today, thanks to my careful planning.

But God wasn't going to let me have my way. After the last of the round tables were unloaded and just as the truck pulled away, the skies opened up *again* with great force, rain and storm winds lashing the roof and sides of the new (weather-proof??) backyard tent, just erected by a small crew an hour earlier. Within ten minutes, inches of water filled the inside. We started with frantic phone calls to the tent guy, asking him to come back, but he wouldn't help. We'd paid for the tent, and he was off taking care of another project. There would be no time to do anything about it before Shabbat. We begged and pleaded with him to come help us, but he simply refused. We asked a local handyman to come and see if he could fix the problem. He came. But try as he might, he couldn't get the flooding under control. It seemed hopeless.

Unwilling to give up on my dream of a perfectly comfortable Shabbat, we jimmied up impromptu gutters and drainpipes, hoping to send the water in another direction. When that didn't work, we tried washing down the insides of the tent—at least that might help get rid of all the mud.

An hour later, I was stamping my feet in frustration, still apparently incapable of learning my lesson. Every time the rain slowed down, and I started hoping, it picked right back up again. Our big tent and once beautiful lawn were nothing but sloshy mud. Instead of an elegant dining space, we had the perfect setting for a game of mud wrestling.

With only an hour or two left until Shabbat we called in the big guns: my in-laws, who were at their Jerusalem apartment getting ready for Shabbat (vacated by Sara and Ron, who had moved into Ron's parents' home for the duration of my in-laws' trip). I picked up the phone.

"Mommy!" I whined like a baby as my mother-in-law picked up the phone. "I need you over here now. It's a disaster!!!"

If anyone could help, it was them. My in-laws love to throw a good party and had hosted countless events in their home and in backyard tents over the years. They were *experts* when it came to home celebrations.

"Ok, Susannah, it's going to be okay," my mother-in-law reassured me. "We are coming right now."

And I knew she would—shower or no shower, ready for Shabbat or not, my in-laws would come to the rescue. By the time they arrived I was teary-eyed. Yet another storm had descended, and the rain was pummeling the tent, seeping in though its "winter proof" walls on all sides.

My in-laws' pitying looks made it all clear, and in my heart of hearts, I had already known what the answer was. I just hadn't been ready to give up on my plan for the perfect Shabbat, which had included this (expensive) outdoor tent. It was a great idea, but it just wasn't going to happen. We were going to have to move this party inside.

With nervous angst shaking me to the core, I started to clear out our furniture, with help from my husband and in-laws. We called friends, borrowed more rectangular plastic tables since the round wooden ones in the tent wouldn't work inside, and arranged them into one loooooooong dining table which stretched from one side of the house to the other. We put aside our rented round tablecloths and gathered every rectangular tablecloth we could find. Then we squeezed in all the folding chairs. And we had it—a table for sixty, inside.

My father-in-law looked at me with a playful grin. "Didn't we tell you when you built the house that it would come in handy to leave a long space from your dining to living room?"

I laughed, finally calming down. Yes. Yes, they had told us that, ten years earlier. We had never really used the space that way, before. I guess this was our big opportunity.

With the house taken over by the long table, the play-room, originally allocated as a bedroom for elderly grand-parents, became our backup living room, and we moved them down into one of the basement bedrooms, relocating Avi's parents into the Gottesman's last available guest room. As we closed the door to the backyard, we took one last wist-ful look at the big tent, withering in the rain. So much for plan A.

And how did Shabbat: Plan B go? Actually, it was

awesome. It wasn't as convenient or comfortable as originally planned, but strangely enough, our extended family seemed to enjoy the novelty of squeezing together indoors while the rain poured outside. After all of the drama and disappointment, nobody was any worse for the wear. Happily, by the time Shabbat dinner was underway, we were able to wholeheartedly thank God for bringing us to this moment, when we could look around at the people who loved us and wanted to be there with us as we celebrated our son's transition to adulthood. My parents had come over from Kochav HaShahar for Shabbat with my sister and her family. My in-laws were there, along with all of my husband's siblings, their spouses, and children. Avi's grandparents, and some aunts and uncles were there too. All at one big table, in the very same room. I watched from the head of the table next to Avi as kids skidded from place to place, looking for somewhere to play, and eventually ran upstairs to nearly-dark bedrooms. Our hired waitresses (two teenagers from the *yishuv*) carried platters and plates back and forth, held up high to avoid colliding with the many children. It certainly was a *balagan* (big mess), but it was exactly the kind of *balagan* that I loved. Our family was all together, celebrating in our home in Israel.

Shabbat morning, we woke up to sunshine. We surveyed the damage in the tent: the giant tarp we had placed on the ground was still kind of wet and muddy, but the tables were standing where we had left them. All they needed was a wipe down and some round tablecloths. We decided to try to use the tent for lunch and began to haul the sixty plastic chairs back outside from our dining room. As long as nobody minded dirty shoes (and the dirty house that would go along with it), this tent would now suit our purposes, and give us more space to spread out during the long afternoon meals.

We all left for shul together, and as I sat there listening to my bar mitzvah boy sing the Torah portion aloud, I felt pride: in his flawless singing, his beautiful Israeli-accented Hebrew. My parents were there listening too, my mother glowing under her fancy hat, a smile on her beautiful face, while my father took it all in from the men's section. I had a feeling that despite the previous day's disaster, my son's reading of the Torah would be all that they remembered.

We moved out to the still-damp tent for lunch. It was a gorgeous day outside. We barely needed the heaters that had been pumping out hot air since the beginning of Shabbat. Our family was in good spirits and didn't seem disturbed by the muddy walls or the sloshing underfoot.

That Shabbat taught me an invaluable lesson. I had planned one thing and, as is so often the case, God had given me another. We had planned a party expecting the dry season to continue, but God had, instead, granted our daily prayers for rain, in extremely generous abundance. There is good to be found in every plan gone awry. Rather than perfection, I was given a lesson in resilience, and a chance to make the most of a less than ideal situation. I was also reminded of just how amazing and supportive our family and friends really were. And I realized that that was all that really mattered.

Looking back, Eitan's bar mitzvah was indeed a success. Through (miraculously victimless) terrorist attacks and pouring rain, we were reminded that God is in charge. We pray to Him all winter for the gift of rain, a hope we know will involve bad weather and last-minute changes in plans. We ask for something that is a national blessing, even though we know it will cause some minor inconveniences along the way. Through these prayers, we connect with God in a deep and practical way.

Mashiv HaRuach u'Morid HaGeshem. The One Who makes the wind blow, and makes the rain descend. Maybe it was inconvenient. Maybe it was a little disappointing. But in truth, God gave us what we really needed.

XVI.

THE WORLD ON OUR SIDE

"My House will be called a house of prayer for all the nations." –Isaiah 56:7

L IFE CAN BE surprising sometimes. Within the everyday routine, unexpectedly inspiring things can happen. Sukkot 2016 was just another typical holiday for us in Israel. We had planned the usual excursions for the intermediate days of *Chol HaMo'ed*: hikes, activities, and beach trips all chosen to suit the interests of our now large and varied brood, aged one and a half to sixteen. What I was most looking forward to was the second day of *Chol HaMo'ed*; that day we would be going grape harvesting on Har Bracha with some close friends. Grape harvesting anywhere sounded like fun for the whole family, but this particular grape-harvesting excursion was going to be something very different than anything we had experienced before.

Har Bracha is a mountaintop in the Shomron (Samaria), as in Judea and Samaria, the two large areas that make up what is known to some as the West Bank (Gush Etzion, where we live, is in Judea). There are many noteworthy landmarks near the community of Har Bracha. Right below the mountaintop lies the well-known valley of Shechem. This ancient city, named after a rapacious prince from biblical times, is now a ruin. The modern Palestinian city of Nablus is nearby. Just across the way are Har Eival and Har Gerizim, described by Moses in the Torah: "When your God brings you into the land that you are about to enter and possess, you shall pronounce the blessing at Mount Gerizim and the curse at Mount Eival" (Deuteronomy 11:29). The Samaritans, a tiny sect who have been preserving a modified version of the Torah for thousands of years, believe that Har Gerizim was the location chosen by God for the Temple. There is a Samaritan museum on Har Gerizim, and a town called Kiryat Luza, where several hundred Samaritans live (the only other Samaritan community still in existence is in Holon).

But these landmarks were all incidental to our day out grape harvesting. What I was looking forward to about Har Bracha was something else entirely.

A large tent sits atop Har Bracha, a short distance from the main town. It's the kind of tent that you'd put up for an event, weatherproof (I think theirs actually is!) and white. But on Har Bracha, the tent stays up all year-round. Rows and rows of dining tables line the wooden floor inside the large structure, and there is also a snack bar and a big white board.

This is the gathering hall for HaYovel, an organization which helps pioneer and plant the land of Israel. The founding members of HaYovel believe that the modern-day existence of the State of Israel is a fulfilment of the ancient biblical prophecies. They believe the redemption is happening right now—through the flourishing fields and blossoming vineyards all over Israel, and the Jews streaming back to settle the land.

HaYovel wants to help this phenomenon. But what makes them different than all other religious Zionist organizations is this one pertinent detail: HaYovel is staffed entirely by non-Jews. Not only that, but they've brought in *thousands* of non-Jewish volunteers to help build up and plant in Israel.

Before being introduced to HaYovel, we had heard of Evangelical Christian groups who support the Jews and want them to return to Israel, but most of these groups believe that they themselves are God's new chosen people, and that Jews returning to the land is what will bring about the *Christian* final redemption. The people of HaYovel are different. They *don't* believe in replacement theology. They believe that the Jews are still God's chosen people, a light unto the nations, and they want to spread the word to other non-Jews and play an active part in the redemption.

I was full of anticipation for our day out at Har Bracha. What would these "righteous gentiles" be like? Was this going to be a totally flaky experience, or were these people really genuine in their desire to help the Jews?

Our friends, Jeremy and Tehila, knew the people at HaYovel well. They were going to take us to meet some of the organization's founding members. We started early that morning; it took us two long hours to drive over with our friends. As we pulled up to a lookout spot near Har Bracha, we heard sounds of the shofar blowing. Hundreds of Asian-looking non-Jewish tourists were streaming towards us. As we passed through the throngs of people, they shouted words of greeting.

"*Shalom*!" called a few.

"*Tishmor et Haaretz*!" shouted one. Guard the land. We had come to the right place.

My kids began asking questions, lots of questions. "Ima, who are those people?" asked Elie, now sixteen years old, very familiar with Israel, and encountering non-Jews blowing the shofar for the very first time.

"Why are they blowing the shofar?!" Eitan wanted to know.

By the time we reached the lookout spot and Caleb Waller, the guide who was going to be escorting us that day, all of my children were dying to know the answer to this question.

"Ask him," Jeremy said, nodding in the direction of Caleb. "He's the guy with all the answers."

Caleb stood six feet tall with strawberry blond hair. He was young, maybe twenty-five years old. That day he wore a big cowboy hat and a Magen David Belt buckle. To outsiders, he might easily pass for a good-looking Jewish tour guide with a southern accent.

"My job," he explained to our children, "is to explain Jews to the Christians, and Christians to Jews."

He went on to explain how these non-Jews (the Nations, as he called them), were blowing the shofar because they thought it might help penetrate evil forces at work in the valley of Shechem below. The shofar has gained popularity amongst Evangelical Christians in recent years; they view the sound of the shofar as an eschatological act, something more than a simple call to repentance. Caleb also gave us a little history of the area, reviewing the stories of biblical Shechem and getting us up to speed with the situation of the Palestinian refugee camps that exist on the edge of Nablus today.

After Caleb's little talk, we all caravanned over to the HaYovel campus that surrounded the big white tent atop Har Bracha, stopping for a look at Samaritan Har Gerizim along the way. The idea of a Samaritan city seemed exciting, but in truth it was quite anti-climactic. Rather than a graceful old-world city with a temple, it looked like any other rather dilapidated modern town, full of crowds, and with trash on the streets. Even on that pretty day, you couldn't call it a thing of beauty.

We left the somewhat depressing setting behind. As we drove away, I couldn't help but feel slightly sorry for Caleb Waller and his extended family, who had all left their homes in America to live in this sad place. What self-sacrifice must it have taken for non-Jews to spend part of their lives in a difficult area like this one, and just for the sake of supporting Israel, a people not their own? While I was mulling this over, we pulled up at "Base," which is what the Wallers call the HaYovel center, right next to the yishuv of Har Bracha. They all live there for six months out of the year.

It felt like I was entering an alternate universe. In a good way. Gone were the trash-covered hills and decrepit homes. We were out in a quiet, natural area of rock-covered hills under a blue sky filled with puffy white clouds. We stepped out of the car and walked down a path, past the main tent, which boasted beautiful vineyards on one side and neatly kept caravan homes on the other. The vineyards were reminiscent of a Napa Valley landscape...endless, orderly, fruitful, and mottled with fall color. And next to each caravan home stood a little sukkah.

Caleb led the way to his caravan, and we all followed behind. We entered through his sukkah, which he explained, "Is not exactly kosher."

"It's kosher style—like dill pickles," I joked.

His blonde wife Kendra came out to greet us wearing a headscarf and a long skirt. It was so strange for all of us; she looked just like a typical Israeli settler. In her arms, over her pregnant belly, she held one-year-old baby Geula. Caleb and Kendra's other two children, Chaya and Shifra, played nearby on the wooden deck.

This wasn't our first time meeting the Wallers (they had spent Shabbat in Neve Daniel a few months earlier, at Jeremy and Tehila's house), so we weren't totally surprised by their Jewish names and style of dress, but as we left Caleb's home and walked through rows of caravans, meeting Caleb's brothers and friends, I felt a new level of awe. Every single man looked like Caleb, tall and blond and wearing a hat. Dozens of blonde children were playing between the small homes. The women were modestly dressed, headscarves and all, according to orthodox Jewish standards. The Sukkot were neat and clean, almost military, each one containing a bunk-bed or two, and a small table and chairs. We met Caleb's brother, Joshua (they record a podcast together, the Joshua and Caleb report—pun intended) who described the scene at Har Bracha on Erev Sukkot, when they had all built their sukkah huts together. It sounded quite similar to holiday preparations in our town.

We were full of questions, so Caleb and Joshua obliged us with a little interview.

Why do their people (the Nations, as they refer to themselves, which is the literal translation of *goyim*), follow a version of Jewish law? Why do they support the Jewish People?

Joshua explained to us with patience that they were trying to lead a *Godly* life. They believe that God gave the Jewish people the formula to do so. Whatever is good for us, therefore, must be good for them too, at least on some level.

In addition, Joshua explained that they believed that it was clear that God was bringing the Geula, the final redemption, now. And they wanted to be a part of it.

After our talk and sukkah tour, we headed off to the grape vines. Every day during harvest season, busloads of non-Jewish volunteers spend the early hours of the morning picking grapes. They treat this as a holy task and care for each cluster with great reverence. Besides serving the purpose of beautifying the land and providing grapes to one of the local Jewish wineries, these righteous non-Jews feel that they are holding onto the Land of Israel for future Jewish settlement. Which to them is, "*obviously*," as Caleb put it, the most important thing.

Caleb pointed out the next hill in the distance. It was rocky and barren, typical of the landscape you often see around Israel, especially in the settlements—the type of mountain that's hard to envision as a place of fertile growth. "You see those hills over there?" he asked. "When we got here, this whole place looked like those mountains. Our volunteers spent months just picking up rocks."

It was hard to internalize. I could see that the vineyards were beautiful, the land neat and well-kept, the grape vines full of fruit. I had never connected Israel's rocky rolling hills with lush fertility and productive farming. Was it possible that, with hard work, much of the country could be as green and fruitful as a Napa Valley vineyard?

Our six kids went on to spend an idyllic hour running down the rows of grapes, enjoying the beauty of the area and picking leftover bunches. At some point, the Wallers left us to wander the vineyards on our own; they set off to get ready for the local Udi Davidi concert in Har Bracha. The rabbi of Har Bracha, Rav Melamed, enjoys a close relationship with the people of HaYovel so, of course, they were welcome to take part in the Sukkot festivities in the town.

When we were done exploring and picking, we said goodbye to Jeremy and Tehila's family—they were off to Har Bracha, themselves. Then, we found a kosher sukkah at HaYovel and had a picnic dinner. As we sat there with our sandwiches, I allowed my feelings of disbelief to wash over me. The entire experience had been so strange. After thousands of years of persecution, we Jews are almost trained to be distrustful of religious non-Jews. Now it seemed like that would have to change, in order for the prophecies of the redemption to come true. After all, at some point in time all of the nations of the world are supposed to recognize God and come to serve Him in the Third Temple.

And here we were: modern Jews experiencing this strange new version of serving God. I, for one, never would have imagined that one day, I would be eating dinner with my family in a non-Jewish sukkah in Israel. Who would have thought that such a thing even existed? The fact was, it was neater and prettier than some of the Jewish-built sukkot I had seen in my life. I let these thoughts sink in over omelet-filled sandwiches and cut up cucumbers.

After finishing their dinner, Gabi and Benzion, ages four and a half, and one and a half, started to get antsy. Gabi's golden blonde hair flopped as he ran around after Benzi, who was desperately trying to escape from having a hat placed on his own head full of blond curls. It was time to move on before we wrecked this nice, clean sukkah. So as the sun began to set in the sky, we piled the kids back into our car and drove off to join our friends at the Udi Davidi concert.

That Sukkot, the CD we played in our car was a collection of songs based on some of the Psalms, performed by Ben Tzion and Tali Waller. Ben Tzion is the oldest son in the Waller clan, and Tali is his wife. Our favorite song on the CD was Psalm 126, the one we recite every Shabbat at the end of each meal, before *Birkat Hamazon* (Grace after meals).

We listened to the words that described the coming of

the Geula, so artfully sung by Ben Tzion and Tali, "Then they'll say among the Nations, 'Hashem has done great things for them.' Hashem has done great things for us. And we are glad."

These prophecies from the Tanach were actually coming true. This struck us in a profoundly real way that day as we rocked down in our beautiful land to "Shir HaMa'alot," sung by The Nations. A land which was being changed before our eyes from a place of desolation to a land of plenty. A land returned to us by God. A land where "those who sowed in tears" now "reap with songs of joy."

At the Udi Davidi concert, it was hard to keep our eyes off the Wallers—they were dancing and singing along with the Hebrew words as if this popular religious Israeli singer were Justin Bieber. These people inspired me to be better—to be a better Jew and a better person. If they could be so devoted to God, shouldn't I be doubly so?

I thought of the miracle that is Israel, a land reclaimed after millennia of lost hope and suffering. Seeing the Wallers' farmland made me realize that it wasn't just the early pioneers who had had a mission to rebuild the destroyed land: it's something that *anyone* in the world can be a part of today. As strange and foreign as it seems, people like this have the ability to empower us on our mission to return the Jewish nation to its land, and its people to God.

It Says So in the Psalm

WHEN IT COMES to descriptions of the time of redemption, there's nothing more beautiful than Psalm 126:

A Song of Ascents. When God returns the returnees to Zion, we shall be like dreamers. Then our mouths will be filled with laughter and our tongues with songs of joy; then they will say among the nations, 'God has done great things for them.' God has done great things for us; and we were glad. Turn our captivity, oh God, like streams in the Negev. Those who sow with tears will reap with songs of joy. He who goes along weeping, carrying his seed, will return with song, carrying his sheaves.

Was it not like a dream for me as a twelve-year-old girl, and for so many others, to walk by night on the holiday of Shavuot to the Kotel, surrounded by other "sleepwalkers," our destination the holiest place in the world? We walked freely to that spot, streaming forth, surrounded on all sides by other worshippers, a far cry from the Jews' experiences since the beginning of their exile from the Holy Land. Nowadays in Israel, our mouths are filled with laughter and songs of joy: We live in our land, the land God gave to us, and in it we are free to celebrate our Jewish holidays and re-joice in our nationhood. We set off fireworks and blast Israeli music on Yom HaAtzmaut.

"Then they will say among the nations, 'Hashem has done great things for them.'" There are even non-Jews here in Israel, recognizing the miracles that God has performed for the Jews and helping to fulfill prophecy. Israel is recognized as a state in the family of nations, has a seat at the UN, and is allied with the greatest democracies of our time. Moreover, some old enmities are fading, with our newest alliances being made with Arab and Muslim nations through the Abraham Accords.

"Turn our captivity, oh God, like streams in the Negev." Through how many centuries did Jews utter these words with no concept of what they really meant?? But those of us lucky enough to live in modern-day Israel know all about these Negev streams. They appear out of nowhere: in the winter-time, a dry desert canyon can turn into a gushing river in a matter of minutes. This is a metaphor for how God will re-deem the Jews. And this metaphor has become a reality: only nineteen years after officially gaining independence, the new State of Israel faced the threat of another holocaust during the Six Day War. But Israel's unexpected and rapid victory was like a stream flowing in, providing salvation with great rapidity.

We once sowed in tears, now we gather our land's abun-dant produce with great joy. We gather wheat, oranges, avocados, bananas, tomatoes, cucumbers, lettuce, grapes, and just about everything else that can grow in the ground—and even above it, on hydroponic farms!

This psalm is a clear depiction of modern-day Israel. God has returned the captive Jewish people to our homeland in Eretz Yisrael.

XVII.

True Pioneering

"The surviving remnant of the house of Judah will again take root downward and bear fruit upward." –Isaiah 37:31

I⊤ was Hoshana Raba, the last day of that same Sukkot. Our family always had a plan for every single day of vacation, and this day was no different, even with Shemini Atzeret starting that evening. The morning would begin with brunch at the Erdfarbs, in Efrat, with some other relatives who were visiting. Then we would drive to "The Farm," a nearby piece of land that our friends and neighbors, Jeremy and Tehila Gimpel, were in the process of cultivating.

Both Jeremy and Tehila had moved to Israel at the age of fourteen, with their pretty typical American families. But they are not living out the typical American dream. The Gimpels had been trying to convince us to come and visit their farm for a while. At lunch on Shabbat, a few days earlier, Tehila had waxed prolific about the beauty of the place. "It's like Gan Eden," she'd said. That was enough to make me curious. She also mentioned that this farm was conveniently located only ten minutes away from Efrat.

After pancakes and scrambled eggs, and hugs and warm wishes for Avi's visiting aunt and uncle, we got ready to go.

"What is this farm place again?" Avi's uncle asked us.

"Oh, we have no idea," we replied, unsure of exactly what we were getting into, "Our friends say it's beautiful. All we really know is that it's in the middle of nowhere."

We pulled the kids away from their cousins and piled back into the car for our short journey to the farm.

We met the Gimpels with their five small children at the entrance to Efrat and followed them in the direction of nowhere. On the way, we passed by small Arab villages, familiar Gush Etzion rocky terrain, patches of grape vines, and more bits of nothing. Surprisingly, it was a *really* short drive to the middle of nowhere. It was kind of amazing to see how quickly we became so isolated. There were hills after hills of no-man's land, so close to home.

After a ten-minute drive, we reached a small Jewish outpost called Ibei HaNachal. The area was rocky and desolate save for the forty or so white caravans that made up the mountaintop town. We saw a few mothers peeking out from their doorways, calling out to their children playing in front. There was dust and dirt everywhere, and I couldn't stop thinking about how messy it must be to live in a place like this with children. No one there looked like they minded, though; the mothers looked more than content, they looked happy. Minimalism at its finest.

We continued on to the outer border of the *yishuv* and

pulled up at a big gate secured with a padlock. Jeremy hopped out of the car to unlock it and we continued through, and there we were, at "The Farm." Or at least, that's what Jeremy and Tehila said. From my car window, it wasn't looking quite like the Garden of Eden they had described.

Jeremy pulled over to the side, and we all got out of our cars. He explained the vistas that surrounded us. Tehila stretched her arms wide, smiling, actually jumping up and down with excitement, her headscarf bopping along with her. "Look at this! Isn't it beautiful?"

The truth? It wasn't *exactly* beautiful at first glance. We were looking at the all-too-familiar scene of rocks and mountains… and more rocks and mountains. Bare, with patches of thorns. Maybe it would have been a cool case study for a geologist. But Jeremy continued with his explanation, pointing to where their property line ended: "Over there, you see that little cave in the side of the mountain? And that valley there is Nahal Arugot." And as he pointed to the Dead Sea on one side and Jerusalem on the other, I slowly began to see the isolated beauty of the place. If I zoomed out, past the thorns and stones, I could see the rolling hills, deep valleys, and a dramatic sky. I could feel our friends' positive energy having its effect on me. Jeremy continued with his descriptions from our lookout, "Imagine this place filled with rows and rows of grapevines, wheat fields, and orchards of olive trees. One day we'll get there…"

Just as I was beginning to adjust my perspective, we got back in the car to continue our tour. The next stop was the "yeshiva," an empty shell of a building that had been built with no specific purpose in mind. When Jeremy's partners started building at The Farm, they weren't exactly sure what to use it for. Along came Jeremy, and he assigned this building a purpose. "It's a yeshiva for non-Jews," he explained. "They'll come here to stay, learn about the Jewish mission, volunteer, whatever."

Of course, I remembered HaYovel, and the Wallers. Only a few days ago we had seen what could be created on our land by purpose-driven, God-fearing people. This "Farm" could almost become a sister campus to the place next to Har Bracha. A place where non-Jews could come to give help and support Israel. A place where Jews could come to teach them and guide them. After all, the surrounding community of Gush Etzion was filled with rich Torah personalities, all of whom with so much wisdom to share.

After our pit-stop, Jeremy and Tehila got back in the car for the next short drive. They had brought a picnic, and it was easier for them to transport it in the car. Our kids had come that morning expecting a hike, so rather than drive, we climbed up to the newly constructed house on a hilltop, passing an ancient-looking olive press on the path.

As we reached the house and walked onto the patio, complete with a romantic stone pergola, I was finally fully struck by the beauty of our surroundings. Sure, it may have been undeveloped and rough around the edges. But looking through the pretty stone pergola framing the view, I could see that this place had an incredible structure.

Another memory floated into my mind. In 2013, we had visited the only kosher winery in Italy, which was in Tuscany. In those vineyards, endless rows of golden grapevines were complemented by a few structures: the wine making and storage facility, the owners' home, and a guest house, complete with an infinity pool and a stone pergola, similar to this one. As I sat down at a wooden table and took in the jaw-dropping views around us, I could almost picture endless rows of symmetrically laid out vines on these barren hills just as Jeremy had described, their leaves changing color in the gentle autumn light.

Tehila pulled out plastic containers of cut-up cucumbers, cherry tomatoes, guacamole, and crackers. Jeremy opened up the front door to give the kids a tour of the dusty guesthouse. "You guys should put in an infinity pool," I joked, staring off into the wild and rocky distance.

"You see that big stone all the way out there?" Tehila pointed. "That's where the pool will be when this place is finished." As opposed to me, she was totally serious.

The kids ran around the little house, in and out, enjoying the echoes to be found in an empty construction site. They careened through the small living room, bedroom, bathroom (with a Jacuzzi), and slid around on lots of dust. Gabi and Benzi were particularly enjoying that day's activity, feeling the freedom of running through an empty house on a remote hilltop, making tracks in the dust, and shouting. Eitan and Noa, now thirteen and eight, followed after them, purportedly to keep them safe. After exhausting themselves, they all scooted over to Tehila's picnic to join the rest of us and replenish their energy.

Avi was gazing around in open admiration. "This could be a bed and breakfast. It's beautiful here!"

We were in awe that this barren nothingness full of potential was basically here for the taking, only ten minutes away from our home. And as we looked out on the little rows of baby olive trees that Jeremy and Tehila had planted a few weeks earlier, the truth dawned on us—with a lot of work, this farm could be better than Tuscany, a veritable holy land of vineyards and olive groves. Maybe a winery too.

My kids wanted to explore some more, so Jeremy's oldest son led the way, taking us on a long walk through rocky hills that led to a multi-level cave. Jeremy likes to tell stories, and as we walked, he quoted passages from Tanach that told the tale of King David hiding in a cave in the area of Nahal Arugot. Perhaps it had even been this exact cave that we were about to explore. The kids were wide-eyed, hanging on his every word.

When the history adventure story was finished, all the kids ran in and then back out of the cave, shouting to each other as they emerged through the different exits. They were like moles in a tunnel. "It's so much fun here," Eitan said. "When can we come back?"

Before we were even ready to leave, our family wanted to be sure that this place would become a permanent fixture in our lives. *I* was already having fanciful visions of my dreams of farm living coming true. For years, I had followed blogs of a couple of different women who lived out in the boonies in America, one in Oklahoma and the other in Wyoming. They homeschooled their children, took beautiful pictures at sunrise and sunset, shared gardening and cooking tips, and wrote about the rewards and challenges of simple living. Although

I was happy in Neve Daniel, a quiet life in a more natural setting was something I had always been drawn to (I had even once toyed with the idea of starting a blog of my own, called Homestead in the Holyland. Problem was, I didn't exactly *have* a homestead). Maybe *we* could find a piece of land like this, and *we* could work it and care for it until it became beautiful. Of course, building a life like that would take a tremendous amount of hard work, something I wasn't so sure I had time for in addition to my regular child-rearing responsibilities. And for Avi, it would be a giant leap to turn from a traditional career to full time farming.

Dream aside, at the very least we could support Jeremy and Tehila through the process as they built up and moved to *their* farm. Besides being beautiful and vast, it was also located in a place of strategic importance for Jerusalem and Gush Etzion. If they didn't cultivate it, who would? Their dream was one I could definitely get behind.

In this land, it feels like almost anything is possible. Not too long ago, it was war-torn and desolate, full of swamps and disease. Looking through old pictures of Israel, the realities of the past spring to life. Not long ago, Jerusalem, Haifa, Tel Aviv, looked more like the Wild West than the metropolitan centers that they are today. The Jerusalem mountains didn't magically turn into the beautiful, well-forested land that they are now. Early Jewish settlers toiled with a common vision to make Israel a fruitful and beautiful homeland for their nation.

It was a miracle that God gave us the opportunity and inspiration to come back and work the land after so many

years. It was a miracle that he made those efforts successful. But it certainly didn't come easy. Being at Jeremy and
Tehila's farm reminded me once again that the responsibility
for restoring the land didn't end with Israel's first pioneers.
Our generation must continue the process. Israel still needs
us.

Jeremy and Tehila told us about their five-year plan.
Jeremy, co-founder of the Land of Israel Network, already
had a large following, built up by years as a radio show and
television host. The majority of his followers were non-Jews,
inspired by Jeremy to support the Land of Israel and Torah
values. Tehila, mother of five and a successful family lawyer,
also had plenty of experience and knowledge when it came
to living simply. At home in Neve Daniel, she raised her
own chickens (the only flock on the block), grew her own
vegetable garden, and sprouted her own wheat. Together
with their partners on the farm, Jeremy would encourage
his many followers to help on their mission to build up the
property, perhaps even arranging volunteer groups for rock
clearing and planting the land. Once the basic infrastruc-
ture was ready, they would build their own home there, close
enough to Ibei HaNachal so that they could be part of the
community, but far enough away to enjoy the peace and quiet of farm life. They would raise animals, grow wheat, and
cultivate vines and olives. They would produce olive oil and
yogurt and wine. And then they would invite people in to
learn about Torah and the Land of Israel.

It's definitely not the two car, white picket fence American
Dream. But reclaiming and rebuilding the Holy Land has

been the dream of the Jews for thousands of years. Beyond God's miracles, it will take hopeful feet on the ground and persevering hands in the soil to bring it to full fruition.

XVIII.

BACK TO LIFE

"We must accustom ourselves to the understanding that the world has a Master." –Rav Tzvi Yehuda HaCohen Kook, Torat Eretz Yisrael

I T's A NEW day. Sunrise, feet pounding on the treadmill, fingers tapping words onto a computer screen. An early morning goodbye as Eitan steps out the door into first light, on his way to school.

A refreshing shower, a soft toddler hug, sweet smiles and greetings from little bed-headed children getting ready for the day.

It's lunches packed: Cucumbers sliced and sandwiches made. Clean dishes put away and cereal bowls into the dishwasher. Tea with Elie before she heads out for her day. She's almost an adult. A break to reach out to God as little boys play. And a thank you for the smile on each child's face. For the blessings of our life.

Then off they all go, except for Benzi, who tags along with me each day. Together, we head to my morning Torah class and then for a walk with Avi. Next, Benzi and I go grocery shopping and run some errands. During naptime, I help a friend, play some guitar, write, or clean up the house. And before we know it, the bright morning light has faded to a gentle afternoon glow.

The younger children return from school: first Gabi, then Noa and Dalya. On nicer days, we play outside. We get through homework and practice and go places.

Then, when the big kids come home, it's dinner time: a bowl of black bean soup and a loaf of freshly baked bread, or salad and pasta, or vegetarian chili with a dollop of sour cream. Sunset spatters the sky with awesome pink clouds, a photo-worthy view more nights than not.

These are days—routine days. They're special because they're ours. They're important because they belong to the Jewish people. And they happen here: In Israel, the land God has returned to our nation.

It is Tuesday. In our house, Tuesday means family time. It's the only day of the week when all eight of us are able to clear our schedules to be together and discuss what's important, embark on a family project, or just pop some popcorn and try to have fun.

Today, we are baking. I pull out the good stuff: Hershey's kisses, pretzels, white chocolate, and away we go. Flour and sugar fly everywhere. From sixteen months to sixteen years old, all the children work together with me to create our masterpieces: Two butter pound cakes, one pan of white chocolate pretzel brownies, and a pan of blondies studded with Hershey kiss chocolate chips.

"My turn to mix!" insists Dalya.

"Where's the cocoa powder?" asks Eitan, who has taken on the pretzel brownies as his own personal project.

After much commotion, mixing, pouring (and yes, a little bit of fighting), I place our creations in the oven. The kids clean up the kitchen table. While the cakes bake, we eat dinner: tonight, that's vegetarian tacos, with extra Hershey's kisses for dessert. After dinner, we all pile into the car and drive off, each child holding a cake fresh from the oven.

Ten minutes later we've arrived at the little caravan in the back of a parking lot at Tzomet HaGush known as the Pina Chama. The Pina Chama, or "Cozy Corner," is a rest stop for the young soldiers stationed in Gush Etzion. These young soldiers fight for us and protect our nation at all hours of day and night, risking their lives in any condition and every type of weather. So, to make their task a teeny tiny bit more pleasant, the residents of Gush Etzion have organized a constant coffee and cake supply in this sweet hangout room with tables, couches, and a popcorn machine. As we pull up to the Pina Chama and pile out of the car, we pass a tall soldier on his way out.

"*Todah!*" he says to our children. The kids are glowing with pride.

"*Todah lecha!*" Avi replies. Thank *you*.

The children hand the cakes to the volunteers behind the counter (most of them moms, like me), who thank us profusely. Three and a half-year-old Gabi smiles shyly at a young soldier enjoying his babka and coffee. The soldier seems to find my little blond son endearing, and waves back.

Our children are experiencing the deep inner happiness that comes with helping others. If, by working together for an hour, we can contribute our four cakes to this effort and give our kids something to feel good about, then family time has been a success.

I feel this way because my children understand, with a strange mixture of sadness and pride, how much we need our soldiers. Without their commitment and protection, without their conviction and will to fight for our country and our people, we would *have* no country. And, most likely, much less of a people.

It is only by the grace of God that we have our nation. God, and the sacrifice of hundreds of thousands of young Jews who gave, and continue to give, themselves over to the Jewish people. "I'm willing to sacrifice," they say, as they begin their service to our country. "Take my innocence and youth, take some of my best years, so that our people, our nation, can continue to survive."

That's a message we can all learn from. After all, on some level, isn't our covenant with God all *about* sacrifice? The real question we have to ask ourselves is this: What are *we* willing to sacrifice for the sake of our commitment to God and to our people?

It's another typical Tuesday afternoon. This Tuesday, I am decorating a cake at the kitchen counter and my husband is taking a little break from working in his downstairs office. He is standing by the kitchen table multitasking—he has a basket of laundry which he is folding (okay, maybe this really isn't so typical) and he is talking on FaceTime with his mother, 'Ma' as our children call her. The little kids are running around in the backyard with our border collie, Rio, beyond the open screen door. Thirteen-year-old Eitan stands nearby.

Ma turns from Avi to Eitan and asks him what the cake I'm decorating is for.

"It's for Bookworm," he replies.

"What's Bookworm?" she asks.

"Bookworm? It's, like, this thing that we do every summer," he explains. "We all read books and write the titles down on a big chart. At the end we have a party. There are still a few more spots left on the chart, but Abba read a bunch of books that he didn't write down."

"What books did you read, Avi?" Ma wants to know.

"I read lots of books," Avi replies, folding a pair of toddler shorts in half and placing them neatly in the pile. "First I read *Snow Crash*..."

"What's that about?" Ma asks.

"*Snow Crash* is, well, it was written as science fiction but it's no longer really science fiction," Avi replies, with animation in his voice. "It was the first book of its kind. It describes a world where people can spend time—even live—in a connected virtual reality."

"When was it written?" asks my mother-in- law.

Avi looks at me to confirm, as I spread the frosting, "I guess, around twenty years ago?"

"Twenty years ago?!" I am skeptical. "It was written in the Nineties!"

"Yeah, that *was* twenty years ago," Avi reminds me with a smile.

Oh yeah…I guess that was *twenty years ago!*

"Anyway," Avi explains to his mother, "The book describes a world that could almost be a reality."

Eitan looks interested, "Abba?" he asks, "Is that kind of world—the world in the book which is almost like our world—do you think that's good or bad?"

"What do you think?"

"Well, it feels like it's bad…."

"That's right," Avi agrees as he balls up a pair of socks, "it does feel bad. But why do you think it would be bad?"

"It is *definitely* bad!" my mother-in-law pipes up through FaceTime, from thousands of miles away.

Avi is never one to give up on a lively argument with his mother. "Ma, why do you say that? Why is it bad? Do you think FaceTime has made your life better or worse?"

"Better," she agrees. "But what does that have to do with it?"

"In a world of interconnected virtual reality, I wouldn't only be able to see you. I'd be able to visit your house. Shake your hand. Throw you a ball."

"It's like FaceTime times a thousand," Eitan exclaims! "It'd be like we live right next door to you. Whenever we wanted, we could just come inside, open the fridge, lie down on the couch. It'd be like we live right next to each other, instead of so far away!"

Avi looks amused. "So, why is that bad?" he asks Eitan again.

"Doesn't sound like its bad!" my mother-in-law answers.

"That does sound great," Eitan agrees. "But it still *feels* bad. Why do I feel like it's bad?"

"I'll tell you why it would be bad," says Avi, getting ready to make his point. "It's bad because in a world like that there is no room for God."

"Right," my son agrees readily. "Like, we wouldn't be able to build the *Beit HaMikdash*."

"Well, we *would* be able to build the *Beit HaMikdash*—" Avi says.

"Yeah, but where would we build it?" Eitan insists. "In the virtual reality world? Or in the real world? You could build it whenever you wanted in the virtual reality world, but would it be the real *Beit HaMikdash*?"

I, for one, am loving the turn this conversation has taken. I'm making dinner, my husband is folding laundry, and my teenage son is talking about virtual reality and its connection to the *Beit HaMikdash*. As a very important, imminent problem we need to sort out. What shall we do when we want to build the *Beit HaMikdash*—where will we build it? Like, tomorrow, or next year…when that happens.

It's conversations like these that remind me how lucky we are to be living as part of a community that takes the *Geula* (Redemption) completely seriously. And not just from a let's do mitzvot and bring Mashiach perspective. My son believed that this was going to happen soon, in his lifetime, in the imminent future; that he was a part of it. And he, like other kids his age around here, had seen pictures and read about how the Temple structure would be built, down to the last beautiful detail. We are here, ready to bring the *Geula*. It is that sense of purpose which influences our every day and, sometimes, makes run of the mill conversations meaningful.

So, what was the verdict?

"In a virtual reality world, God doesn't exist," my husband insisted. And although my mother in-law and I argued with him on this point, he continued. "What would have to happen for God to affect humankind in virtual reality? Miracles. How would he break your leg; cause you to lose your fortune; even cause a natural disaster? In a virtual reality world, everything within is controlled by computer algorithm. The only way to make it happen would be a revealed, obvious miracle."

The kids in the background become a little louder and more boisterous. The laundry pile is folded. And then Noa and Dalya run in, Noa for a snack, Dalya for help with her English homework. FaceTime ends. The rest of the conversation will wait for another day. In the meantime, we'll just go on living our regular lives, in a land and community where redemption is an everyday topic of conversation.

Establish a Just Society in Israel

FAST DAYS ARE never easy. Throughout the Jewish year, we are required to keep four different fasts to commemorate the destruction of the Holy Temple. As a young adult, I don't think I even understood the purpose of these fasts; I definitely devoted more attention to my hunger than to thoughts of the Beit HaMikdash on those days.

It seems this aversion to fast days has been around for a while. During the time of the rebuilding of the Second Temple, Jews from outside of Israel sent emissaries to the land with important questions for Zechariah, the local prophet. These emissaries brought monetary gifts with them, for the rebuilding of the Temple. They also asked Zechariah for a halachic ruling for their communities back home: would they have to continue keeping the fast days held every year to mourn the destruction of the First Temple, now that the Temple was being rebuilt?

First, the prophet rebuked them for not moving back to rebuild the nation in Israel. And he told them that the fast days should continue to be observed for as long as Jews choose to stay in their communities abroad, rather than return to the Jewish homeland.

Then, Zechariah offered a picture of what *real* redemption would look like: "Thus spoke God, saying: Execute true judgement, and show loyal love and mercy, every man to his brother. And do not oppress the widow or the orphan, the stranger or the poor. And let none of you devise evil against his brother in your heart" (Zechariah 7:9–10). True redemption will occur when the Jewish people have, together, established a just society in Israel: one that cares for its orphans, its widows, and its poor.

In modern day Israel, this prophetic vision is no longer a distant dream. Here, we have health care and welfare systems that support all types of people: widows, orphans, and the poor. Jews stream in from around the world and are embraced and cared for. Israel, established and run by Jews, leads the world in medical advances and technology. We aren't perfect but, for the most part, we have rectified this ancient problem in our society.

Zechariah continued his prophecy:

Old men and old women shall yet again dwell in the streets of Jerusalem, and every man with his staff in his hand for his age. And the streets of the city shall be full of boys and girls playing in the streets.... Behold, I will save my people from the east country, and from the west country. And I will bring them in, and they will dwell in the midst of Jerusalem... (Zechariah 8:4–8).

This poignant description could be about any street in modern-day Israel. It wasn't always like this but, *today*, boys, girls, old men and old women fill the streets. Jews stream in from the east, west, north, and south to dwell in our Holy Land, in Israel's holy city, Jerusalem.

The last words of Zechariah's message from God describe

the ultimate goal for redemption. When the time comes: "…
they will be my people and I will be their God, in truth and
righteousness."

It's interesting to note that the story of Purim occurred
right around the time of Zechariah's prophecy. The penul-
timate chapter of Megillat Esther makes mention of a letter that was sent out to Jewish communities throughout
the Persian empire, with "words of peace and truth" (Esther
9:30). What exactly were these words of peace and truth?
According to Rabbi Menachem Leibtag of Yeshivat Har
Etzion, these words of the Megilla were meant to reinforce
those uttered by Zechariah—they were a call for Jews to return to Israel and establish their own peaceful and just society in their homeland.[1]

Only about ten percent of the exiled Jews returned to
Israel during the Second Temple period. Perhaps this is what
is being referred to obliquely at the end of the megilla, when
it says: "These days of Purim shall be observed at their proper time, as Mordecai the Jew—and now Queen Esther—has
obligated them to do, and just as they have assumed for
themselves and their descendants the obligation of the
fasts, with their lamentations" (Esther 9:31).

We know that the fasts mentioned in this verse can't be
the Fast of Esther (one of the only fasts not related to the
destruction of the Temple), because lamentations and fasts
are referred to in plural, indicating more than one day. There
was one thing that was even harder for the Jews in *Galut*

---

1   "Megillat Esther, it's 'Hidden' Message," Rav Menachem Leibtag, https://www.etzion.
    org.il/en/holidays/purim/megillat-ester-its-hidden-message.

than keeping a few fast days to commemorate the destruction of the Temple: uprooting themselves from the foreign lands they had begun to call home. From these last lines of the megilla, we understand that rather than return to Israel and help build a renewed nation, the majority of the Jews at that time chose, instead, to remain in exile, where they had built their lives.

Back to modern times, we can see the ancient prophecies of Zechariah beginning to take form in our own society, in Israel. Anyone who visits Israel today can see his words being fulfilled right before their very own eyes, on the streets of Jerusalem. Perhaps this time around, the Jews will be able to free themselves from the shackles of exile and return to the land of redemption, where, one day, our fast days will turn into days of celebration.

XIX.

PASSION

FOR THE FIRST decade or so of our lives in Israel, we would fly to America every summer. There were people to visit: my parents, and my brother Jesse (who had married Tracy in 2009 and now had a daughter, Lila), my in-laws, all of Avi's siblings, and our old friends.

As the years passed and our family grew, that all changed. With so much of Avi's family having moved to Israel, there was no real need to fly to America *every* summer. My parents and in-laws visited on a regular basis, so we got to spend plenty of time together. Avi's siblings had all married, one by one, so there were no more weddings left to attend back in New Jersey. And with the majority of Avi's family here, Schild Family Vacation had officially moved to Israel. So, with no international demands on our summers, we were ready to branch out. Of course, we loved Israel, but the country was close in proximity to many beautiful places we had never seen. And we certainly were not opposed to visiting a foreign country in the summertime.

In the summer of 2018, fifteen years after making aliyah,

we decided to take our first real family trip in Europe. Avi and I had traveled there together (to Italy, Spain, and the UK) many times, but we had never made Europe our summer family vacation destination. With the help of David, our Scottish friend in Neve Daniel, we planned out a family trip to Scotland, a country known for its natural beauty and plentiful hiking trails.

During the days before the trip, we packed two-and-a-half-weeks' worth of cookware and clothing into six small, rolling carry-ons. We were going to live as minimalists on this journey (much to the dismay of our fashion-loving teenage daughter, Dalya). Thanks to the strict luggage policy enforced by the budget airline we chose, there would be no schlepping of oversized suitcases on this lightweight trip through Scotland. With our gear stripped down to the very basics, we loaded our six children into the car and headed for the airport. Many flight delays later, we had landed in London, the first stop on our summer adventure.

Elie, Eitan, and Dalya were huge Harry Potter fans at the time. We slept in the hotel for just a few hours and then embarked on our morning's escapades in the city of London, including a visit to Buckingham Palace. Then we boarded a bus and surprised the kids with a visit to the Harry Potter Studio Tour; seeing the thrill on their faces made the pit stop in London well worth it. The next morning, we boarded the scenic train to Glasgow—we were on our way to Scotland.

The next two-and-a-half weeks were indescribably wonderful. We met David in Glasgow, where he was staying for a few weeks to visit his elderly mother. He showed us around the city, helped us stock up on kosher supplies, and then escorted us to the car rental agency where we picked up a huge van. With that, we drove off into the Scottish Highlands towards Loch Lomond. The place was just as green and beautiful as we had imagined, perhaps even more so. I had just finished reading all of the *Outlander* books (a series of novels which take place in Scotland in the eighteenth century), so my brain was full of images of reflective lochs (lakes), green valleys, and verdant hills. These were all truly present in the Highland landscape. While we hiked through Glencoe and Fort William, we immersed ourselves in the deep natural beauty, only slightly disturbed by the swarming and biting midges that came out whenever the breeze died down. Thick moss grew in every crevice, and colorful mushrooms, purple heather, and red berries adorned the hiking paths.

It rained a lot in Scotland. We had stuffed lightweight rain jackets into our tiny carry-on bags and worn waterproof hiking boots right onto the airplane, so we were well equipped to continue our travels despite the wet weather that came and went, seemingly at random. A thermos full of tea or soup accompanied us on every adventure. Despite the persistent drizzle, our kids couldn't have been happier. Elie, who had just finished up high school as an art major, brought along a small sketch book and portable watercolors everywhere we went. She painted the scenery when we stopped for (yet another) picnic. Eitan loved everything about the place, especially the challenging hikes. And Benzi couldn't get enough of the fluffy Highland cows and sheep that were just about everywhere. The natural world we wandered through was so beautiful that even the little kids couldn't help but notice. We were on an outdoor adventure, all together.

In addition to the natural beauty, Avi and I were drawn to the Scottish people, culture, and history. After a couple of weeks in Scotland, we were talking about Bonnie Prince Charlie and the Jacobite rebellion. We found ourselves browsing through the plaid kilts and blankets at gift shops, listening to bagpipe music, and practicing words in Gaelic. Tea with milk and shortbread cookies became our afternoon snack of choice while we traveled. As we hiked past castles and ancient battlefields, we became totally absorbed in the Scottish experience.

For many summers running, we had been quite the outdoorsy family. When visiting our family in America, we liked to try to go on our own family vacation too, just the eight of us. Somewhere along the way, we had realized that the most universally loved activity by all of our six children was hiking and spending time in nature. The bigger ones liked the walking, and the littler ones were easily transported on our backs and shoulders, so hiking and outdoor adventures had become our main focus on those vacations. Scotland is known to be a hikers' paradise. From the West Highland Way to the John Muir Way and beyond, there were many incredible outdoor places to explore. To guide us on our journeys that summer, we used a popular local website called Walk Highlands. With this online resource, we were well equipped for our day trips, with maps, descriptions, and info about every trail in the country.

The highlight of the trip may have been Ben A'an, a small mountain peak in the Trossachs that presented quite a challenge for our family. On the day we climbed it, the sky was threatening rain (as usual). It took a lot of coaxing and piggyback rides to get the kids up that steep ascent. Avi carried Benzi the whole way, and Eitan and I took turns with Gabi on our backs. The older girls pushed through, putting all of their energy into conquering the slopes of Ben A'an.

Just before we reached the top, it started to storm; a violent wind and rain accompanied our last steps. We arrived at the summit, in a surge of exhilaration, to find a pillar of cloud surrounding us, obscuring our final reward: the magnificent view. The cold wind bit at our faces. I felt a wave of disappointment wash over our crew. And then, just as quickly as the storm had arrived, it faded away, leaving behind a magical rainbow and a jaw-dropping panoramic view out to the shimmering lakes and the green Scottish Highlands down below. We were in heaven.

After two-and-a-half weeks of hiking in Scotland, none of us could bear the thought of leaving. Avi and I made an impulsive decision: we would extend our trip for one more week. We visited a reindeer reserve in the Cairngorms, scoped out more castles, and hiked towards the coast in Cruden Bay. On our last Shabbat in Scotland, we rented an unbelievably inexpensive Airbnb. Our hosts had once used the giant home as a bed and breakfast, renting out rooms individually and cooking for their guests. As they aged, they found that they were no longer up to the caretaking and cooking tasks, so they decided to rent the little hotel out as one large house. We took over the entire place, cooking in the industrial kitchen, stacking our games behind the check-in counter, and eating our Shabbat meals all by our-selves in the oversized dining room filled with round tables. It couldn't have been more memorable.

Three-and-a-half weeks after leaving home, we returned to Israel. We felt the same way we felt at the end of every sum-mer: Our summer had been incredible, but it was still good to be home, back in Israel. But this time, there was a new feeling sitting somewhere deep in my heart. I wasn't quite sure what it was. But I knew that, in some unidentifiable way, my life had been forever changed by that summer experience in Scotland.

Right after our Scotland vacation, I had what some might describe as a mid-life crisis. It was September 2018. There was no red convertible and no plastic surgery. I didn't give up on my values, or drastically change my life at all, really. But in my own organized way, I was going through an internal storm. I was thirty-eight years old. Benzi, my youngest son, was three years old at the time, and I was pretty sure that he was going to be my last. My oldest daughter, Elie, was now living in an apartment in Jerusalem, completing her nation-al service. The demands of parenting six children were not small, and I was not floating about aimlessly, by any means. But I did have five straight childless hours every morning. For so many years, I had put my talents and capabilities on the backburner to be a stay-at-home mom, struggling with feelings of inferiority that so often came up when I com-pared myself to more career-oriented friends. I had watched with a tinge of jealousy as my old friend, Peggy, grew in popularity as a musician, her band, *The Pains of Being Pure at Heart*, eventually playing on the David Letterman Show. I believed that my decision to stay home with the kids was the right one for my family, but that hadn't meant that it was always easy. Over the years, I had searched for small creative and intellectual outlets, always keeping my main focus on the little ones at home. But now, almost twenty years after having my first child, life looked different.

It's not as if I hadn't given my future profession any thought. I had taken some classes at Herzog, a local college, during the previous few years, including an intensive class in beginner's Talmud. While pregnant with Benzion, I had studied the laws of family purity with Rabbanit Taragin and had become a certified "*Kallah* Teacher," trained to prepare new Orthodox brides for the mitzvot of *Taharat HaMishpacha* (family purity), including monthly immersion in the ritual bath, along with other practices. The previous year, I had investigated the possibility of beginning a training course to become a *Yoetzet Halacha*, to become one of the women who serve as halachic guides in the laws of family purity for other women.

But now, with the prospect of day after day of Talmud study staring me in the face, I hesitated. It was a big investment, especially for someone like me, with so little experience in Talmud. And I just wasn't sure that this was the life path I was destined to take. So, during the first week of September, I made a decision: I would embark on a journey of discovery and give myself as long as it took to actively figure out what I wanted for my future.

That autumn, I spent morning after morning on our

playroom couch, sunk deep in the faded denim upholstery and plaid pillows. Armed with a notebook, pens, and my laptop, I was ready to discover my life's path. To start the process, I laid out every profession that could possibly interest me: from doctor, to midwife, to photographer, to interior designer, to travel planner, to writer, to *yoetzet halacha*, to singer, and beyond. This took some time.

Then, before figuring out the pros and cons of any one of these many possibilities, I thought about *why* any of these things interested me. Was there some childhood baggage I was carrying around, some expectations that I hadn't let go of? Doctor got a checkmark for this one—with two physicians as parents, it sometimes felt like medicine was the only truly honorable career. I gathered my thoughts and feelings about every possible life path and wrote about them all. The next part of the process was to break each potential profession down into several components. Aside from my internal feelings about, for example, becoming a doctor, I had to figure out how it would actually fit into my life. What would it give me in terms of personal fulfillment? What about lifestyle? Would the many years of schooling required be a fair price to pay? How would my chosen path help the world? How would it affect my family?

Every day, when it was time to pick Benzi up from preschool, I would shut my computer and congratulate myself on a morning well spent. Even with the many long hours that I devoted to the process, I felt that I was doing something necessary, and important. If I didn't stop to think about my life now, when would I?

A few weeks in, I felt that I was finally approaching a conclusion. I had dozens of careers mapped out in front of me, complete with score charts. Just looking at my notebooks and computer screen, I could see that becoming a doctor was not going to happen. Aside from the obvious emotional baggage I was carrying, there was also an unreasonable learning curve, and no guarantees when it came to lifestyle. I could expect long hours, at least at first, during internship and residency. In essence, I was still a stay-at-home mom, and I wasn't willing to give that up in my search for personal fulfillment. One morning, after our usual routine of *shiur*, walk, and breakfast, I returned to my place on the couch to tabulate my results. I was shocked by the outcome. According to my research, my correct life path was not what I had expected it to be. I wasn't destined to become a professional singer, a midwife, or a *yoetzet halacha*. I was going to become a writer.

I had added it to my list almost as an afterthought, with the same amount of feeling as I'd had when I wrote down "interior designer." Writing had to be on there somewhere—in fact, I had worked as a part-time content writer while pregnant with Noa years earlier, and I had already written bits and pieces of two different books. I *loved* to write for fun. I constantly wrote in notebooks, had filled stacks of blank pages over my many years of adulthood. When Avi and I were engaged, I had written poetry, filling my little red cloth-covered journal with rhymes and metaphors.

But to choose "writer" as a career? What did "being a writer" even mean? There were a million different ways of doing that, from content writing, to book writing, to news-paper reporting.

Yet, it was clear that writing would allow me time with my family. It could bring me personal fulfillment—I loved language and word play—as well as enable me to give some-thing back to the world. While the financial prospects were slim, there was at least *some* possibility of being paid for my work. And with Avi as the main breadwinner up until that point, financial concerns were pretty low on my list.

I guess I would have to figure out what being a writer meant for me.

At the same time that I was working through my midlife crisis, my family was feeling inspired by our recent trip to Scotland. Our time spent traveling had been so incredible, we had *so* loved hiking and fully immersing ourselves in na-ture. Upon our return to Israel, we decided that we want-ed more vacation-like experiences like that in our lives. We started to explore.

First, we returned to our favorite hiking trails nearby. We hiked through Nahal Prat one morning, on our way to visit Sharon and the kids in Kochav Hashahar. For the first time, we noticed wild mint growing on the trail, and the late sum-mer figs that hung from trees growing out of the stream. We hiked the loop around Mount Eitan, a favorite Jerusalem Mountain trail we had discovered in a photo essay years ear-lier. And we returned to the little trail near Beit Shemesh we'd been hiking since we made aliyah, affectionately known by our kids as "The Schuster." Eitan, who had recently received a new Canon camera as a present, took professional-looking photos, zooming in on pine needles, wildflowers, and waterfalls. We brought along thermoses filled with iced coffee, a nice replacement for the hot tea which had always accompanied us on our trips in Scotland.

One Friday morning, with the kids all (finally!) in school after a long summer, Avi and I decided to try a totally new hiking trail. With a couple of hours of internet research, we managed to find a local trail called Caesar's Way, only twenty minutes from home.

Using Google Maps to guide us, Avi and I pulled up at the trailhead, then followed the path along an ancient Roman road, through a thick forest. This part of the hike was really lovely, and we congratulated ourselves on finding a nice new trail close to home. After an hour or so of walking, we stopped for breakfast, drinking our thermos of iced coffee and consuming our carrot muffins from the new bakery with relish. And sitting there, out in Israel's nature on a Friday morning, we felt almost like we were back in Scotland. True, it was a lot drier in this part of the world, especially in early September. But the birds were chirping, and the bees were buzzing. A gentle, late summer breeze blew through the overhanging oak trees. And most importantly, it was quiet, just like it had been in Scotland, where there were so many places to hike that it never got too crowded on any given trail.

To make the hike circular, we had to cut back along a differently marked path. We didn't have any of the cool navigational tools we had used in Scotland for this hike. And of course, we got lost. We ended up climbing a mountain of dirt and rubble, along an old water pipe which we used to help us shimmy up the hill.

"Are you sure this is the right way?" I shouted up to Avi, who was peering over the last little bit of water pipe towards the path beyond.

"No!" he replied, "but at this point, it's the only way. Let's give it a try!"

I'm pretty sure it wasn't the *right* way. But eventually, we were back on Caesar's Way, only a little the worse for wear. Tired, sweaty, and covered with dust, we returned to the trailhead with mixed feelings.

Clearly, there were lots of places to hike in Israel, places near home that we'd never even known existed. But why was it so difficult to find them? And to find our way on the trails?

Meanwhile, back on the playroom couch, I was giving my new profession as a writer a lot of thought.

A few months earlier, Elie and I had taken a three-day graduation trip to Romania, mostly chosen by virtue of the fact that the tickets to Cluj-Napoca, capital of the Transylvanian region, cost only a hundred dollars, total. For that price, we were willing to go just about anywhere. Elie and I packed our carry-on bags and set off for an adventure through Romania, just the two of us. On the first day of our trip, I hired a guide for a bike tour named Iancu. He and his partner Levi took us around the country in a big van, and together we biked from the beautiful Belis Lake towards the border with neighboring Hungary. Sharing cookies in the car after our bike trip, Iancu had told us about his other job as a travel writer. Every winter, he travelled around Europe to photograph and report on various skiing events and destinations.

For some reason, back in Israel months later, this conversation was playing on repeat through my head. As a content writer, I had been asked to write about many vacation destinations, some of which I had never even been to. Writing about traveling was something that I could do. And if I could become a travel writer…well who would say no to more vacation? Especially after an epic trip to Scotland?

With my plans still unformed, I sat down and wrote an article about traveling to Scotland. Then I wrote an article about visiting Romania. And then, for good measure, I wrote an article about our favorite local gem that we had just recently hiked through: Nahal Prat.

On the Sunday evening after our hiking trip to Caesar's way, I gave Gabi and Benzi their daily bath. Sitting there on a plastic stool next to the tub, I mulled over my writing, our vacations, hiking, and our trip to Scotland. I thought about the difficulty Avi and I had experienced hiking the previous Friday morning. And also, the beauty of it. Benzi and Gabi were fully engaged in their game of generously "washing" each other's hair, each taking turns with the blue plastic bucket.

"Why was hiking so much easier in Scotland?" I muttered under my breath.

Wait. I knew the answer to that question.

Hiking was so easy in Scotland because we had used an *awesome* website to guide us on our journeys. Featuring plenty of photos and descriptions, along with maps and navigational tools, Walk Highlands had taken most of the difficulty out of our hiking trips and allowed us to focus on our experiences in nature.

The wheels in my head started spinning. I thought about other trips we had taken—trips to Sedona and Sequoia during our summers in America, planned with the help of detailed blog posts written by other parents. I thought about the time Avi and I had gone away to the Lakes region in Italy in search of fall foliage. We had tried so hard to hike on that trip, but for some reason, the only information we could find was in Italian. My ability to decipher Romance languages was pretty good, but it wasn't good enough. We had driven to one national park and had spent hours looking for the trailhead before eventually giving up and having a picnic near an old, abandoned church.

I loved to hike. And I wanted to write. And Israel suffered from the same exact problem. Israel had no English language hiking resource like Walk Highlands.

My brain was suddenly on fire. I shouted down to Avi who was doing post-dinner clean-up. "Avi, can you come here?!"

Avi barreled up the stairs to the kids' bathroom, looking slightly panicked.

"I have an idea!" I exclaimed. "Remember how I want to become a writer? I think I should write about hikes in Israel for English speakers! Israel has sooooo many tourists. And we don't have an English hiking site like Walk Highlands. Maybe I can start a blog?!"

I paused for breath, giving Avi a chance to reply. He smiled with relief, "That's a great idea!" And as he helped me (actually) wash Gabi and Benzi's hair and get them out of the tub, I chattered on and on.

Who knew? Perhaps it was just a pipe dream. But I already had one article written, about Nahal Prat. And Eitan had taken lots of pretty pictures I could use for a first post. All I really needed was a website. I had once been a computer programming *major*. Of course, decades had passed, and I hadn't kept up with my skills at all. But we were living in modern times, when almost anyone could start a blog. How hard could it be?

The next morning, after the kids were in school, I took up my now traditional spot on the playroom couch and did a Google search: "How to Start a Blog." According to the articles that came up, it could be accomplished in a few simple steps. I needed a hosting service—that would only cost $3 a month. I needed a logo, a signature, all easily designed using free tools on the Internet. But before getting started, I would need to choose a web address, and in order to do that, I needed a name.

I thought back to the blogs I had followed years earlier, about farm life and simple living. Once upon a time, I had wanted to start my own blog, Homestead in the Holy Land. Inspiration came to me. I knew *just* what my new website would be called. I began filling out the first form, ready to name my new website. "Site Title," the form requested. I typed my new name out in a flurry of excitement, "H-I-K-I-N-G-T-H-E-H-O-L-Y-L-A-N-D."

"Hiking the Holyland, here we come!"

During the fall of 2018 and the winter of 2019, Avi and I felt like we were on our own magical vacation. Instead of traveling by airplane to a foreign land for weeks at a time, all we had to do was hop into our gold Toyota Sienna minivan every Friday morning, coffee and muffins packed away in our backpacks.

We began with local trails—in Gush Etzion, Tzur Hadassah, and Jerusalem. There, we discovered archeological remnants, echoes of our people's past, hidden between natural springs and pine forests. I was already starting to feel like exploring Israel would be, in some ways, quite similar to what we had experienced in Scotland. It was easy to fall in love with the history of a land while hiking through it. Instead of Jacobite battlefields, we passed by battlefields of King David and Goliath, in Adulam Reserve and in Park Britannia. In Gush Etzion, we hiked near Givat HaSelaim, where Jewish soldiers had gone down fighting in battle in 1948.

Next, we branched out further, to Makhtesh Ramon, the Sorek River Estuary, and Nahal Arugot in Ein Gedi. We took in the wonders of the desert in the wintertime, a

beautiful world of stark natural beauty and impressive geo-
logical formations. It was quiet there—even quieter than
Scotland. And we found birds, reptiles, and mammals that
I hadn't known one could see around Israel. Occasionally,
our hikes were miserable failures (which we didn't really
mind—we felt like it was our job to take one for the team!).
But more often than not, we were completely blown away by
what we discovered on our Friday excursions.

Finding hikes wasn't easy. If it had been, then I would
have questioned the need to start Hiking the Holyland in
the first place. But we became more and more proficient in
the use of online mapping tools. Israel actually *did* have a
really neat app, called Amud Anan (Pillar of Cloud, words
used in the Torah to describe the miraculous cloud cover
that accompanied the nation of Israel during their forty
years in the desert). On this map, we could see *all* of the
hiking trails in Israel, in addition to points of interest noted
by thousands of users. It was all in Hebrew, and sometimes
there were no notes along a trail; we didn't necessarily have
any real idea of what we were getting into much of the time.
But it didn't really matter. My goal wasn't to have a smooth
hike every time, but rather to create a resource that other
people could benefit from. It would be my job to filter out
the good from the bad.

There was *so* much more good than bad. As the rainy season worked its magic on Israel, I almost felt like I was back
in Scotland. One misty morning, we drove to a trail twenty
minutes from home to witness a river that flowed only on
rainy days. As we sat by the rapidly-flowing water we drank

steaming hot coffee, enjoying the cool drizzle in our faces. Luckily, we had come ready with the rain jackets we had purchased for our trip that summer. As we hiked back up through the valley, I took in the sights of green moss and mushrooms growing on rocks. Between the rainy weather and the thick greenery, this trail was reminding me a lot of our summer vacation.

I took pictures of our adventures using Eitan's camera. If my articles were going to help people on their travels, photos would be useful. I also snapped pictures of important trail markers and took down notes about the journey. Then, I would return home and throw myself into the writing, sharing my experience in a blog post.

It wasn't difficult to wax rhapsodic about the wonders of Israel's nature as I saw them. Avi and I felt truly blessed to be able to have these encounters with nature in our very own land, the land we'd left home for back in 2003. The same one we had grown to love deeply over many years. All I had to do was communicate these feelings in each twelve-hundred-word blog post. Simple.

Of course, it turned out that there was a bit more to it than that. I took an online photography course, read eBooks on web design, and downloaded plugins to improve the look and functionality of my site. One thing I really wanted was a truly useful map, one that would be very different than all of the maps I saw on other Israeli sites. They were difficult to navigate, zooming in and out without much rhyme or reason, making it difficult to see the different regions and attractions located within. I wanted a map that was clean, easy to use, functional, and pretty. I knew that a project like that was slightly out of my league, from a technical perspective, but Avi had endless patience and, with his technical background, the ability to figure out almost any problem. So, I put him to work on my Hiking the Holyland hike map in his free time.

In addition to giving prospective hikers interesting information and inspiration to capture their imaginations, I wanted all of my hikes to be easy to follow. I didn't want hikers following my instructions to have experiences like our misadventure at Caesar's Way. After playing around with a few different concepts, Avi helped me create a table at the top of each post just like the ones we'd found so useful on Walk Highlands. In each table, I listed basic facts about the trail: its level of difficulty; grade of ascent; its length; the time it would take to complete and, of course, a link to the trail map we had created while hiking, plus links to navigation that would get hikers to the trailhead.

I had taken concrete steps towards achieving my vision. I had a pretty website (with a catchy name!), useful hike posts, and functional maps. I was spending my time doing the things I loved: writing and hiking through Israel. And my entire family was enjoying the benefits of this, too. It was good for Elie, who joined us on hikes when she found herself needing a break from the drudgery of city life. Our new pastime was good for our other kids, who enjoyed discovering Israel's natural world on our now frequent adventures near home. And it was good for Avi and me, suddenly blessed with large quantities of quiet time together. Not only that, but even though

Hiking the Holyland was *my* project (at least back then), Avi found himself almost as passionate about it as I was.

That November, Avi's family flew in for our nephew Koby's bar mitzvah. On the Friday after they all arrived, my in-laws suggested that the adults go out to breakfast at a café, a fairly typical Friday morning outing for the Schild family. Avi and I had a great idea: There was a hike that we had been wanting to document in Jerusalem, one that led from the neighborhood of Ein Karem on the outskirts of Jerusalem, through the countryside, to Beit Zayit, a neighborhood in a completely different part of the Holy City. There was an excellent outdoor café in Beit Zayit, Café Derech HaGefen. Perhaps we could have our Friday morning breakfast there?

Avi got his parents on the phone, "Sure," his dad replied, "But can *we* go on the hike too?"

We readily agreed. The other siblings, many of them with babies and toddlers at that point, would meet us at the café. We would hike to Derech HaGefen together with my in-laws.

Avi and I met his parents in a parking lot in Ein Karem. That Friday morning in autumn, the cute neighborhood was at its best. The leaves on the trees had started to change color. Tourists and locals were exploring its shops and cafés. We left behind urban life as we made our way down a set of stone steps onto the Israel Trail, following trail markers past pink bougainvillea and red ivy. Soon, we were out in the countryside. I snapped lots of pictures, as was now my custom whenever we went hiking. Avi's parents looked on with confused expressions. For some reason, I felt so *awkward* about sharing Hiking the Holyland. It was still my secret, something that I wasn't completely confident about. A great idea, perhaps, but one whose future success was still in question. Perhaps it was because I had "just" been a stay-at home mother for so many years. Maybe I had an inferiority complex; with little professional experience in writing, blogging, or hiking, for that matter, I just didn't think that I would be taken seriously. Or maybe it was something about the public nature of writing a blog. Although I had always loved writing, *sharing* was not my strong point. But the moment to get over my inhibitions had come. I had already told my mother and sister about Hiking the Holyland. In fact, they were my only regular readers! And if I couldn't tell Avi's parents about Hiking the Holyland, then how could I possibly share it with people all over the internet?

"Guess what, guys?" I began, then rushed in, without pausing for a moment, "I started a website, a blog. It's called Hiking the Holyland. The idea came to me after our trip to Scotland. They had a great website there which helped us throughout our trip. I decided to try to create my own website to help people hike in Israel."

"Really?" said my father-in-law, his eyebrows raised, a look of pleasant surprise on his white-bearded face, "That is so neat!"

My mother-in-law had her own questions too. Like, was it really true that there was no English language hiking site out there already? Who would this site be for? And was I going to write about *this* hike on the website?

Avi stepped in, to my great relief, and filled in all the details about my new project. His excitement was far more convincing than my awkward reservedness anyway. By the time he had finished telling them all about it, we had reached the café, where we joined Avi's siblings, who were already seated around a big table under a pergola.

We ordered Israeli breakfasts aplenty, with eggs scrambled, fried, and in omelet form. My father- in-law ordered his favorite, green shakshuka, and my mother-in-law requested coffee and a butter croissant. Hot cappuccinos and platters of salads and cheeses arrived, and a moment of silence descended upon our talkative crew, until Ilana broke it. "How was the hike?"

"Wonderful, wonderful. Did you guys know about Susannah's new blog?" my mother-in-law asked with a smile.

I wanted to retreat inside of myself, and I raised my own cup of coffee to my lips in an attempt to hide behind it. But Ilana and Ari and the rest of the siblings hadn't known, of course, and they wanted to hear what this new blog was all about. Between us, Avi and I managed to get out the complete story. And although Ilana was confused about the purpose of the blog, "Did you just feel like you wanted to share?" she asked, I finally managed to explain all about Hiking the Holyland, how I chose to write it in blog format, and what I hoped it would do for Israel.

It had to be a blog, because I didn't yet have complete information on all the hikes available. I would write as I explored. My readers would discover Israel right along with me. And besides, I liked the personal nature of a blog, and felt that it could be a useful format, especially for parents who were looking for practical advice on hiking with their kids. I hoped that, eventually, the site would prove useful for tourists, allowing them to fully explore the country using information provided in English, the international language. I imagined that new *olim*, like the Erdfarbs, would be able to use the website to access places of hidden beauty, places that would make their aliyah feel a lot easier, places that they never knew existed.

Two cups of coffee and one mushroom omelet later, the deed was done. Hiking the Holyland was no longer my secret, and it certainly was no longer just an idea. Avi's entire family was now on board, and they were excited to get started hiking with us right after Koby's bar mitzvah.

Now I just had to share Hiking the Holyland with the rest of the world.

I sat in front of my computer, on the playroom couch once again. This time, I wasn't writing. I wasn't working on site design. And I wasn't planning out a hike. Instead, I was scrolling through Facebook, reading through posts on a group that was popular with Anglo *Olim*.

I knew that getting Hiking the Holyland out there would involve the use of social media. And while I wasn't much of a social media user, my main problem was that I never, and I mean never, posted on Facebook groups. If I had a question or needed a recommendation, I would ask friends or family. I never shared any information about my life publicly. So how could I possibly start sharing my new Hiking the Holyland posts on Facebook?

As I scrolled through the feed, looking at recommendations, questions, and advertisements, something caught my eye. It was a blog post about a trip to an archaeological site, written by a young student. His post simply said: "New blog post about Tel Megiddo and Tel Hazor in Northern Israel. Enjoy!"

And then he had pasted a link to his post right beneath.

That was it. It was so simple. I didn't have to write anything fancy or self-promoting. All I had to do was post one of my articles as a public service. I picked out a new post about the Sorek Estuary, a beautiful coastal hike towards a series of craggy cliffs. Avi and I had hiked there on a rainy morning and had been taken by the wildflowers along the stream, the beautiful sea, the treasure trove of seashells, and cool rock formations. As far as I was concerned, it was a trail that every Israeli family should know about. I pasted in a link to the post and added my introduction: "New blog post about a hike at the Sorek Estuary at Palmahim. Enjoy!"

Enter. Click. Done.

My heart somersaulted as I thought about what I'd just done: I'd put myself and my dreams out there for the world to see. And on Facebook, no less. I immediately ran downstairs to report to Avi. "I just shared a post on Facebook," I told him, feeling shell-shocked.

"Great!" he replied.

"Not great!" I said, "What if it's horrible?! What will people think?"

"Chiquites," he replied, using his pet-name for me, and a calming voice, "it's going to be okay. It's not horrible. It's amazing. And everybody will think just that."

He was probably right. But still, I wasn't used to this sort of thing. I went through the rest of my day in a mild panic, feeling like I had stepped majorly out of my comfort zone.

And there I remained, for weeks after. Every Sunday, after spending a Friday morning hiking, I wrote a post, edited pictures, added maps, and hit publish. And then, every week, I shared my new blog post on Facebook. At first, it felt like a huge challenge to share these posts—not to write them, that was easy and enjoyable, but to share them! But then a funny thing happened. I started getting feedback—lots of it.

Aside from posting thankful comments on Facebook, people began emailing me directly. Sometimes, they had questions about the trails I posted, or feedback about their experiences. But often, they wrote in simply to say thank you. I heard from Anglo locals, and from tourists from all over the world, exactly the crowds I'd been hoping to reach. I heard from young moms who were now hiking with their kids, German tourists who were excited to see a different side of Israel, and experienced hikers who were expanding their playbooks. And I watched as my newly established email list started to grow.

As that year passed, our repertoire of hiking trails around Israel grew. We traveled north and south, exploring the Golan and Galilee with the kids and the Negev desert by ourselves. The more we hiked, the more there was to see. We were constantly discovering new areas of hidden beauty and peeling away layers to learn about the history of the land.

On one January trip to Nahal Tavor, in the Galilee, we felt like we had *actually* returned to Scotland, as we took in the verdant hills from above and crossed over the snaking river in the valley, all while surrounded by worlds of multicolored wildflowers. I couldn't believe that this place existed—and that I had never been there before.

Nahal Tavor was absolutely gorgeous, but it was also so much more than a beautiful place. Mount Tavor, visible just above the stream, had been the site of a famous biblical battle between Deborah and Barak and the (Canaanite) general, Sisera. As with so many things in Israel, this place had a story. During our lunch break, we sat next to the Basalt Canyon waterfall, in the middle of the stream. Grey clouds began to gather in the sky. I imagined a fierce storm and an overflowing stream, just what Sisera's troops would have had to contend with when their chariots wheels got stuck in the mud during battle.

This place was incredible.

Thankfully, the rain clouds didn't burst that day, and we left Nahal Tavor feeling exhilarated. Those first forays into a less-traveled part of Israel (for us) showed us a world of hidden beauty, a place that I could dream about and connect to. I couldn't wait to bring this beauty, this history, into other people's lives.

Over the course of that year, my hopes and dreams for Hiking the Holyland expanded. I wanted to inspire more people with a love for the Land of Israel. The more I hiked through and learned about our beautiful country, the more I felt that I wanted to share my love with others. I made plans for the future.

One day, I would write eBooks, make videos, perhaps even start a podcast. I would run group hikes, in order to share outdoor experiences in Israel with those who didn't feel comfortable hiking alone. I wanted Israel's history brought to life on hiking trails, and its rich natural world to reach as many people as possible, both Jews and non-Jews. I wanted people to form a deep connection with the seasons, the plants, the wild fruits, the flowers, and the trees, and to get to know the land like they did an old friend. Through images of nature and time spent outdoors, perhaps others would connect to Israel as we had connected to Scotland the previous summer. Perhaps even more deeply. I wanted to share the gift of Israel's nature with all those who could be inspired by it.

XX.

A NEW BEGINNING

"Do not be frightened, and do not be dismayed, for the Lord your God is with you wherever you go." –Joshua 1:9

"IMA, I MET a guy," said eighteen-year-old Elie over the phone, in her typically forthcoming style.

I could tell she was a little nervous about this topic, since she stopped there, the story not spilling out in her usual flood of chatter. I closed my laptop to pay closer attention. "Yeah? Who?" I asked.

"His name's Moshe. I met him a couple of days ago at…" here she paused, and giggled, "…the piano in town."

Town meant Jerusalem, where Elie was living. She was in the middle of her first year of national service after high school.

"And…?" I prodded.

Elie told me the story. She had been having a really bad day, and wasn't in the mood to hang out in her apartment with her ten roommates (that's right, ten). On an escape into the center of Jerusalem to buy some necessities—toilet paper, of all things—she decided to stop and play piano at the open baby grand in Safra Square. While she was waiting her turn, a young guy came over to wait too. When it was Elie's turn, she played some of her favorite songs.

"And then Ima, he played too. But he was amazing!!!" she said.

Then, she carried on, the two of them had played together, which put her in a much better mood. They talked for a few minutes at the piano, and when she got up to leave, they had exchanged numbers.

Elie wasn't quite sure what this all meant. This boy, Moshe, was a religious guy from Beit El. He seemed nice enough, but she hadn't actually been looking for romantic involvement. Moshe had called her the next day: He wanted to go for a walk together in the Jerusalem Forest. Just the two of them, and his guitar.

"Do you think this is a date? Should I go out with him?" Elie asked me. She told me that she definitely wasn't ready to get into a relationship with this Moshe, but she did think he was a nice guy, and she was thrilled to have a new friend who was also a musician.

I wasn't sure what to say. This kid was a perfect stranger. On the other hand, he was a religious Jew from a religious family. According to my daughter, he seemed like a really good guy, with good *midot* (character traits). He shared her talents and interests. And he was only nineteen—how bad could he be?

So, I advised Elie to trust her instincts. As long as she

wanted to hang out with him, it was okay—if they were in a public place and she felt safe. I wasn't sure whether the Jerusalem Forest at night fit that description, but I trusted her to make the right decision. "If he wants to know if this means you're dating, just be up front," I said. "Tell him you aren't ready to officially go out with him, but you're happy to get together and see what happens."

I hung up the phone and went back to editing photos. Soon, I'd forgotten about the whole conversation. It was safe to assume that she'd go out with Moshe, find out that he wasn't for her, and move on with her life. I mean, what were the chances of anything else?

Two weeks later, Elie called with an announcement: she and Moshe were now officially going out. I was excited for her, but I continued to adopt a hands-off approach, offering a listening ear and advice when it was asked for, but refusing to worry about whether or not Moshe was the right one for Elie. My husband had a harder time with this. And when my close friends found out about the relationship, they thought I was crazy. How could I be willing to let a random stranger off the street go out with my daughter? I didn't even know his parents. What if he was an axe murderer? (This scary question was repeated a few times by my good friend, Anita.)

The truth is that, somewhere along the way, I had learned that God works in mysterious ways. He had clearly done so in my life. Who was I to say where Elie's future life partner might come from? Was I all-knowing? (Um…no.) Would I be willing to limit the pool of candidates to children of friends and acquaintances? As long as my daughter was committed to intellectually analyzing the suitability of the match, which she was, I believed she could feel out the situation herself, with my guidance.

Months passed, summer rolled around, and one thing became clear: Moshe was here to stay. Once we met him ourselves, we discovered that he was bright, funny, and a pleasure to have around. He was kind and caring towards everyone, but especially to Elie. It touched my heart to see the way he treated her. He worshipped the ground she walked on.

Moshe was also totally and completely Israeli. So, we made an effort to speak more Hebrew at home when he was around. After living for the past sixteen years in places where I could get away with mostly speaking English, I was happy to have an opportunity to work on my fluency.

As August approached and things got more serious, we made plans for Moshe to join us on the Schild Family Vacation with Avi's entire family. This year, for the first time ever, we were headed to a foreign destination, a sprawling villa in the countryside on the outskirts of Rome, just the twenty-nine of us in one big house with a pool.

It would be Moshe's first time on an airplane.

By this time, Avi had come around to the idea of Moshe as Elie's boyfriend, but once again, my friends thought I was completely crazy. Was I sure that taking him on family vacation was a good idea?

Instead of arguing, I invited them all over for *Seuda Shlishit* (Saturday dinner) one Shabbat when Moshe and Elie were with us. We sat around in the backyard as the sun set on a beautiful summer day, and they got to know my daughter's mystery man. He charmed everyone. By the time night fell, he was sitting in a circle with my friends' teenage sons, chatting and laughing in his sweet, easy-going way.

After Shabbat, my friends came over to me one by one. They finally got it—this guy was amazing. "He seems just perfect for Elie," said one friend. "So easygoing, so relaxed, so sweet."

We looked over at Elie. She sat there in her floor-length colorful skirt and brown leather sandals, watching Moshe with a smile on her face, "And just *look* at Elie," added another friend, "She's so great."

So, Moshe came along to Italy with us. It was his first time leaving Israel. And even with the awe he felt at the whole experience, he turned out to be an asset on that summer vacation. We visited my aunt, my mother's sister, who lived in Florence, and on the nearly three-hour-long late-night drives back to our villa, Moshe was the one who kept me awake at the wheel, playing music and chatting from the backseat while Elie (and everyone else) slept. He spent a lot of time preparing food in the kitchen and sharing it with everyone. Moshe got along really well with our entire extended family (it's possible that his inability to hold long conversations in English may have helped).

Four short months later, an engagement was in the works. Elie had waited long enough—she and Moshe loved each other. They both felt like they inspired each other to be better people. They were ready to start the rest of their lives together.

For the big proposal, Moshe took Elie up to the rooftop

of Yeshivat Aish HaTorah, overlooking the Kotel, where he had set up a candlelit dinner. He played Elie a song he had written especially for her. She said yes, of course. A few days later, we celebrated their engagement with a small party in our home, where the two families got to know one another.

What can I say? I was thrilled. Some of my friends wondered if it was challenging for me to marry my daughter into a completely Israeli family. It was the opposite of challenging. I *did* break my teeth over high-level Hebrew while conversing with Moshe's parents and siblings, and we *had* come from very different backgrounds—Moshe's parents are Israeli nurses, originally from Russia. But their values were similar to ours. Moshe's parents were religious Jews and kind people; their priorities, which they had inculcated in their son, were exactly what I would have wanted for my firstborn daughter.

Still, Elie was only nineteen, as was Moshe. They both had years of schooling, growth, and development ahead of them. I could have spent their entire engagement in a state of panic, wondering if these youngsters could possibly know what they wanted out of life, but as the wedding planning began, I didn't feel scared or nervous. Just grateful. I had long ago learned that God has His own plans for people's lives. Things often play out differently than one might hope or expect. Judging by Elie and Moshe's fortuitous meeting, Hashem had a hand in this match. My daughter was going to marry someone incredible, who loved her deeply. She had found her life partner: a steady soul who brought out the best in her. What more could a parent want for their child?

Sometimes I thought that maybe I was a deficient mother for not worrying enough, but that is how I honestly felt.

As the winter months passed, we began planning the first wedding in the family, for late March. Elie and Moshe wanted a simple affair. Food was unimportant to them, and the outdoors seemed like a perfect event hall in their eyes (which was just perfect for me, of course). Elie's first suggestion was a pot-luck wedding at Jeremy and Tehila's farm. That was nixed—Jeremy and Tehila didn't have the proper set up for a lot of people; no floodlights, no dance floor. We scoped out lots of simple event halls, even driving out to the desert in the middle of a rainstorm to check out one place. I contacted several caterers, and we enjoyed delicious tastings, night after night. And soon, a plan for a simple, elegant (and yes, catered) wedding surrounded by friends and family began to take form.

That was the winter of 2019–2020. None of us had any idea that a global pandemic was coming, one that would change all of our lives—and totally derail our wedding plans.

XXI.

REFLECTIONS REVISITED

"It goes towards the south, and veers to the north; round and round goes the wind, and upon its circuits, the wind returns." (Ecclesiastes 1:6, attributed to King Solomon)

W E STOOD WITH our firstborn daughter, facing the chuppah that had been set up at Arugot Farm, the most unique setting, at this most unique wedding, in the midst of a crazy pandemic, right before the country went into a complete lockdown.

Jeremy and Tehila's farm was no longer a distant dream. They lived here now, with their six kids, flocks of chickens, horses, olive groves, wheat fields and vineyards—and yes, even an infinity pool. The farm, Elie's original wish, had turned out to be the ideal location for our tiny wedding—the only kind we were allowed, since only two separate groups of ten people were allowed to gather in one place. I took one last deep breath, exchanged a glance with my husband, and together we walked Elie towards her chuppah.

The ceremony itself passed in a blur—from the ring, to the blessings, to the glass cup being crushed under my new son-in-law's foot. I had just moments to comprehend the transition that was happening right there on a mountaintop in our ancient land: from daughter to wife; from mother and father to mother-in-law and father-in-law. Before I knew it, we were dancing back to the car and on to the party itself.

When we arrived back home, and stepped into our backyard, I was simply astounded. Our neighbors, our wonderful friends, had decorated our beloved garden. Yellow and white streamers hung from our tall Plane tree and fluttered out to the wall. Flowers were artfully arranged *everywhere*. And the extra tambourines we had left behind when we left for the ceremony had been hand-painted with watercolors, beautifully lettered and decorated by a talented daughter of my close friend and neighbor.

Elie danced into our yard with her new husband within an explosion of confetti.

In the backyards surrounding our home, friends and family took turns dancing along with us. From the streets, all spaced two meters apart, more friends sang and celebrated. Our driveway became the dance floor for a while. The bride and groom sat and watched neighbors who became jugglers, belly dancers, and a dancing bear. Our now Israeli aunts, uncles, and cousins were there too, dancing from a distance. My sister looked on, teary-eyed. And my daughter danced and laughed as if she had three hundred guests at her wedding.

But when it was all over, and we waved goodbye as the new couple drove off to their Airbnb in Jerusalem, I felt horrible. I finally *crashed.* The wedding had been incredible—my daughter was happy. Scrolling through my phone, I could see that the pictures reflected the unbelievable beauty of the location: rolling hills jutting above a gaping valley. Olive groves and vineyards. My daughter and her husband glowing with the innocence of young love. Everything looked perfect.

But Elie was gone now. She would probably never appreciate everything we had done that day, or everything we had done since the day she had been born. She would probably never know how much I missed her, all of my true feelings hidden behind a mask of happiness I kept in place to reassure her that everything was going to be ok. There would be no Sheva Brachot, no week of parties after this pandemic wedding. No hugs from friends and family. It was all over now.

After putting the house back in order, Avi and I dragged ourselves up to bed, late at night, and we found a letter waiting for us on my pillow:

> *To my dear, amazing parents, Ima and Abba,*
> *I honestly don't know where to start. But Ima, you taught me to always be grateful, so I guess I'll start from there.*
> *Ima and Abba, thank you for bringing me into this world, for taking care of me before I could even begin to understand who you are.*
> *Thank you for raising me, for teaching me the difference between right and wrong, good and bad.*
> *Thank you for teaching me how to eat, drink, talk, walk, sit, stand, write, read, and so much more.*

Thank you for putting me into art class and swim class and gymnastics and piano.

Thank you for teaching me how to be a good friend and a respectful person.

Thank you for teaching me what it means to care for someone, to love someone.

Thank you for teaching me what it means to be part of a family.

Thank you for teaching me how to be independent and responsible.

Thank you for teaching me how to love myself and how to be happy.

Thank you for punishing me and rewarding me.

Every part of me is thanks to you.

And I will probably never appreciate it enough, but I will definitely keep trying.

The letter went on. A waterfall of tears poured down my face. Uncontrollable. My daughter's wedding day had been entirely bittersweet. Hard. Beautiful. Happy and sad. A lesson in what's really important. A lesson in gratitude. And my daughter, God, and a crazy pandemic had given me the chance to experience all of it.

She ended her letter with this:

I will miss seeing you every day or at least every week.

I will miss intruding on your walks and on your breakfast.

Thank you for always supporting me, no matter what.

I was not unappreciated, not forgotten. This pandemic wedding experience had a purpose—to teach me an ancient lesson: That perfection is a fleeting thought, a breath of air. It is not attainable, no matter how much money, effort, and work you put into achieving it.

True perfection comes from appreciating what you have, from being grateful, no matter the circumstance. For my daughter, and for me, a bare bones Israeli wedding during a pandemic became a lesson in what actually matters: true friendship, relationships, family. Our beautiful Land of Israel.

We had all of these treasures at our dream wedding. And nothing could have been more perfect.

XXII.

HOPE AND DELIVERANCE

"Relief and rescue will come for the Jews"
(Esther 4:14, Mordechai speaking to Esther).

A FEW MONTHS AFTER my daughter's wedding, I received a text from my mother. She had unearthed an old letter from my great-great uncle on my father's side and thought I'd like to see it.

I printed all ten pages out right before lighting Shabbat candles, then cuddled up on a living room armchair to read the letter at sunset. I found myself completely absorbed—Gabi and Benzi bounced around the living room while I lost myself in the eloquent words on the pages. Until that point, I had never known what this letter revealed: my grandfather's uncle, Ernst, had been a traditional Jew and a Holocaust survivor.

Uncle Ernst had been one of four children. He was born in Vienna, in 1896. His brother, Hugo, was something of a troublemaker, and he was sent abroad to Chicago by his father. In Ernst's letter to Hugo, my great-grandfather, he wrote of the atrocities of 1938 and 1939, when he experienced the systematic antisemitism that was perpetrated against all the Jews of his community; this included beatings, confiscation of property, and the destruction of synagogues and homes. He eventually ended up in Dachau, where constant physical abuse and horrific conditions left a nightmarish imprint on his memory. In the camp, he and the other prisoners were physically and emotionally tortured, but Ernst considered himself to be one of the lucky ones—he watched as many others died from the torture inflicted upon them. Ernst's wife, Jella, advocated for his freedom behind the scenes, on the grounds that he had been twice decorated for valor in combat. Simultaneously, she worked to procure emigration visas and boat tickets. Ernst was finally freed from Dachau after a few unspeakable months. The two then made their way to Chicago, where they joined my great-grandfather.

For years, I'd heard Holocaust stories from Avi's side of the family. Both his parents' families had been through the war, his grandfather actually surviving Auschwitz at the young age of thirteen. My husband was the *real* Jew. I had always felt that I was part of the Jewish story only by proxy; with only one grandparent born Jewish, it felt as though my own Jewish roots were mostly non-existent. I had never even imagined that my own family had been a part of this national tragedy.

It wasn't something to rejoice over, but I took comfort in the fact that at least my great-great uncle had *survived* Dachau. He was one of the "lucky ones." Because his brother, Hugo, had been sent overseas as a young man, Ernst had been able to reach America, escaping the graveyard of Europe for a better life across the ocean.

As soon as Shabbat ended, I texted my mother. "Mama!" I wrote, "What an incredible letter! Has it been circulated?"

My mother replied with all the particulars; how exactly Uncle Ernst was related to us, and which descendants from my father's side of the family lived in Israel. After a thorough and complete explanation, we moved on to my mother's ancestors. I had done some research and discovered that Azevedo, my grandfather's last name, might be a Jewish name. "Mama, did you trace your Azorean ancestors back to the Marranos of Portugal yet?" I wrote.

"I didn't have to do that," she wrote back. "One of my great-great-great grandfathers on my father's side was a Jew from Morocco who moved to the Azores. He was named Moíses Bensabat. And anyway, 45% of Azoreans have genetically-Jewish backgrounds."

I couldn't believe it. It may have taken forty years for me to see it, but I had real Jewish roots.

Later, I couldn't help but think over the strangeness of it all. Somewhere on my journey from American Southerner to Religious Zionist living in Israel, I had come to see the hidden reality of God's plan in our world, his intention for our people. Maybe at some point in our history, His intervention had been outwardly miraculous, like the Ten Plagues or the Splitting of the Sea. But perhaps even then, it hadn't been as obvious as we would imagine.

Now, God *was* intervening. He was turning the page to a new chapter of Jewish history, a new time for our nation. A time during which Jews are flowing back to Israel from all corners of the world: New Orleans, Angola, Ethiopia,

India, Peru, and beyond. A time during which lost threads of Jewish lineage are being picked up again and woven back into the fabric of the Jewish people. Like the lost thread of my very own family. My daughter, my children, are building Jewish lives in a land we had been exiled from for thousands of years. Like the tallit above my daughter's chuppah, our nation was becoming one complete cloth once again.

It took years for me to grasp the full importance of the Land of Israel—decades after I experienced life as a little girl on swim team, a wandering Jew in a foreign land. I had the dream, the feeling that Israel was the place I wanted my children to grow up in, and I followed that dream, full of hope, but it was only now, sixteen years later, as I watched my eldest daughter begin her own family in Israel, that I truly knew, deep in my soul, that my decision had been absolutely right.

I had grappled with the small pains of moving here, and I had discovered big blessings. Again and again, from our first struggles in Ramat Beit Shemesh to the torrential storm at my son's bar mitzvah, I learned that what we *think* we want is not always what we *need*. I grew to realize that it was necessary to sacrifice comfort and familiarity to build up our nation…but that our nation was worth every moment of difficulty I experienced. I learned that this land, *my* land, has a rich history, and that I am a part of it. Most of all, I learned that I needed to give myself over to God's plan for our people to be able to see God's promises coming true here, right before my eyes.

We have reached a time in history when Jews recognize

their importance as a nation and have reclaimed their homeland. A time when our people have rectified so many of the social injustices of the past: in our country, widows and orphans are cared for. The poor are clothed and fed.

For the *first time* since the destruction of the Second Temple, we have a sovereign Jewish state which supports our Jewish values. Where our children can grow up surrounded by inspiring role models, in the wellspring of our ancient wisdom. Where they can experience our most precious Torah as something that is *alive*, not simply words on ancient parchment, however treasured.

We've arrived at a time when our land supports life and is filled with abundant growth: a time when we can sustain ourselves through the earth and build our own destiny with the help of God. When we can read the stories of Tanach and understand their significance in the natural world all around us.

We have the ability to begin preparations for the rebuilding of the Temple. And, at this very moment, the Jewish mission is supported by people around the world, from China to Utah. We can't take this for granted.

In our time, we can redefine what it means to dream.

For the first time in two thousand years, we are a people in a land and a state where independent thought and deep Torah wisdom thrive, forming the character of our country. We live in a place that we can *truly* call home.

In our land, life is not always easy. Sometimes, all of this good is obscured by a less-than-perfect veneer. On some days, it may be hard to see anything but that guy in the shuk smoking a cigarette, the one who tried to sell you rotten strawberries. Or the bus driver who honked and yelled as you crossed the street. There are traffic jams, high costs of living, religious struggles, and even sporadic warfare. Yes, there is room for improvement. That's one of the reasons that we are here. Our imperfect lives here are part of God's greater plan for His people.

Looking at it this way, I couldn't help but wonder: Will Jews around the world recognize that we've entered into a key moment in history? Or will we fail to see that the divine plan is coming to fruition for the Jewish people, right here in Israel?

As Mordechai said to Queen Esther: Salvation will come to the Jewish people one way or another. If there's anything my experience as a Jew in Israel has taught me it's that the prophecies of redemption are being fulfilled around us, every day: in the earth and its nature, the cities and holy sites, and the people themselves. Will we be part of this deliverance? Or will our names perish?

We are all living through the next big moment in our nation's story. We are here. Now is our chance to seize our roles as custodians of the Jewish nation with pride, as a unified people serving God, in this Holy Land, the Land of Israel.

XXIII.

Epilogue

Past the walls of our blue nylon tent, I heard the birds chirping. I felt the day's first rays of sun through my closed eyelids. It was morning. Opening my eyes, I rolled slightly to the left and saw Avi lying there next to me, already awake.

"Good morning, Chiquites," he whispered.

It was time to get going.

Today was the last day of *Yam el Yam*, our three day trek from the Mediterranean Sea to the Sea of Galilee. On this last day, we would hike through Meron Stream and Amud Stream, past cool pools, waterfalls, and beautiful rock formations. In about fifteen hours across twenty-five kilometers, we would reach our final destination. My feet hurt, but my heart was full. I couldn't wait to begin the day.

We unzipped our tent and greeted the morning, still slightly cool at that time of day in early June. After I watched the sun rise past the isolated mountain peak we were camped on, I slipped my sock-covered feet into my muddy hiking boots. Then I set about the task of packing up camp while whispering my morning prayers. Nearby, Avi unfurled a white tallit over his head and shoulders, then wrapped his arm in tefillin.

Twenty minutes later, we were hiking in Meron Stream.

That day was full of beautiful moments. I don't remember them all, but I remember many. I remember sitting perched on a leaf-covered hill under a tree above Amud Stream, brewing coffee and preparing cinnamon raisin oatmeal on our camp stove. I remember staring into the crystal clear pools of Nahal Amud, and then applying my mental and physical energy to conquer the intense challenge of hiking over boulders with a heavy backpack as we walked above the stream.

Midway through our day's journey, we almost ran out of water—a dramatic climax to any hiking story. With empty bottles, we frantically searched for a water spigot that the maps told us was somewhere a little way off the trail, but it was very difficult to find. Eventually, when we were just about to panic, we met some other hikers, and they pointed us in the right direction. We reached a herd of cows surrounding the spigot, and carefully approached, stepping over cow paddies and puddles to reach fresh water and refill every one of our empty bottles. Water had never tasted so good.

We almost didn't make it through that last day. Avi's feet were blistered, and he was in awful pain, done in by three days of him traipsing under the weight of his forty-pound pack without special hiking socks. We stopped at the beginning of Lower Nahal Amud, where I broke out the first aid kit and wrapped his feet in layers upon layers of gauze. And we continued.

On the last stretch of the Nahal Amud trail, I jumped from rock to rock, completely in the zone, imagining that I was a character out of a video game. At the very end of the path, as night fell, we reached the Sea of Galilee. It had swelled to overflowing following the plentiful winter rains we had been blessed with the previous winter. All alone, we stripped down and gleefully immersed ourselves, washing the sweat and exhaustion from our bodies.

One taxi ride and a two hour bus ride later, Elie and Moshe picked us up at the Jerusalem Central Bus Station with our car. They laughed as we emerged from the bus, hunched and hobbling after our intense multi-day trek like the two forty-something year olds that we now were. Elie and Moshe had taken care of everyone and everything while we were gone—we returned to a clean, quiet house and sleeping children.

It was good to get home.

Since the dawn of Hiking the Holyland, I've had dozens of days like this one—memorable days filled with special adventures discovering our very beautiful Holy Land. I don't take this for granted in any way. This path has changed my life, and the lives of those I love best. My children are see-ing Israel as one would see an old friend—with love, deep knowledge, understanding, acceptance, and excitement. It is their home and their playground. Beyond the confines of our garden, they pick wild mustard, za'atar, carob, and figs, tast-ing as they go. They search out animal dens and spider webs. And the ancient stories of holy men hiding from their pur-suers in caves, hidden by webs or nourished by carob, mean something to them. We've traveled through underground cave systems together, exploring Bar Kochba tunnels that are unknown to most, and discovered the ruins of ancient towns from the First and Second Temple periods while we hike. We've played in waterfalls that dry up during the first weeks of spring, feeling their cool spray on the very first hot day of the season. My children are growing up enmeshed in the land.

Over the years since October 2018, Hiking the Holyland has become a well-established entity, Israel's premier English language hiking site, well-known amongst Israelis and tourists of every sort. Avi has taken on an ever more central role. Together, we revamped the site, made videos, wrote eBooks, and started running group hikes—from Friday morning singles hikes to multi-part journeys along the Israel Trail.

To cement Hiking the Holyland's role as an official business, I cleared out our home office, the very same one that I had huddled in with my babies years earlier building Lego towers, the same one that Avi had occupied when Noa was a baby, before moving to his new office downstairs. This became Hiking the Holyland headquarters. After a fresh coat of paint, I hung "artwork" that was dear to me: a quote from Rav Kook, and an extra special letter from a reader. Next to this, I hung a giant map of Israel, along with some of my favorite photos from the trail. And of course, pictures of my treasured family took their place front and center, between the whiteboard and the hooks for photography equipment.

I can't pretend to know all there is to know about my place here, in this land. But as the years go by, I've learned that only one thing is certain: things will keep on changing. With every passing day, my relationship with Israel deepens, as I learn this language of love and land, and approach a more complete understanding of what Israel means to me, and what it means to its people.

I can't wait for the next step.

Acknowledgements

THANK YOU TO my editor, Deborah, who helped me make this book everything I wanted it to be.

Thank you to my friends and family for being willing to experience the raw side of things and for giving me so much time and perspective.

Thank you to my mentors and teachers who have inspired me.

Thank you to my parents and siblings who have been role models to guide my actions since the moment I was born.

Thank you to my wonderful children, who have given me the opportunity to be a better person.

Thank you to my husband, Avi, who's patience, love, insight, and constant support are behind my every achievement.

Thank you, Hashem.